Rockets' Red Glare

Rockets'
R E D
GLARE

Missile Defenses and the Future of World Politics

EDITED BY

James J. Wirtz

AND

Jeffrey A. Larsen

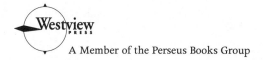

A Member of the Perseus Books Group

Copyright © 2001 by Westview Press, A Member of the Perseus Books Group

Westview Press books are available at special discounts for bulk purchases in the United States by corporations, institutions, and other organizations. For more information, please contact the Special Markets Department at The Perseus Books Group, 11 Cambridge Center, Cambridge MA 02142, or call (617) 252-5298.

Published in 2001 in the United States of America by Westview Press, 5500 Central Avenue, Boul-der, Colorado 80301–2877, and in the United Kingdom by Westview Press, 12 Hid's Copse Road, Cumnor Hill, Oxford OX2 9JJ

Find us on the World Wide Web at www.westviewpress.com

Library of Congress Cataloging-in-Publication Data

Rockets' red glare : missile defenses and the future of world politics / edited by James J. Wirtz and Jeffrey A. Larsen.
    p. cm.
  Includes bibliographical references and index.
  ISBN 0-8133-6450-7 (alk. paper)
    1. Ballistic missile defenses. 2. Ballistic missile defenses—United States. 3. United States—Military policy. 4. World politics—21st century. I. Wirtz, James J., 1958– II. Larsen, Jeffrey A., 1954–

UG740 .R63 2001
358.1'7182—dc21

                                      2001026563

Contents

Foreword

The decision to build a defense to protect the United States from missile attack is a crucial political issue facing the Bush administration and Congress. This is the third time that missile defense has risen to the top of the national policy agenda. In the 1960s, the Johnson administration explored several ballistic missile defense options, including the Safeguard system. President Nixon eventually canceled those U.S. missile defense programs to sign an agreement with the Soviet Union banning national missile defense (NMD). In the early 1980s, President Reagan announced U.S. intentions to pursue a national missile defense under the auspices of his Strategic Defense Initiative (SDI), an ambitious and controversial research program that was transformed into more modest form once the Cold War ended. Today, elected officials are again considering ballistic missile defense in response to the proliferation of long-range missiles and weapons of mass destruction to countries hostile to the United States. In 1999, President Clinton signed into law the National Missile Defense Act, which made it the policy of the United States to deploy an NMD system as soon as technologically feasible. In 2000, the President postponed a pending decision regarding NMD deployment, leaving it to the Bush administration to resolve the NMD issue.

As Secretary of the Navy, I was present at the 1972 signing of the Anti-Ballistic Missile (ABM) Treaty, and served in the U.S. Senate during both the SDI and NMD debates. I am convinced that neither Soviet nor American officials ever believed the Treaty was a static agreement that would forever preclude reassessments of our national security situation. There are substantive reasons why now is the right time to reconsider the ABM Treaty and the role of ballistic missile defenses in U.S. national security policy.

This book describes how the major political and technological changes that have occurred since 1972 have pushed missile defense to the top of the national agenda. Although I may not agree with every viewpoint expressed in this book, I commend it as a thorough and balanced treatment of this important and complex subject.

The United States no longer faces a single monolithic opponent with whom deterrence has been practiced painstakingly for decades. Rather, it now must stand up to a growing number of vague but potentially deadly threats to our homeland and to friends and military forces abroad. The rise of increasingly well-armed "rogue states" that exhibit little willingness to abide by international standards of behavior puts America potentially at greater peril than during the Cold War. The threat we face today is less from a massive nuclear attack than from the launch of a few nuclear, chemical, or biological warheads by dictators whose values—and accordingly, cost and benefit calculations—may be very different from our own. Nor can the threat of an accidental missile firing—either from decaying Cold War systems maintained by the Russians or from new systems being deployed around the world—be discounted.

Compared to the slower tempo of political change during most of the Cold War, the world today is more dynamic, making it increasingly important for U.S. officials to reconsider the continued relevance of policies and institutions that are vestiges of a different era. The ABM Treaty is slowly being undermined by several developments. Technological improvements in both offensive and defensive capabilities have made missile defenses more desirable and attainable than they were thirty years ago. It is also time to rethink strategies developed during the Soviet-American nuclear standoff. Future deterrence policies may call for a different offense/defense force mix than in the past, one that relies on strategic defenses to bolster traditional deterrent threats. At a minimum, elected officials and policymakers must begin to think about new ways to integrate arms control, active defenses, and offensive forces in an overall security package for the country.

This book tackles these issues in an unbiased and informative manner. By standing above the political fray that colors current debate about missile defenses, the well-informed contributors to the volume offer unique insights into the potential consequences of a U.S. decision to deploy defenses and to modify the ABM Treaty. The book explores the range of NMD deployment options facing the Bush administration and the strategic and diplomatic consequences associated with each potential system. As the contributors illustrate, the likely reactions of our allies and competitors should be given serious consideration by those who advocate rapid, large-scale missile defense deployments. Those who call for strict preservation of the status quo, by contrast, should focus on the outstanding discussion of how changing politics and technology are eroding Cold War institutions.

Today, the implications of deploying national missile defense are little understood and, unfortunately, little considered by most Americans and their public officials. *Rockets' Red Glare: Missile Defenses and World Politics* will contribute to an informed national debate about the role of missile defense in the future international security environment.

Senator John Warner
Committee on Armed Services
United States Senate

Acknowledgments

Many individuals and organizations made this book possible. First and foremost, we thank the contributors to the volume who have offered their insights and advice on how to assess the policy and politics behind U.S. interest in missile defense. Our contributors' professionalism and good cheer not only allowed us to meet a series of strict deadlines but also made the project an enjoyable exercise as we debated the theoretical and policy insights drawn from official Washington. Several contributors also helped us gain access to key segments of the policy community, which allowed our project team to conduct a series of extensive interviews and group discussions with key officials and Congressional staffers in November 1999. We met again in May 2000 at the ANSER facility in Crystal City, Virginia, to discuss our preliminary findings and to listen to a critique of our work offered by many of the individuals we had interviewed the previous fall. This book is a distinctly collective enterprise.

We benefited greatly from support offered by many organizations and individuals who encouraged us to reach our own conclusions about the complex issues we were addressing. We are especially indebted to Victor Utgoff, Tony Fainberg, Bill Durch, Alan Shaw, and Steven Boyd, of the Advanced Systems and Concepts Office of the Defense Threat Reduction Agency (DTRA/ASCO); Gilbert Bernabe of the On-Site Inspection Directorate of DTRA; Dutch Miller, Alex Ivanchishin, Kurt Klingenberger, Mike Preston and Don Minner, of the National Security Policy Division of the Air Staff (AF/XONP); Thomas Skrobala at the Navy Treaty Implementation Program; and Jim Smith, Brent Talbot, and Diana Heerdt, at the USAF Institute for National Security Studies (INSS). We also thank Ted Warner, Frank Miller, and Kent Stansberry in the Office of the Secretary of Defense; and David Martin, Lara Gross, and Mike Safrino of the Ballistic Missile Defense Office. Frank Jenkins, Mark Barbour, Jim Rutherford, and Debra Van Putten, of Science Applications International Corporation (SAIC) were generous with their time, describing many of the legal and technical issues embedded in the enormous documentary record surrounding the Anti-Ballistic Missile Treaty. SAIC's Matthew Billingsley provided valuable administrative help during our May conference. We appreciate Dean Wilkening's support for our efforts by inviting several contributors to a conference on international reactions to U.S. ballistic missile defense, held at the Center for International Security and Cooperation, Stanford University, in March 2000. Finally, we thank those officials who offered extensive comments on our work but who wished to remain anonymous.

Special thanks to Elizabeth Skinner of the Naval Postgraduate School for providing administrative support and for offering extensive editorial guidance. Without Elizabeth, we still would be cleaning up footnotes. We are grateful to her for making this a better book.

We also thank our families for tolerating our absence during the many hours we devoted to preparation of the manuscript. We also thank our parents, John and Elizabeth Wirtz and Calvin and Elaine Larsen, for their love and support.

The opinions and analysis offered here do not represent the official policy or positions of the U.S. government, the U.S. Navy, SAIC, or other individuals and organizations that supported us in the preparation of the manuscript. Any remaining errors are, of course, the other editor's fault.

James J. Wirtz and Jeffrey A. Larsen

Acronyms

ABL	airborne laser
ABM	anti-ballistic missile
AF/XONP	Headquarters United States Air Force, Nuclear and Counterproliferation Directorate, National Security Policy Division
ANSER	ANSER Corporation
AST	Airborne Surveillance Testbed
BMC3	battle management command, control, and communications
BMD	ballistic missile defense
BMDO	Ballistic Missile Defense Organization
CEC	Cooperative Engagement Capability
CFE	Conventional Forces, Europe
CIA	Central Intelligence Agency
CONOPS	contingency operations
CTBT	Comprehensive Test Ban Treaty
DCI	Director of Central Intelligence
DoD	Department of Defense
DPRK	Democratic People's Republic of Korea
DSP	Defense Support Program
DTRA/ASCO	Defense Threat Reduction Agency/ Advanced Systems and Concepts Office
FMCT	Fissile Material Cutoff Treaty
Frog	Russian missile
GBI	ground-based interceptor
GBR-P	ground-based radar prototype
GEM	guidance-enhanced missile
GPALS	Global Protection Against Limited Strikes
GPS	Global Positioning System
HALO	high altitude large optics
IAEA	International Atomic Energy Agency
ICBM	intercontinental ballistic missile
IDA	Institute for Defense Analyses
IFICS	in-flight interceptor communications system
IFT	integrated flight test

INF	intermediate-range nuclear forces
IRBM	intermediate-range ballistic missile
IRIS	infrared instrumentation system
JNTF	Joint National Test Facility
km/s	kilometers per second
MAD	mutual assured destruction
MIRV	multiple independently targeted reentry vehicle
MOU	memorandum of understanding
MRBM	medium-range ballistic missile
MTCR	Missile Technology Control Regime
NBC	nuclear, biological, and chemical
NCA	National Command Authorities
NIC	National Intelligence Council
NIE	National Intelligence Estimate
NMD	national missile defense
NPT	(Nuclear) Non-Proliferation Treaty
OSD	Office of the Secretary of Defense
PAC	Patriot advanced capability
PLV	payload launch vehicle
PRC	Peoples' Republic of China
SALT	Strategic Arms Limitation Talks
SAM	surface-to-air missile
SBIRS	Space-Based Infrared System
SCC	Standing Consultative Commission
SDI	Strategic Defense Initiative
SLBM	submarine-launched ballistic missile
SM	standard missile
SRBM	short-range ballistic missile
SSBN	strategic ballistic missile submarine
START	Strategic Arms Reduction Treaties
THAAD	Theater High-Altitude Area Defense
TMD	theater missile defenses
TOM	target object map
UAV	unmanned aerial vehicle
UEWR	upgraded early warning radar
UHF	ultra-high frequency
UNSCOM	United Nations Special Commission
WESTPAC	West Pacific Missile Defense Architecture
WMD	weapons of mass destruction
XBR	X-band radar

Introduction

JAMES J. WIRTZ

The United States is developing missile defenses that will offer some protection against ballistic missile warheads launched against the American
homeland.[1] While the goals of these limited defenses are modest, the U.S.
effort to deploy a national missile defense (NMD) constitutes a major departure in American defense strategy.[2] Since the signing of the Anti-
Ballistic Missile (ABM) Treaty by the United States and the Soviet Union
in 1972, the United States has refrained from developing an active defense capability against ballistic missiles and has continued to rely on the
threat of retaliation to deter missile attacks. Faced with emerging threats
produced by the proliferation of long-range ballistic missiles that can be
armed with chemical, biological, or nuclear warheads, however, the idea
of using active defenses to destroy warheads launched against America
and to bolster deterrence is gaining domestic political support within
the United States. Americans can expect to have some form of national
missile defense by the end of the decade.

There is no shortage of scholarly or political interest in the issue of deploying missile defenses and revising the ABM Treaty, with most attention being directed toward issues of *immediate* concern. Debates focus
on whether a particular weapon is "treaty compliant," whether or not
new weapons will actually work against current or hypothetical threats,
and when domestic political forces might coalesce and overcome obstacles to the creation of a national missile defense. It is virtually impossi-

ble, however, to move beyond first principles. Seemingly simple questions (for example, is the airborne laser under development by the U.S. Air Force treaty compliant?) can elicit a plethora of plausible answers based on likely versus maximum weapon performance; broad versus narrow interpretations of the ABM Treaty; or references to judgments offered by Department of Defense, congressional, arms control, allied, or even Russian sources. The restrictions created by the ABM Treaty have been debated so heavily by individuals, epistemic communities, institutions, and governments with competing normative and political agendas that a consensus no longer exists about the very meaning of the Treaty itself.[3] Since nearly everything related to NMD is disputed, technical analyses of an evolving strategic balance, or scholarly discussions of the way the Treaty might be interpreted to better fit today's international circumstances or emerging technologies, cannot resolve the debate over whether or not the United States should deploy missile defenses.[4]

To take a fresh look at the missile defense issue, we asked the contributors to our volume to assume that the United States will deploy missile defenses and that it has either modified or abandoned the ABM Treaty. We then asked them to give their best estimates of how these changes might transform the international strategic landscape, affecting policies and politics globally. By assuming that the United States will soon deploy missile defenses, we do not suggest that critics of U.S. NMD are necessarily incorrect, that new technologies will work flawlessly, or that only positive developments will flow from the deployment of missile defenses. Instead, we believe that by asking our contributors to imagine that a deployment decision had already occurred, we can begin to identify the unanticipated or unintended consequences of a U.S. decision to deploy NMD.

WHY WORRY ABOUT THE ANTI-BALLISTIC MISSILE TREATY?

Much consternation has been aroused by the possibility of U.S. deployment of even modest national missile defenses, which necessarily would involve U.S. modification, violation, or abrogation of the ABM Treaty. Ratified by the U.S. Senate by a vote of 88 to 2, the Treaty entered into force on 3 October 1972. The ABM Treaty prohibits the deployment of nationwide missile defenses or systems that might serve as components of national missile defenses. The ABM Treaty was not the first Cold War arms control treaty. The Partial Test Ban Treaty, Nuclear Non-Proliferation Treaty, and Outer Space Treaty all had been negotiated by the early 1970s. The ABM Treaty, however, emerged as the cornerstone of the evolving Soviet-American arms control regime. The Strategic Arms Limitation Talks (SALT) of the 1970s and the ongoing Strategic Arms Reduction Treaties (START) are based on the premise that strategic nuclear forces will not have to overcome defenses if deterrent threats are executed. Russians and Americans still hold each other's cities hostage to strategic nuclear attack, even though the political motivations to launch a strike evaporated with the end of the Cold War.

The ABM Treaty was revolutionary because it reflected the controversial idea that cooperation with an adversary might produce mutually beneficial results, in this instance conserving economic resources and preserving crisis stability (that is, minimizing incentives to use nuclear weapons first during a crisis). Opponents of strategic defenses argued that a decision to move forward with an effort to protect the American or Soviet population from nuclear missile attack would set off an arms race between offensive and defensive systems that would be expensive and unlikely to work. They suggested that after the expenditure of enormous resources to build the offensive forces necessary to overcome an ABM system, this offense-defense arms race would simply return to a situation of mutual assured destruction, albeit one at extraordinarily high force levels. In other words, defenses would never be able to eliminate the threat posed by the opponent's land-based or sea-based missiles; cities would remain hostages to destruction because opponents could be counted on to do everything in their power to overcome newly constructed missile defenses. This was a marked change from traditional thinking, which held that strong defenses raised the cost of war, thereby reducing both the fear of surprise attack and motivations to attack preemptively. Critics also charged that this arms race would be unstable in crises: at various points in the competition, one side or the other might believe that they could obtain a significant military advantage if they used nuclear weapons first. The ban on missile defenses has thus taken on a privileged position in American strategic thought and policy. The ABM Treaty not only is viewed by many as a triumph of arms control but as evidence that ideas about fighting, winning, or prevailing in a nuclear war are hare-brained.

The strategic importance of the ABM Treaty, however, has waned with the end of the Cold War. On the one hand, few believe that a renewed Russian-American nuclear arms race is likely. On the other hand, a new threat is emerging. Nations and groups hostile to the Unites States, so-called "rogue states," are acquiring long-range missiles and attempting to equip them with chemical, biological, or nuclear warheads. The issue has become a political hot potato. The November 1995 national intelligence estimate "Emerging Missile Threats to North America During the Next Fifteen Years" predicted that new missile threats to the forty-eight contiguous states and Canada would not emerge before 2010 and that U.S. intelligence would be able to detect missile development programs long before missiles were deployed. These estimates were proved mistaken when the U.S. intelligence community apparently was caught by surprise by North Korea's 1998 launch of a three-stage Taepo Dong missile. That same year, a bipartisan Commission to Assess the Ballistic Missile Threat, headed by Donald Rumsfeld, now Secretary of Defense in the first Bush administration, painted a highly alarming picture of the proliferation problem. The Rumsfeld Commission identified new threats from Iran, Iraq, North Korea, China, and even Russia (in terms of exporting missile technology). The Commission further suggested that the United States could face new missile threats with little warning.

While the ABM Treaty remains important to both domestic and international audiences for its symbolic and political value, emerging threats are beginning to undermine the strategic logic behind the Treaty. The Treaty stands as an early and critical achievement of the U.S. arms control community (an informal coalition that includes academics, bureaucrats, elected officials, members of the U.S. armed forces, and policy activists). Many members of this community are unwilling to tamper with the Treaty because to them it symbolizes the benefits of a cooperative approach to international security. Even though it might be preferable to start from scratch and negotiate a treaty suited to today's circumstances, for them it would be unthinkable to redraft this diplomatic milestone to suit current tastes.[5]

The Treaty also serves as a sort of political litmus test to gauge the degree of international acceptance of any U.S. decision to deploy national missile defenses. If the Treaty can be modified to accommodate U.S. missile deployments, then a U.S. national missile defense might prove far less destabilizing than critics charge. A new multilateral treaty, which might include efforts to curb missile proliferation, could even signal the start of a new, more cooperative effort to deal with the spread of long-range missiles armed with nuclear, chemical, and biological warheads. Alternatively, if the ABM Treaty is abandoned, it will indicate that all concerned now consider it prudent to end cooperative efforts to integrate missile defenses into their national strategies. It would reflect an increasing turn toward unilateralism not only on the part of the United States, as most critics of NMD point out, but also on the part of Russian leaders. Additionally, an end to the ABM Treaty could be interpreted as a consequence, not a cause, of changes that have occurred in the world since the end of the Cold War. If the U.S. backed away from the Treaty, it would indicate not only that the Russian-American strategic balance no longer was the primary driver of U.S. nuclear policy but that emerging missile and proliferation threats had come to take center stage in U.S. defense planning. An American decision to deploy defenses in the absence of Treaty constraints would mark a fundamental departure from Cold War policy and indicate that new forces were beginning to shape world politics.

THE POLITICS OF ESTIMATING CONSEQUENCES

Determined critics and advocates of NMD deployment often appear certain about what will happen if the United States deploys missile defenses. For instance, critics suggest that missile defense cannot be achieved with today's technologies and that U.S. officials will realize this at the worst possible time—during a crisis, when those defenses are put to the test. For some critics, defenses are all cost and no benefit. They charge that missile defense produces arms races and alliance acrimony or simply will not work.[6] By contrast, NMD supporters highlight benefits while downplaying costs and technical uncertainties. For example, they suggest that the costs of NMD would be forgotten if the system stopped an accidentally launched missile from hitting an American city.

One-sided estimates are unrealistic. At a minimum, they ignore the opportunity costs involved both in deploying and in not deploying missile defenses. Such commentaries often are based on political rhetoric and lack even rudimentary analysis. Those involved in political advocacy feel no compulsion to explain the downside of their policies to their audience. Yet rarely do public policies produce consequences that are all good or all bad. At most, one can say that some course of action will produce more good than harm, but there is always a price to be paid for whatever course of action is taken. Policies inevitably have multiple effects, most of them unintended or unanticipated.[7]

Two important observations suggest that it might be unusually difficult to predict the consequences of deploying national missile defense or altering the ABM Treaty. First, because the superpowers agreed to limit missile defenses, the ABM Treaty constituted a *de facto* global ban on missile defense. The Treaty's effects reached across the entire international community. Once the United States and the Soviet Union had decided not to deploy missile defenses, it was unlikely that their allies would have the political will, to say nothing of economic or technical resources, to develop defensive systems. Many governments based their foreign and defense policies on the absence of missile defenses. British, French, and Chinese leaders, for example, could more easily decide the appropriate size of their offensive missile force, knowing that they would have to penetrate only a very limited Soviet missile defense around Moscow. However, the efforts of so-called rogue states to acquire long-range missiles are encouraged by banning significant missile defenses. The North Korean decision to produce a limited number of long-range missiles, for instance, can be well justified only in the absence of missile defenses.

Two decades ago, Kenneth Waltz, a prominent political scientist, explained that one of the consequences of bipolarity (the presence of only two superpowers) was a high degree of "international management" and predictability in world affairs.[8] This clearly was the case in terms of strategic defenses. Soviet and American leaders agreed to live with mutual assured destruction so as to avoid an expensive arms race between offensive and defensive systems. Other states have been free riders on the absence of strategic defenses ever since. With the Cold War long over, however, the United States has become more sensitive to the costs of preserving this global regime banning missile defenses, especially when small, hostile regimes brandish long-range missiles armed with chemical, biological, or nuclear warheads. Whether or not growing

American disenchantment with the ABM Treaty reflects a "unipolar moment" of American global dominance or an increasingly multipolar world is a question best answered in hindsight. But the Cold War regime banning missile defenses is under pressure.

This leads to the second observation. Because the ABM Treaty has affected strategic relationships and policies across the international community, altering the Treaty will produce systemic effects.[9] Systems are said to have "emergent properties": the whole has fundamentally different qualities from the sum of its parts. Introducing defenses into strategic relationships might change the general tenor of world politics.[10] In place of deterrence, offense-defense arms races might spring up globally, creating a hellish world of crisis instability and small nuclear wars. Alternatively, missile defenses might initiate a transition away from deterrence based on mutual vulnerability to missile attack and towards a global strategic defense regime or other cooperative national security policies. Because most states have responded in some manner to the presence of the ABM Treaty, their collective behavior creates a global context for strategic interaction. Alter the Treaty significantly, and this global strategic context will change. But in what direction?

Systems are composed of interconnected elements. When these interconnections are dense, system effects can defeat purposeful behavior. This type of outcome was clearly on the minds of many of our contributors. For example, several note that it is within the realm of possibility that Chinese or Russian officials, angered by a unilateral American move to deploy missile defenses, could provide other states with the advanced technology necessary to overcome limited U.S. defenses. Such a reaction could leave the United States effectively facing more incoming warheads after NMD deployment than it faced before deployment—clearly an unintended and undesirable consequence. Moreover, interconnections can make a system resistant to change, and that resistance can lead to instability or cascading effects when change does occur.[11] Analysts who worry that missile defense will produce arms races and crisis instability, or foster missile proliferation, clearly are worried that missile defenses will be destabilizing. By contrast, analysts who expect that NMD will reduce proliferation incentives or strengthen deterrence believe that missile defenses will constrain the options available to other states, resulting in greater security.

A systems perspective highlights the fact that the ABM Treaty, for better or worse, has become an integral part of the strategic landscape. It in-
fluences U.S. foreign and defense policy in ways that are difficult to discern even for policymakers and experts. Because it has been a cornerstone
of U.S. strategic planning for so long, altering the ban on strategic defenses
is likely to produce myriad unintended or unanticipated consequences.

WHICH NATIONAL MISSILE DEFENSE?

Any effort to estimate the effects of missile defense deployment on the
ABM Treaty and worldwide strategic relationships would confront an immediate obstacle. There is considerable uncertainty about the size and capability of the missile defense that eventually will be deployed by the
United States. President Clinton endorsed no definitive NMD plans in the
final months of his presidency. It was unlikely that his preferences would
have survived long in the next administration in any case. During the
2000 presidential election, George W. Bush described his vision of a robust
and far-reaching missile defense system: "It is time to leave the Cold War
behind. America must build effective missile defenses, based on the best
available options, at the earliest possible date. Our missile defense must be
designed to protect all 50 states—and our friends and allies and deployed
forces overseas—from missile attacks by rogue nations, or accidental
launches."[12] Indeed, debate about NMD and the relevance of the ABM
Treaty to U.S. national security can be expected to continue long after the
Bush administration announces specific plans to deploy missile defenses.
Given this evolving policy and political milieu, estimates of the impact of
U.S. missile defense deployment must consider a range of policy options.

We have attempted to overcome this obstacle by asking our contributors to explore the consequences of three missile deployment and treaty
options. The options vary in several ways. First, deployment options differ in terms of the number of incoming warheads they can destroy and
their ability to defend American territory regardless of the direction of
the incoming attack. Second, they vary in terms of where interceptors
are deployed. Third, they vary in terms of their *prima facie* impact on
existing strategic relationships. Some systems do not significantly interfere with the ability of great powers to target the United States; others

are so extensive that they might even call into question the situation of mutual assured destruction that still exists between the United States and Russia. Fourth, the options reflect different international political climates. Minimal deployments are assumed to occur in a relatively benign diplomatic setting. More ambitious missile defense deployments are assumed to produce international acrimony—in one case, leading to the abandonment of the ABM Treaty.

One final caveat is in order. Although the options considered here are based on policies under consideration or systems under development, they reflect general types of missile defenses that are not entirely dependent on specific systems. As several of our contributors note in their chapters, these options reflect an American perception of missile defenses because they vary substantially in terms of the degree of protection they provide to U.S. territory, as well as in the degree to which Americans are willing to act unilaterally to achieve their security objectives via these options. Assessing the impact on American security alone might not be the best way to measure the international impact of U.S. NMD, but it does provide a way to characterize missile defenses that will remain relevant in the years ahead. Our chapter authors sometimes found it necessary to deviate from the basic plan described here, particularly in those chapters dealing with foreign reactions to American NMD deployment. These deviations imply that common assumptions among Americans about international reactions to U.S. decisions may not be comprehensive enough to capture the nuances of thinking outside the United States.

Threshold Capability 1:
Limited Defense in a Cooperative Setting

The first scenario we consider is a "threshold" deployment of between 20 and 100 interceptors in a new base located in central Alaska, which could be put into place fairly quickly (i.e., sometime before 2010). This deployment option is similar to the initial operational capability of the missile deployment plan (dubbed the "C1" option) advanced by President Clinton in the last years of his administration. Although Clinton's C1 option evolved to include 100 interceptors, we asked our contributors to focus on 20 interceptors as the minimal initial operating capability to be deployed by the

10   James J. Wirtz

United States. The deployment also would include construction of a new X-band radar and three new command and control facilities, and would require upgrading five existing early warning radars, including the U.S. early warning radar located at Fylingdales Moor, United Kingdom.[13] C1 also would use two new space-based infrared early warning satellites (SBIRS-High) for early detection of missile launches. Depending on the firing doctrine used in the defense (the number of interceptors that are fired at each incoming warhead), the lowest-level, threshold system could engage a maximum of somewhere between five and ten warheads flying towards the United States over the North Pacific Ocean.

A threshold defense deployment would provide the United States with a capability to protect itself against an accidental missile launch or very small, deliberate attacks that approach U.S. territory from the northwest. In other words, this deployment option poses no realistic threat to the Russian or Chinese ability to strike the United States with warheads carried by intercontinental ballistic missiles (ICBMs). This option would provide the United States with a significant denial capability, however, against an emerging North Korean missile threat to American territory—especially if combined with the preemptive use of U.S. conventional precision-guided weapons to destroy the majority of North Korean missiles before they are launched.

Although threshold defenses provide very limited capability against missile attack, they nevertheless pose a fundamental challenge to the ABM Treaty. Estimating the impact of any NMD deployment scheme on the ABM Treaty is highly contingent on the exact capability and location of the missile defense deployed. Moreover, the way individual Treaty articles, amendments, negotiating records and operational histories are used to interpret the interaction between defensive missile systems and the Treaty greatly affects judgments about how the Treaty would need to change to accommodate a specific system.[14] It would be safe to assume, however, that Article I of the Treaty (which prohibits defense of one's entire national territory) would have to be amended to allow national missile defense. Although the Treaty allows the deployment of a single missile defense site, it specifies that defenses need to be situated near national capitals or ICBM deployment areas. Thus, Article III (which limits where defensive systems can be deployed) would have to be amended to allow construction of the Alaskan missile defense site and the new X-band radar on Shemya Island, Alaska. Articles V and VI of the Treaty also would have to be modified to permit the use of space-based sensors in the missile defense architecture (SBIRS-High and the terminal-guidance sensors on the hit-to-kill interceptors) because they are based on "other physical principles," prohibited by the Treaty. Article VI(a) would require modification because the booster for the planned NMD interceptor is also used for commercial purposes, and the Treaty forbids giving non-NMD systems the ability to intercept strategic missiles.

Revising the ABM Treaty to allow these limited missile defenses would create some tense moments in Russian-American relations. But since a threshold defense would not present a credible threat to the Russian nuclear deterrent (even at the reduced force levels envisioned in a START III agreement), Russian leaders probably would see it as being in their national interest to continue to constrain U.S. defense deployments in an arms control regime. Ideally, a bilateral decision to revise the ABM Treaty could lead to improved Russian-American relations if the give and take over NMD led to greater security cooperation. However, it could also lead to deadlock and acrimony. Both sides would look to their negotiating partner to compromise over NMD deployments and might interpret a lack of progress in negotiations as evidence of some fundamental, potentially dangerous departure in strategic policy. This book assumes that cooler heads will prevail. Russian and American negotiators will find some way to accommodate the deployment of a modest interceptor force within the arms control regime limiting strategic defenses.

Capability 3 Plus:
Enhanced Defenses and the Limits of Cooperation

The second scenario we consider is more speculative, even though it also is based on a plan proposed by the Clinton administration (the C3 plan) and on systems that are already under development. It encompasses several systems that realistically could not be deployed before 2011, and would provide a more robust defensive capability than the Threshold C1 system. A C3 Plus-type deployment might be a logical answer to critics who charge that a C1 deployment comes with all of the drawbacks and few of the potential benefits of missile defenses. It also includes systems that were not necessarily intended to defend American territory but that could be included in U.S. missile defenses to create a layered defense or to supplement NMD systems in a crisis. For example, it might be possible to integrate the Navy Theater-Wide missile defense system into a national missile defense to increase its ability to defeat a missile attack. Barring some unprecedented scientific or engineering breakthrough, this C3-Plus plan probably constitutes the most extensive defense the United States would be physically and fiscally able to deploy over the next fifteen years.

Capability 3 was proposed by the Clinton administration in 1999 as a long-term option; the C3 Plus option we describe here is based on this Clinton proposal. These enhanced defenses would include 250 interceptors based in Alaska and in Grand Forks, North Dakota. Grand Forks basing would improve the ability of the system to protect against missiles approaching the United States from the northeast and would help provide overall coverage of the United States. The system would include a total of nine new X-band radars, upgrades to six early warning radars, and construction of five command and control facilities. The system would rely primarily on a constellation of five SBIRS-High and twenty-four SBIRS-Low warhead tracking satellites to track missiles in their boost phase and incoming warheads as they reenter the atmosphere. Placed into low-earth orbit, the infrared sensors aboard SBIRS-Low would look upward to track the hot missile warheads against the cold expanse of space. If all worked as planned, SBIRS-High would provide early warning information to U.S. strategic forces, national missile defenses and theater missile defenses, passing information to the SBIRS-Low satellite constellation and ground-based missile radars. SBIRS-Low would help distinguish incoming warheads from advanced countermeasures and create a quick estimate of the warhead trajectory, allowing the C3 Plus to fire its first salvo of interceptors more quickly than the threshold C1 system. These ground-based interceptors would be supplemented by the U.S. Air Force's airborne laser and the Navy's Aegis-radar-based Theater-Wide missile defense system. If moved close enough to an opponent's missile field (e.g., off the coast of North Korea), the airborne laser could destroy missiles while still in their boost phase. Navy warships also could be deployed off America's shores to bolster defenses along likely threat axes. Given expected intercept rates, C3 Plus might be able to stop upwards of 100 warheads from reaching the United States.

U.S. deployment of a C3 Plus system would have a significant impact on the international strategic landscape. C3 Plus would defend the United States from attacks launched from a variety of directions and would "raise the bar" for states interested in targeting U.S. urban areas for ICBM attack. Small states such as North Korea, Iran, and Iraq would be forced to look for alternative delivery methods to attack the United States. Without outside technical or financial help, it would be unlikely that these small states could build or launch enough warheads and countermeasures to penetrate this system. Similarly, Chinese leaders could no longer free ride on the Russian-American agreement to forego missile defenses. They would face significant technical and quantitative challenges in any effort to create a secure second-strike force directed against the United States.

The enhanced capability of the C3 Plus system would come at a significant price in terms of arms control. In addition to the changes made to accommodate a C1 deployment, Article III of the Treaty would have to be amended to allow for construction of two ground-based interceptor sites, and Article V would have to be amended to allow air-based and sea-based NMD. Because SBIRS-Low can act as a missile defense engagement radar, its use would require modification of Articles III, IV, and V.

Revising the ABM Treaty to permit a C3 Plus deployment probably would strain Russian-American cooperation in arms control to the breaking point. Although it would still be in the Russian interest to constrain U.S. missile defense deployments in an arms control agreement, critics might correctly charge that a C3 Plus system would provide the United States with a "break-out" capability. In other words, by quickly adding interceptors to an existing defense architecture, U.S. forces could greatly reduce Russian second-strike capabilities against the United States. No matter what the final outcome, Russian-American treaty negotiations to allow a C3 Plus deployment would be highly acrimonious. Even if an agreement about the Treaty were finally reached, Russian leaders would feel that they had been strong-armed by their American counterparts. At a minimum, they would communicate to a global audience that U.S. leaders were unilaterally endangering international stability in order to achieve their selfish objectives.

Unlimited Defenses, Unconstrained By Treaty

The third scenario our contributors consider assumes U.S. withdrawal from the ABM Treaty. Defense deployments would no longer be constrained by an arms control regime. In this scenario, we posit that efforts at revising the Treaty have failed. The failure might have come about because highly robust defenses were necessary and simply could no longer be accommodated by the existing Treaty. Alternatively, Russian and American negotiators might somehow have overplayed their hands, expecting that the other side would compromise rather than risk an end to the regime constraining strategic defenses. This scenario also assumes that any breakdown in negotiations will be acrimonious. The opportunity to increase Russian-American cooperation by creating a revised arms control regime is unlikely to emerge under these circumstances.

American officials then would be free to deploy whatever weapons or sensors they considered necessary or technologically feasible. But given the long lead times involved, it might be nearly two decades before revolutionary kinds of systems—for example, the space-based laser—could be deployed. In all probability, U.S. leaders would attempt to deploy the most robust defense possible, as soon as possible, otherwise why would they be eager to eliminate the ABM Treaty? It is difficult to say, however, how robust those defenses might actually be, given the long time-frame required to deploy even limited defenses based on relatively proven technologies.

THE WAY AHEAD

Our examination of the issues surrounding U.S. deployment of national missile defenses and the effort to modify the ABM Treaty unfolds in three stages. In Part I, our contributors examine the background of today's debates. Kerry Kartchner explores the origins of the ABM Treaty by identifying alternative views of the motives, interests, and objectives that drove the United States and the Soviet Union to the negotiating table in the early 1970s. Kartchner suggests that these attitudes will continue to shape Russian and American approaches to treaty revision. Robert Joseph identifies the new strategic challenges and domestic political developments that are pushing American policymakers toward deployment of missile defenses and revision of the existing arms control regime. His analysis suggests that missile defense is really a matter of politics and strategy, not technology, and serves warning that missile deployments or Treaty revisions in the absence of a new strategic vision for global stability are exercises in futility.

The construction of missile defenses in the late 1960s seemed beyond the limits of existing technology. Today, a variety of systems based on multiple technologies hold out the promise of providing highly effective defenses, especially against limited attacks. Dennis Ward identifies these new technologies and systems. He also explains how technology itself—sensors, command and control networks, and increasingly capable computer and communication systems—is eroding the rationale behind the ABM Treaty in ways never envisioned by its originators.

In Part II, our contributors explore the systemic consequences of missile defense deployment and modification of the ABM regime. Michael O'Hanlon describes the various types of NMD systems that are under consideration and their domestic political proponents. He also identifies how American political alignments are likely to form behind various missile defense options. Richard Harknett explores how U.S. deployment of missile defense will affect the global arms race and crisis stability. He explains how the nature of deterrent relationships and the general tenor of international relations might change following missile defense deployments. He also identifies the types of missile defenses and treaty regimes that would enhance U.S. national security in the years ahead. Julian Schofield explores the future of arms control in the aftermath of a U.S. decision to deploy missile defenses. He also identifies the circumstances in which a bilateral approach to Treaty modification would be more productive than multilateral negotiations.

In Part III, we explore regional responses to U.S. missile defense deployment. Will U.S. missile deployments have a domino effect in terms of regional rivalries, leading to a proliferation of missile defenses or offensive arms races? Ivo Daalder and James Goldgeier explore Russian reactions to the missile defense issue and the way Moscow likely will approach negotiating changes to the ABM Treaty. Bradley Roberts examines the Chinese reaction to NMD, especially in terms of China's ongoing effort to modernize its strategic nuclear forces, and its relations with Taiwan. Timothy Hoyt suggests several ways missile defenses might affect the enduring Indo-Pakistani rivalry. He points out the unintended international consequences of potential Chinese reactions to U.S. decisions, and the impact they would have on Indian policies. Charles Ball identifies allied reactions to missile defenses, focusing on Western Europe, Japan, South Korea, Taiwan, and Israel.

In the Conclusion, Jeff Larsen captures the crosscutting themes that emerge in this volume, and draws conclusions regarding the likely result of the American debate over missile defenses.

NOTES

1. For a concise description of the Clinton administration's plans for national missile defense, see "Remarks of the Honorable Walter B. Slocombe, Under Secretary of Defense for Policy, to the Center for Strategic and International Studies Statesmen's Forum, November 1999," published in *Comparative Strategy*, Vol. 19, No. 2, 167–174.

2. The estimated cost will be approximately $1 billion per year, according to the Congressional Budget Office. See *Budgetary and Technical Implications of the Administration's Plan for National Missile Defense* (Washington, D.C.: Congressional Budget Office, April 2000), 2.

3. Michael O'Hanlon, "Star Wars Strikes Back," *Foreign Affairs*, Vol. 78, No. 6, 68–82. The argument that the Soviets (now Russians) have systematically violated the ABM Treaty to construct a robust national missile defense has reappeared in support of abandoning the Treaty. See William T. Lee, "The ABM Treaty Was Dead on Arrival," *Comparative Strategy*, Vol. 19, No. 2, 145–165.

4. Dean A. Wilkening, *Ballistic Missile Defense: How Much Is Enough? How Much Is Too Much?* Adelphi Paper No. 334 (London: International Institute for Strategic Studies, 2000).

5. Several government contractors and officials remarked in interviews conducted in the fall of 1999 that given the enormous volume of documentation involving the Treaty, it was nearly impossible to reach defini-

tive judgements about what was permitted by the ABM Treaty regime. They suggested that under these circumstances it was better to start from scratch. Interviews by James J. Wirtz and Jeffrey A. Larsen, November 1999, Washington, D.C.

6. Stephen W. Young, for example, sees only a downside to national missile defense: "By building national missile defenses, the U.S. may stimulate new threats, unraveling the entire post–Cold War structure for controlling nuclear and missile technology and weapons. U.S. withdrawal from the ABM Treaty would jeopardize four nonproliferation and disarmament treaties—the NPT, the CTBT, and START I and II—as well as the potential for START III, for even deeper cuts, and for the ban on fissile material production. Russian officials have even hinted that the Intermediate-range Nuclear Forces (INF) Treaty, which completely eliminated nuclear-tipped missiles with a range of 500–5,500 kilometers, could come into question. Prospects for mutual, cooperative steps to reduce nuclear dangers outside the treaty process would also diminish sharply." Stephen W. Young, *Pushing the Limits: The Decision on National Missile Defense* (Washington, D.C.: Coalition to Reduce Nuclear Danger, April 2000), 25.

7. Robert Jervis, *System Effects: Complexity in Political and Social Life* (Princeton: Princeton University Press, 1997); and Charles Perrow, *Normal Accidents* (New York: Basic Books, 1984).

8. Kenneth Waltz, *Theory of International Politics* (Reading, Mass.: Addison-Wesley, 1979).

9. This discussion is based on Jervis, *System Effects.*

10. Because of a lingering bipolar mind-set, U.S. policymakers often fail to consider the impact of their actions on other states when it comes to issues of nuclear weapons and strategic deterrence. See Brad Roberts, Robert A. Manning, and Ronald N. Montaperto, "China: The Forgotten Nuclear Power," *Foreign Affairs,* Vol. 79, No. 4, 53–63.

11. I have labeled these cascading effects elsewhere as nuclear multilateralism. See James J. Wirtz, "Beyond Bipolarity: Prospects for Nuclear Stability after the Cold War," in T. V. Paul, Richard Harknett, and James J. Wirtz (eds.), *The Absolute Weapon Revisited: Nuclear Arms and the Emerging International Order* (Ann Arbor: University of Michigan Press, 1998), 137–165.

12. "New Leadership on National Security," speech by George W. Bush, Washington, D.C., 23 May 2000. Available on line at http://www.georgewbush.com/News.asp?FormMode=SP&id=2 (accessed 9 February 2001). After he became president, Bush reiterated this vision in a major speech on 1 May 2001. The text of the speech is available on line at http://www.washingtonpost.com/wp-srv/onpolitics/transcripts/bushtext050101.htm.

13. The other radars are located at Clear, Alaska; Beale Air Force Base, California; Cape Cod, Massachusetts; and Thule, Greenland.

14. For a discussion of how various NMD systems would require changes in the existing ABM Treaty regime, see Dean A. Wilkening, "Amending the ABM Treaty," *Survival,* Vol. 42, No. 1 (Spring 2000), 29–45.

PART ONE

The ABM Regime

1

Origins of the ABM Treaty

KERRY M. KARTCHNER

ENCOUNTER AT GLASSBORO

The United States first proposed negotiating limits on anti-ballistic missile (ABM) systems at the summit meeting between Prime Minister Aleksei N. Kosygin and President Lyndon B. Johnson at Glassboro, New Jer-
sey, on 23 June 1967. U.S. officials had discovered that the Soviet Union
was deploying a substantial ABM system around Moscow, and U.S. Secretary of Defense Robert S. McNamara was convinced that the United
States would be forced to respond by deploying additional strategic offensive weapons. McNamara had just won a series of political battles
with the Air Force and Navy to curtail growth of the U.S. strategic arsenal, and he was loath to respond to the new Soviet ABM challenge with
an offensive missile buildup.[1] He concluded that the only alternative to
spending billions of dollars on a pointless offensive arms buildup was to
convince the Soviets that ABM deployments were destabilizing, and to
get them to agree to strict limits on defenses. Accordingly, he persuaded
President Johnson to place the ABM issue high on the agenda for the
summit meeting at Glassboro.

Johnson at first tried to convince Kosygin that limiting defenses could
help head off an arms race in offensive weapons. When his own efforts
failed, Johnson invited McNamara to explain the U.S. rationale for wanting to place limits on defenses. McNamara proceeded to lecture Kosygin

on the inexorable action-reaction dynamic that he believed would govern the emerging U.S.-Soviet strategic arms competition. He asserted that if the Soviet Union deployed an ABM system, the United States would be forced to respond, not by matching the Soviets' ABM system with one of its own but by increasing its arsenal of offensive weapons to overcome whatever Soviet defenses were deployed. McNamara insisted that the United States and the Soviet Union had to agree to limit defenses to head off this senseless arms race. Evidently infuriated by McNamara's indictment of defenses, Kosygin "absolutely exploded," according to later recollections by McNamara. "The blood rose into his face, his veins swelled, he pounded the table and he said . . . 'Defense is moral, offense is immoral!'"[2]

Notwithstanding this rebuttal at Glassboro, a year later Soviet leaders reversed their position and called for negotiations with the United States to limit ABM systems. When those negotiations commenced in 1969 under the rubric of the Strategic Arms Limitation Talks (SALT), the United States and the Soviet Union had completely traded positions: Soviet negotiators focused steadfastly on limiting ABM systems, whereas the United States put top priority on negotiating a halt to a massive Soviet strategic offensive arms buildup. Eventually the two sides produced a formal treaty, signed on 26 May 1972 in Moscow, placing strict limits on ABM systems but relegating limits on offensive weapons to a temporary executive agreement that greatly favored the Soviets.

What had transpired since the Soviet rejection of ABM limits at Glassboro in June 1967 to bring about such a change in the positions of the two sides? What did the Soviet Union hope to gain from the negotiations to limit ABM systems? Had Soviet leaders come to accept McNamara's view that defenses were futile and destabilizing? What were U.S. objectives? This chapter suggests that the reversal in positions evident in late 1968, and the Treaty that ultimately resulted from the Soviet decision to accept limits on its own ABM system, were the culmination of two different roads to the ABM Treaty. The courses these separate roads followed were determined by each side's strategic culture, domestic and foreign policy objectives, institutional imperatives, and political circumstances. This chapter explores the conceptual and historical context of these two negotiating paths.

THE MAKING OF THE ABM TREATY

The Soviets were the first to begin a substantial ABM research and development program, and the first to deploy an operational ABM system. The Soviets began ABM development efforts in the early to mid-1950s. Preparation of ABM deployment sites around Moscow was detected by U.S. intelligence in late 1962. In November 1964, long-range, nuclear-tipped Galosh ABM interceptor missiles were paraded through Red Square.[3] By early 1967, it was becoming difficult for U.S. officials to ignore the fact that the Soviet Union had embarked on deploying a major ABM system around both Leningrad and Moscow. The Soviets intended eventually to surround other major Russian cities with ABM interceptor missiles, and some estimated that the Soviet territorial ABM system ultimately would consist of up to 10,000 interceptor missiles.[4] It was in the face of this looming challenge that McNamara and Johnson went to Glassboro and pleaded for negotiations to limit these deployments.

In the aftermath of the failure to interest the Soviets in mutually limiting ABM systems, and despite his own reservations regarding deploying an American ABM counterpart, Secretary of Defense McNamara announced the administration's intention to seek Congressional approval to begin deploying the Sentinel ABM system. In a speech to the editors of United Press International in San Francisco on 18 September 1967, McNamara explained at length why he believed that the United States should not deploy ABM systems, and summarized his views of assured destruction deterrence, the dangers of an action-reaction arms race, and the destabilizing qualities of ABM systems. Near the end of his speech, McNamara cited "marginal grounds" for proceeding with a "light deployment" of the Sentinel ABM system. He noted that the system would be relatively inexpensive; would help discourage nuclear weapons proliferation; would provide some defense of Minuteman ICBMs, thus allowing the United States to forego "a much more costly expansion of that force;" and would give the U.S. population some protection against the accidental or deliberate launch of an ICBM (by, say, China).[5] It went without saying that the decision to deploy Sentinel had the added benefit of defusing the "emerging ABM gap" as a potentially explosive issue in the 1968 presidential campaign.

Despite these announced U.S. plans, the Soviets remained uninterested in talks to limit ABM systems. On 24 June 1968, after a lengthy and divisive debate, the U.S. Senate approved funding for the Sentinel ABM system by just one vote. This action had an immediate impact on Soviet interest in ABM negotiations. Three days later the Soviets reversed their Glassboro stance and signaled readiness to begin discussions on ABM limitations as well as on constraints on offensive arms.[6] Formal agreement to hold the talks was announced on 19 August 1968.[7] The following day, Soviet armored columns invaded Czechoslovakia, and Johnson was compelled to cancel the talks. In view of the impending presidential elections, negotiations were deferred until after the new president was inaugurated.[8]

The Safeguard Program

The newly installed Nixon administration postponed any plans to begin arms talks with the Soviets until after it had made a thorough study of U.S. force posture, policy, and arms control. Upon completing this review, the administration agreed to seek strategic arms limitation talks with the Soviet Union, while at the same time pressing forward with a revamped plan for ABM deployments, under the name Safeguard.[9] President Nixon stated the following as objectives for the new ABM program:

- Protection of our land-based retaliatory forces against a direct attack by the Soviet Union.
- Defense of the American people against the kind of nuclear attack which Communist China is likely to be able to mount within the decade.
- Protection against the possibility of accidental attacks from any source.

Using criteria remarkably similar to those employed by the Clinton administration some thirty years later, Nixon stated that the program would be reviewed annually in light of (a) technical developments, (b) the evolution of the threat, and (c) the diplomatic context, including progress in any arms limitation talks. The primary difference between Safeguard and Sentinel was the new program's emphasis on protecting ICBM silos rather than population centers. The administration made it clear that Safeguard was intended primarily to provide a local defense of selected Minuteman missile sites and an area defense designed to protect bomber bases and command and control authorities, prompted in part by concerns that their survivability would soon be threatened by newly confirmed Soviet efforts to test and deploy multiple warheads on the SS-9 ICBM.[10] As an explanation for its having eschewed a population defense, the administration noted, "In view of the magnitude of the current Soviet missile threat to the United States, and the prospects of future growth in quantity and quality, we have concluded that a defense of our population against that threat is not now feasible."[11]

The Department of Defense provided a more elaborate list of considerations behind the decision to deploy the Safeguard ABM system, including:

- Continued Chinese progress in nuclear weapons deployment.
- The evolving and increasing Soviet offensive weapon threat.
- Technical progress and budgetary factors.
- The current international situation.
- A U.S. desire to place emphasis on strategic *defensive* systems rather than being forced to deploy additional *offensive* weapons.[12]

The administration also emphasized that the decision to deploy Safeguard was intended to underwrite the U.S. position in SALT: "An orderly, measured, flexible but ongoing Safeguard defense program will help maintain our relative positive position in SALT and improve the chances for a successful outcome."[13] This bargaining chip rationale would figure prominently in the campaign to win and sustain Congressional support for the Safeguard ABM program.

As part of a broad foreign policy of détente, on 11 June 1969, the Nixon administration extended an invitation to the Soviet Union to engage in preliminary discussions regarding the agenda for strategic arms control negotiations. After having first seemed anxious to hold talks with the United States, however, the Soviets now temporized, apparently awaiting the outcome of Congressional deliberations on the Safeguard program, which was encountering stiff opposition in the U.S. Senate. Opposition in the Senate was driven not only by technical doubts about the proposed system and concerns about its potentially negative impact on strategic stability and U.S.-Soviet relations but also by the unpopularity of the war in Vietnam, which had generated a backlash against all things military. Nevertheless, on 27 June 1969, the Senate Armed Services Committee approved a defense appropriation bill containing funds for Safeguard deployment. On the Senate floor, on 6 August 1969, amendments intended to delete or restrict the Safeguard funding portion of the defense bill were narrowly defeated, and the bill was passed. The House of Representatives later approved the legislation by a 3-to-1 majority, the Soviets relented, and on 25 October 1969, the Nixon administration announced that it had accepted a Soviet offer to begin preliminary strategic arms talks on 17 November.[14]

1969-1972: The SALT Negotiations

Once agreement to hold talks had been reached and the negotiations actually had actually begun, two key issues related to ABM confronted the delegates: What limits should be placed on ABM systems; and whether, and how, limits on offensive and defensive weapons should be linked.[15] The first round of talks was purely exploratory. Neither side tabled any formal proposals. Much to the surprise of the Americans, however, the Soviets suggested that the parties explore three ABM options: a total ban, a light deployment, and a dense defense of a specific area. Although they made no specific proposal, it became clear that they preferred the light deployment option. U.S. negotiators, recalling the Soviet reaction at Glassboro to the idea of limiting ABMs, were astonished that the Soviets were even interested in discussing such options. Indeed, the Soviets were "most eager" to discuss ABM limits, and contrary to expectations, seemed uninterested in any offensive weapons limits at all.[16]

When the next round of talks began in April 1970, the U.S. side tabled a proposal to limit ABM systems to a defense of National Command Authorities (NCA) only, by which was meant national capitals. The U.S. position also called for strict linkage of offensive and defensive weapon limits—that is, no ABM limits would be agreed to without an agreement on offensive limits. The Soviet negotiators, obviously under instructions to protect the Moscow ABM system and limit to the extent possible any other ABM deployments, accepted the NCA-only option "with amazing and totally unprecedented speed."[17] This left the U.S. negotiators in a quandary; they had made what Henry Kissinger later referred to as "a first-class blunder."[18] There was a fundamental inconsistency between the bargaining position adopted by the U.S. delegation in the arms talks and the ABM program approved and supported by Congress. Congress had approved a Safeguard program whose first phase involved the deployment of ABM systems designed to protect Minuteman ICBM fields—a program that would only later encompass a site to protect the national command authorities. Yet the U.S. position in SALT was to forego all but one ABM site to protect its NCA. Furthermore, Congress was unlikely to approve an NCA-only ABM program. This no doubt added to the appeal of this option to the Soviets, since if accepted and codified in a treaty, it would almost certainly have meant that the United States would end up with no ABM system at all, while legitimizing and preserving the Moscow ABM system then nearing completion. The awkwardness of the U.S. position was exploited by the Soviets, who dug in on the NCA-only position.

Anxious to extricate itself, the United States reconsidered its initial proposal and, when the next round of talks resumed in the summer of 1970, the Americans tabled a series of alternatives similar to those first presented by the Soviet delegation in the exploratory round the previous year, including a total ban, an NCA-only option, or an option providing for both an NCA site and an ICBM defense site (essentially formalizing the existing ABM programs of the two sides). The Soviets, however, continued to press for approval of the initial agreement on NCA defense, and showed little interest in either a total ban on ABM systems or limiting them to defense of ICBM silos. They also continued to reject U.S. attempts to link agreements on offensive and defensive weapons, and insisted that an agreement on ABMs must be reached before they would even discuss limits on offensive weapons.

Domestic disenchantment with Safeguard continued to accumulate, led by groups of scientists who were convinced that a large-scale ABM system designed to protect the U.S. population was technically infeasible, economically prohibitive, domestically wasteful, and dangerously destabilizing. This swelling resistance, and the intensity of opposition in Congress, convinced the Nixon administration to modify its negotiating position. The U.S. delegation subsequently tabled a position that would essentially codify the programs then being pursued in the United States and Russia respectively, permitting the United States to pursue the Minuteman ICBM protection aspect of Safeguard (or "hard point defense"), and allowing the Soviet Union to retain its Moscow NCA deployment. This would be accompanied by a freeze on offensive strategic weapon deployments.[19] In due course, the Soviet Union agreed to drop its NCA-only requirement, and the two governments jointly agreed to concentrate "on working out an agreement for the limitation of the deployment of anti-ballistic missile systems." They also agreed that, "together with concluding an agreement to limit ABMs, they will agree on certain measures with respect to the limitation of offensive strategic weapons."[20] This formulation meant that the two sides would achieve some form of agreement on defenses in parallel with an accord on offenses, and the delegations were instructed to fashion treaty language codifying this arrangement. Eventually, a formal and permanent treaty limiting ABMs was worked out, accompanied by a more limited, temporary executive agreement on offensive weapons (leaving a formal, comprehensive offensive arms agreement to SALT II negotiations). This package of documents, collectively referred to as the SALT I accords, was signed at a summit meeting in Moscow on 26 May 1972.

The ABM Treaty permits each side to have 100 launchers and interceptor missiles at each of two ABM sites. This was later reduced to one site for each side by the 1974 Protocol to the Treaty. The Treaty bans mobile and air-, sea-, and space-based ABM systems. It also places strict limits on the numbers and locations of ABM radars. It allows modernization of ABM systems within the Treaty's numerical and qualitative limits. It prohibits transfer of ABM systems or components to other countries, and deployment of ABM systems or components outside each party's national territory. It allows amendments to be proposed by either side; and it establishes a Standing Consultative Commission, chartered to "consider possible changes in the strategic situation which have a bearing on the provisions" of the Treaty, which was to be of unlimited duration. Under the terms of the 1974 Protocol, the United States kept its right to the one ABM site at Grand Forks Air Force Base, and the USSR kept its Moscow ABM site. The treaty that was signed in Moscow validated and embodied McNamara's original Glassboro proposal by establishing a link between offensive and defensive weapons, and by trading a halt in further ABM deployments for the promise of limits on strategic offensive weapons.

THE U.S. ROAD TO THE ABM TREATY

The conceptual origins of the U.S. road to the ABM Treaty are found in the theology of the "absolute weapon." Beginning with Bernard Brodie, who along with other contributors compiled the 1945 publication *The Absolute Weapon,* civilian academics in the United States had come to the conclusion that nuclear weapons were fundamentally different from conventional weapons.[21] According to Brodie and his colleagues, nuclear weapons were "absolute" in the sense that there was no defense against them. Consequently, the advent of nuclear weapons had rendered traditional military strategy obsolete. Brodie's characterization of the political implications of nuclear weapons laid the foundation for the paradigm of "absolute vulnerability" that was later institutionalized in the ABM Treaty.

This paradigm rested on four key concepts. First, no defense against the bomb existed, and the possibilities of creating such a defense in the future were deemed exceedingly remote. This was the keystone tenet of the new paradigm. Only offensive forces and offensive strategies were possible. Second, cities were deemed the only logical target for nuclear weapons. Brodie claimed that "under the technical conditions apparently prevailing today, and presumably likely to continue for some time to come, the primary targets for the atomic bomb will be cities." Since no defense against atomic bombs was possible, efforts to protect cities would be futile. Third, military superiority had lost its traditional significance. According to Brodie, "We can say that if 2,000 bombs in the hands of either party is enough to destroy entirely the economy of the other, the fact that one side has 6,000 and the other 2,000 will be of relatively small significance." Fourth, traditional military strategy—which has both an offensive and a defensive component—was no longer valid, partly because the main purpose of armed forces had changed from warfighting to deterrence. Brodie noted, "Thus far the chief purpose of our military establishment has been to win wars. From now on its chief purpose must be to avert them. It can have almost no other useful purpose." Nuclear forces had to be sized, composed, and postured for maximizing their deterrent value, not their war-fighting value.

Each of these tenets is found also in the ABM Treaty and the accompanying offensive arms accord. Thus, the Treaty codifies societal vulnerability to ballistic missile attack as a legitimate means of preserving peace. At the same time, in signing the Treaty, the United States willingly accepted a strategic offensive arms accord that ceded strategic parity to the Soviet Union, and thenceforth solidified an approach to national security that relied exclusively on offensive forces and abandoned traditional military strategic considerations.

The notion that there was no defense against nuclear weapons did not immediately translate into a sense of strategic vulnerability on the part of the United States. Although nuclear weapons were considered absolute, their initial means of delivery was restricted in the 1940s and 1950s to slow-flying heavy bombers. Defenses against bombers had become highly developed during the war, and a bomber's relatively long flight time meant that an early warning network could provide substantial warning time. Having deployed such a network, the United States enjoyed a certain sense of security. That sense of safety was stripped away in the aftermath of the 4 October 1957 launch of the first artificial satellite, Sputnik, which demonstrated the Soviet Union's ability to use a ballistic missile to deliver a nuclear warhead at intercontinental ranges. Nuclear weapons could now be carried high above the extensive U.S. air defense network and delivered to their targets in minutes rather than hours. Absolute weapons coupled with intercontinental ballistic missile (ICBM) delivery systems now meant absolute U.S. vulnerability to a devastating surprise nuclear attack.

Arms control theory emerged in the early 1960s as a direct response on the part of Western scientists and intellectuals to the surprise attack scare precipitated by Sputnik. Arms control made reducing the risks of war by reducing incentives to launch a surprise nuclear attack its guiding objective. Theorists suggested that such risks could be contained through cooperatively negotiated arms control accords.[22] Three ideas were central to this theory of arms control: (1) arms control was not an end in itself but a means to enhance security, especially by moderating the threat of surprise nuclear attack; (2) the superpowers shared a common interest in avoiding surprise attack that could be the basis for arms control; and (3) arms control should stabilize a condition of mutual nuclear deterrence between the superpowers. Together with Brodie's paradigm of "absolute vulnerability," these would become the conceptual foundations for the U.S. road to the ABM Treaty.

McNamara and Assured Destruction

McNamara should be considered the intellectual godfather of the ABM Treaty. McNamara defined the terms of the ABM issue and fashioned an approach to the Soviet Union that was entirely consistent with Bernard Brodie's paradigm of "absolute vulnerability," and that incorporated the major concepts of modern arms control theory. McNamara believed that the ability to assure the destruction of an opponent's society—not the ability to limit damage to one's own society—was the basis of deterrence. That is, offensive forces alone provided sufficient deterrent effect. McNamara's thinking about deterrence and the role of ABM systems was the result of a systematic search for "criteria of sufficiency" to determine the optimal size and composition of U.S. strategic forces. Initially, he asserted that two criteria should be used: the ability of U.S. forces to assure damage to an opponent's assets and to limit damage to U.S. assets. McNamara eventually discarded the damage limitation criterion out of a conviction that it was inherently destabilizing and increased force requirements by obligating the other side to deploy offsetting offensive forces to maintain its own assured destruction capability. He also concluded that the defensive forces necessary to limit damage were not cost-efficient; defensive forces were more expensive than were offensive forces. U.S. missile defenses could not be fielded without provoking the deployment of additional, and cheaper, Soviet offensive forces that would be able to overwhelm those defenses, resulting in no net gain to American security. Since the Soviets could offset and neutralize whatever defenses the U.S. deployed with much less costly offenses, the Soviets could turn any action-reaction arms race to their advantage.

McNamara eventually determined that assured destruction alone would have to bear the full burden of U.S. deterrence requirements. In his own words: "'Damage Limiting' programs, no matter how much we spend on them, can never substitute for an Assured Destruction capability in the deterrent role. It is our ability to destroy an attacker as a viable 20th Century nation that provides the deterrent, not our ability to partially limit damage to ourselves."[23] McNamara was increasingly alarmed at how the U.S. armed forces were using the damage limitation mission to justify an ambitious force acquisition program. McNamara emphasized assured destruction to contain pressures on both Soviet and American policymakers to acquire more and more strategic offensive forces.[24]

Second, McNamara believed that the Soviet Union shared a commitment to maintaining its own assured destruction capability. He believed that a mutual ability to assure the destruction of the opponent's society in a second strike provided the United States and the Soviet Union with the strongest possible motive to avoid nuclear war. McNamara stated in Congressional testimony: "We believe the Soviet Union has essentially the same requirement for a deterrent or Assured Destruction force as the United States. Therefore, U.S. deployment of an ABM defense which would degrade the destruction capability of the Soviets' offensive force to an unacceptable level would lead to expansion of that force. This would leave us no better off than we were before."[25] He stated on another occasion: "If our assumption that the Soviets are also striving to achieve an Assured Destruction capability is correct, and I am convinced that it is, then in all probability all we would accomplish by deploying ABM systems against one another would be to increase greatly our respective defense expenditures, without any gain in real security for either side."[26]

In making this assumption, McNamara and his staff apparently believed that the Soviets either had not thought systematically about nuclear weapons, or had reached the same conclusions they had. Yet, there is little evidence that McNamara took actual Soviet strategic thinking about nuclear weapons into account in determining what was required to deter Soviet leaders or how the Soviet Union might react to American deployment of ABMs. McNamara had difficulty explaining the heavy Soviet investment in strategic defenses, which contradicted his assumption of a Soviet commitment to assured destruction.[27] And he dismissed Soviet resources spent on air defense as "wasted."[28] In fact, the Soviets had thought seriously about nuclear war prior to being introduced to

American thinking about deterrence and arms control at Glassboro, and had formed their own doctrine to deter a nuclear surprise attack by the capitalist powers.[29] They had not, however, reached the same conclusions about stability and deterrence, nor had they arrived at a similar paradigm of absolute vulnerability. In any event, McNamara assumed that the Soviet Union eventually would recognize the logic of the vulnerability paradigm and the value of ABM limits through negotiated arms control.

Third, McNamara believed that the U.S.-Soviet strategic arms competition was characterized by an action-reaction arms race dynamic. As McNamara stated in a September 1967 speech in San Francisco:[30]

What is essential to understand here is that the Soviet Union and the United States mutually influence one another's strategic plans. Whatever be their intentions, whatever be our intentions, actions— or even realistically potential actions—on either side relating to the buildup of nuclear forces, be they either offensive or defensive weapons, necessarily trigger reactions on the other side. It is precisely this action-reaction phenomenon that fuels an arms race.

Moreover, McNamara argued, the reaction triggered on the other side would not necessarily be the same as the provocation. Prior to the encounter at Glassboro, both U.S. and Soviet leaders assumed that defensive deployments by one side would be matched by incremental increases in defenses by the other side. In fact, when Johnson announced in his State of the Union address in January 1967 that the Soviet Union had begun to deploy an ABM system around Moscow, he implied that this would necessarily be met on the U.S. side by the deployment of an American ABM system.[31] It was at Glassboro that American officials first insisted that the arms race was, in fact, characterized not so much by this tit-for-tat process as by an *asymmetrical* action-reaction process: if one side deployed defenses, the other side would be compelled to deploy more offenses.

Fourth, McNamara believed that the action-reaction phenomenon inevitably led to "overkill," or the acquisition of more forces than needed for an assured destruction capability. He attributed U.S. nuclear superiority in the mid-1960s to inflated perceptions of a "missile gap" earlier in the decade. It therefore made sense to counteract the momentum of an escalating action-reaction arms race by negotiating arms limits. These convictions formed the basis of his approach to the Soviets at Glassboro.

The ABM Debate

If McNamara laid the policy foundations for the U.S. road to the ABM Treaty, a vigorous debate over the wisdom of deploying ABM systems that arose in the mid-1960s gave it added momentum. Following the 1964 publication of an article in the journal *Scientific American,* a view began emerging among some American scientists that the U.S. deployment of missile defenses would lead to a costly and dangerous escalation in the arms race and would be doomed by deficiencies in existing technological capabilities.[32] While this view was vigorously challenged by other scientists and defense experts, the 1960s debate over missile defenses provided an important context for government deliberations regarding the value of ABM systems, and reinforced McNamara's policy of emphasizing assured destruction as central to deterrence and to measuring U.S. strategic force sufficiency. This debate helped reinforce a general predisposition against ABM systems among Americans, including many in the scientific community.

The ABM debate revolved around two questions: (1) *could* the United States deploy a cost-effective and technically feasible ABM system; and (2) *should* the United States deploy such a system?[33] The first question raised issues of technological capability and system lethality, including the ease of developing countermeasures, the potential contribution of ABM to Minuteman ICBM defense, and the effects of endo- and exoatmospheric nuclear detonations. The second question concerned the impact of ABM on strategic stability and whether strategies based on defenses were morally superior to offensive strategies.

Arguments against deploying ABM included the assertions that an American ABM system would fuel the arms race and oblige the Soviets to react with a buildup of offensive nuclear weapons, would undermine arms control efforts, and would divert resources needed for more pressing domestic priorities. In addition to these central arguments, a number of more esoteric themes emerged:[34]

- There was no need to deploy ABM because there was no appreciable threat to the U.S. deterrent capability. The Soviets were not planning a first strike against the United States.
- There would not be sufficient time for the President to authorize firing an ABM interceptor in the event of a first strike.
- An ABM system would not work because advanced technology (especially computer technology) was unreliable. Defensive systems were too complex.
- It would be easy to overcome an ABM system by fitting offensive warheads with penetration aids.
- A decision to deploy an American ABM system would upset the balance of power in Asia, forcing the Chinese to build a larger nuclear arsenal.
- U.S. missile defenses would destroy the North Atlantic Treaty Organization by decoupling the United States from the defense of Europe.
- Missile defenses against a Soviet first strike were unnecessary because U.S. intelligence organizations could detect any buildup of forces preparatory to such a strike in time to allow an appropriate diplomatic response.
- An ABM system would encourage nuclear proliferation.
- The United States should bow to pressure from other nations and forego deploying missile defenses.
- The Soviets could mount a surprise attack to prevent the completion of an ABM system.

ABM proponents had corresponding counterarguments for each of these points.[35] They argued that an ABM system was technologically possible, would provide the U.S. side substantial bargaining leverage in negotiations with the Soviets to place limits on offensive weapons, and was needed to reinforce the survivability of the U.S. nuclear deterrent. These advocates also noted that a ballistic missile defense of Minuteman ICBMs was not incompatible with maintaining an assured destruction capability. They suggested that:

- Missile defenses would bolster deterrence by introducing uncertainties into an opponent's attack calculations.

- An American ABM defense was necessary to offset Soviet strategic offensive superiority.
- Devoting resources to defense was morally superior to relying on the threat to destroy an opponent's cities.
- Vulnerability to attack would encourage other nations to acquire nuclear weapons. Missile defenses would discourage proliferation.
- The United States would gain defensive technological expertise in developing an ABM system, and operational experience in deploying it.
- Missile defenses would contribute to crisis stability by reducing first-strike incentives.

Although ABM proponents won many political battles, the ideas championed by ABM critics ultimately appealed to a wider audience. The American public accepted a treaty limiting defenses that was designed to institutionalize their vulnerability to nuclear attack for the sake of mutual deterrence.

The Strategic Arms Race

During the mid-1960s, it was generally assumed that U.S. missile superiority would remain unchallenged and that the Soviets would not commit the resources necessary to match U.S. ICBM force levels.[36] The Soviet offensive force buildup that came to light in the late 1960s was consistently underestimated by U.S. intelligence. It soon began to pose a threat to the survival of America's ICBM and bomber forces, and thus to America's assured destruction capability.

The total number of U.S. strategic bombers, intercontinental ballistic missiles, and sea-launched ballistic missiles leveled off in 1967 and then began a gradual decline, which accelerated with the end of the Cold War. At its peak, this force consisted of 1,000 Minuteman I and II ICBMs; 54 Titan ICBMs; 41 Polaris ballistic missile submarines (SSBNs), which could carry a total of 656 submarine-launched ballistic missiles (SLBMs); and about 500 bombers. Ironically, the same year that U.S. force numbers began leveling off, U.S. officials began taking note of what was described as "a massive Soviet ICBM buildup."[37] The pace of

TABLE 1.1   Annual Deployment of U.S. and Soviet ICBMs, 1964–1974

	1964	1965	1966	1967	1968	1969	1970	1971	1972	1973	1974
U.S.:	410	20	50	50	50	0	0	0	0	0	0
USSR:	100	70	130	160	340	250	250	210	17	0	0

SOURCES: John M. Collins, *American and Soviet Military Trends Since the Cuban Missile Crisis* (Washington, DC: Center for Strategic and International Studies, Georgetown University, 1978), 92, 98, 105; John J. Barton and Lawrence Weiler, eds., *International Arms Control: Issues and Agreements* (Stanford: Stanford University Press, 1976), 179; and Thomas Wolfe, *The SALT Experience* (Cambridge: Ballinger, 1979), 117.

Soviet ICBM deployments remained more or less steady until 308 10-warhead SS-18s had been fielded, along with hundreds of SS-11, SS-13, SS-17, and SS-19 ICBMs. The CIA concluded, "The striking thing about these programs is not that they have accelerated in the last few years but that they have grown at a more or less steady pace for two decades."[38]

Table 1.1 highlights the pace of the Soviet ICBM force buildup and its phasing compared to U.S. deployments. The U.S. buildup accelerated in the early 1960s but tapered off beginning in 1965 and was virtually complete in 1967. The Soviet buildup accelerated in 1967, reached its highest annual deployment rate in 1968, on the eve of the SALT negotiations, and did not slow down until well after the SALT I agreements were signed. During this period, the United States began placing multiple independently targeted reentry vehicles (MIRVs) on its ICBMs and SLBMs, thus expanding the number of warheads deployed. It also continued intermittent production of modernized versions of its ICBMs, SLBMs, SSBNs, and heavy bombers. But the United States did not increase the overall number of its strategic delivery vehicles.

The Soviets also were devoting resources to deploying an ABM system around Moscow. By 1971, a year before the ABM Treaty was signed, the Moscow system consisted of 64 launchers with Galosh interceptor missiles (the Galosh is a large, long-range ballistic missile equipped with a nuclear warhead and designed for exoatmospheric interception); Try

Add terminal tracking and guidance radars; and Dog House and Cat House large phased array radars.[39] Dog House was oriented to the north, toward the corridor of approach that would be used by U.S. ICBMs; and Cat House was oriented toward the south, to cover the likely approaches of Chinese ballistic missiles. This system was judged at the time to have extremely limited capabilities and to be vulnerable to saturation by a dedicated attack. Try Add radars could track only one object at a time; and because the system relied on exoatmospheric interception, it was thought to be easily confounded by decoys and chaff before these were stripped away by reentry through the atmosphere.

The U.S. Domestic Setting

By the 1970s, U.S. policymakers were disinclined to deploy additional strategic nuclear delivery vehicles, preferring instead to concentrate resources on developing follow-on systems (such as Trident SSBNs and SLBMs, the MX ICBM, and the B-1 bomber) as well as on MIRVing the ICBM and SLBM force. American policymakers were politically ready to accept and codify parity with the Soviet Union, at least in terms of strategic delivery vehicles. Given these circumstances, arms control offered the only way to prevent the Soviets from gaining numerical superiority in strategic launchers.

The high political and monetary costs of the Vietnam War created important disincentives to devoting resources to ABM systems in the late 1960s. Others have noted that the Vietnam War affected the U.S. disposition toward SALT negotiations in general. President Richard Nixon wanted to counter the negative effect of the Vietnam War on the credibility of his foreign policy by improving U.S.-Soviet relations. SALT was an important part of the Nixon administration's policy of détente with the Soviet Union.[40] Moreover, there was a perceived need to respond to growing pacifist sentiment in the United States, which largely represented a backlash against the Vietnam War and general disenchantment with military spending.

By the early 1970s, Congress essentially made pursuing arms control a precondition for funding strategic arms acquisition programs. Thus, arms control became an essential step in the Nixon administration's effort to secure Congressional support for defense programs. There was a real concern on the part of the Nixon White House that without arms control agreements, Congress would cut U.S. forces. Kissinger notes that: "The Administration had to marshal all its strength to keep the Congress from imposing unilaterally what we were seeking to negotiate reciprocally with the Soviets."[41]

Assumptions about Soviet interest in arms control, and a faith in a supposed U.S.-Soviet doctrinal convergence around acceptance of mutual assured destruction as a basis of deterrence, also played a role in encouraging American officials to engage in the ABM Treaty negotiations. Many Americans assumed that the Soviets had notable political and economic incentives for responding favorably to U.S. arms control initiatives and that arms control would be driven by mutual enlightened self-interest. Convinced that common ground could be found for arms control talks, and fearful of a debilitating arms race that the Soviets were winning, the United States by 1967 was ready to enter into serious strategic arms negotiations with the Soviet Union. But the Soviets had not yet fully traveled their own road to the ABM Treaty.

THE SOVIET ROAD TO THE ABM TREATY

The Soviet Union entered the ABM Treaty negotiations in 1969 with a cultural and conceptual background different from that of the United States. First and foremost, military officers were responsible for developing Soviet military strategy and doctrine and for extrapolating corresponding force requirements; civilians played little role in the defense planning process.

The U.S. road and the Soviet road to the ABM Treaty shared at least one central objective, however: to mitigate the surprise attack threat posed by nuclear weapons delivered by ballistic missiles. The United States sought to institutionalize mutual vulnerability, believing it would act as a stabilizing factor in times of crisis and as a brake on the arms race; but the Soviet Union adopted a different approach to the surprise attack problem. Nazi Germany's surprise attack on the Soviet Union early in World II had nearly led to the destruction of the Soviet state. Those responsible for shaping the Soviet Union's postwar military strategy determined never to let such an attack happen again. As one observer of Soviet military affairs in the 1950s put it, "No point is emphasized more consistently [in Soviet military literature] than the need never again to allow themselves to be caught in a surprise attack."[42] According to Herbert Dinerstein, a RAND analyst who undertook a comprehensive study of postwar Soviet military thinking, "Readiness to strike a pre-emptive blow became, early in 1955, a principal aim of official Soviet policy" in the event that the enemy seemed to be preparing an attack.[43] This meant developing a strategy that placed a premium on the ability to preempt a surprise attack before it was launched, or failing that, to limit damage to the homeland from the enemy's attack to the greatest extent possible. Underwriting these twin goals meant developing and fielding offensive and defensive nuclear forces optimized to conduct disarming first strikes and to blunt the enemy's attack.

Moreover, at least until the Soviet Union began engaging the United States in substantive arms control negotiations, Soviet leaders made little effort to study the interaction between offensive and defensive nuclear forces, or how to maintain a stable strategic relationship with the United States. Rather, their focus was on avoiding or managing a nuclear conflict with the West, the inevitability of which was predicted by Marxist-Leninist ideology. The 1950s emphasis on preempting any impending surprise attack, coupled with the deeply rooted goal of protecting the Soviet homeland, created the doctrinal blueprint for the Soviet strategic offensive and defensive buildup of the 1960s and 1970s.

Nevertheless, by the time SALT negotiations began in 1969, Soviet leaders apparently had begun to harbor doubts about the technical feasibility and cost-effectiveness of ballistic missile defenses. These doubts were reinforced by the emerging U.S. lead in deploying MIRVed ICBMs and SLBMs and the prospect that a rapid increase in the number of U.S. warheads would easily overwhelm whatever Soviet ABM systems were deployed. Soviet leaders, according to contemporary Russian accounts of that era, also increasingly worried about the economic burden of the strategic arms competition with the United States. These accounts assert that they were soon ready to turn to arms control to stabilize their strategic planning requirements and to lock in the gains achieved by their offensive and defensive arms buildup.

The Birth of Soviet Missile Defense

Aleksandr G. Savel'yev and Nikolay N. Detinov, who were involved in the making of Soviet arms control policy from 1969 to 1991, claim that Soviet scientists concluded in the early 1960s that it was technically feasible to intercept ICBM warheads during their reentry phase, using nuclear-tipped interceptor missiles.[44] High-altitude atmospheric tests had validated the concept, making a nationwide ABM system appear practical. This techno-logical confidence, coupled with a perception that the United States in-tended to deploy such a system of its own to protect its cities, prompted Soviet leaders to initiate the development of a Soviet ABM system.

Savel'yev and Detinov note that despite this national policy, many So-viet military and civilian leaders understood that victory in a nuclear war was unattainable and would inevitably result in the annihilation of both the United States and the Soviet Union. These officials also realized that despite their ability to destroy a limited number of incoming war-heads with nuclear-tipped interceptors, it was quite another matter to develop an effective nationwide ABM system against a determined en-emy—the same conclusion McNamara had reached. They understood that such a system could be overwhelmed by ICBMs equipped with MIRVs, which the United States was then beginning to deploy. Initially, these reservations about deploying missile defenses were scattered and low-key. By the mid-1960s, however, the Soviet scientific community was generally beginning to mirror its American counterpart's doubts about the technical feasibility of extensive ABM systems. It is not clear whether the ABM debate in the United States was responsible for precip-itating these doubts, or whether they arose from technical obstacles en-countered by the Soviet Union's own ABM research and development ef-forts. But by the late 1960s, according to Savel'yev and Detinov, Soviet leaders began feeling the economic burden of maintaining the pace and scale of the enormous military buildup they had initiated in the early 1960s. Sharp divisions over ABM policy also began to flare up among So-viet military leaders, who were probably wary about diverting resources to ABM systems that could otherwise be used to acquire "real" war-fighting assets.[45] This set the stage for what might be called the Soviet Union's "dual-track" approach: agreeing to negotiate limits on ballistic missile defenses while forging ahead with plans to deploy an ABM system around Moscow—and if necessary, around other major Soviet cities, until a nationwide territorial defense system had been established.

While the United States and the Soviet Union began trading proposals to hold talks, still no serious Soviet effort was made to explore how one side's deployment of strategic offensive arms might affect the other side's decision to deploy defensive arms. Concepts of arms race stability as understood in the West were foreign to the Soviet leadership at this point. Savel'yev and Detinov report that "When the SALT I talks were subsequently opened with the United States in November of 1969, the issue of strengthening strategic stability was not one that formed a cornerstone of the Soviet position." Instead of seeking to institutionalize some academic concept of mutual assured destruction, Soviet leaders pursued much more self-interested objectives. They believed that "negotiations promised to slow the burden of the arms race and promised the attainment of some advantage over the United States."[46]

Competing Interpretations of Soviet Objectives

At the outset of the U.S.-Soviet dialogue on limiting ABM systems, Soviet leaders rejected limiting defenses out of hand. They did not accept McNamara's assertion that defenses were destabilizing, nor did they accept his prediction of a "defensive action–offensive reaction" dynamic. Nevertheless, two years later, when U.S. and Soviet delegations opened formal arms control negotiations in Helsinki, the Soviet Union not only placed highest priority on achieving strict limits on ABM systems but it was distinctly uninterested in offensive arms limits. Why then did the Soviets reverse their stance at Glassboro, and enter into the SALT I negotiations so determined to limit ABM systems?

This dramatic reversal of the Soviet opposition to negotiating limits on ABM systems mystified Americans at the time. In his account of the talks, Gerard Smith, chief U.S. SALT negotiator, admitted puzzlement: "Why did the Soviets agree to enter the negotiations? We do not know for sure."[47] Smith was left to speculate, suggesting that the Soviets "wanted to avoid a competition in ABM systems," that they were satisfied with the strategic balance, that they believed "that the prospects for unilateral constraints on the American MIRV program might be improved once

SALT negotiations got under way," or that they wanted to head off U.S.-Chinese rapprochement. Marshall Shulman, a scholar of Soviet affairs, believes the following reasons underscored the Soviet decision ultimately to enter into strategic arms negotiations with the United States:[48]

- A decade of strenuous effort had helped the Soviet Union overcome the inferiority in nuclear weapons under which it had labored since World War II, as a result of which it could now codify the principle of "equal security" in an arms control agreement.
- Soviet political leaders increasingly realized the limited political utility of strategic weapons and of the futility and high cost of an unregulated strategic competition.
- A preference had crystallized among the Party leadership for obtaining long-term increases in the flow of grain, technology, management, and goods from abroad as a way of addressing economic shortcomings in the Communist system.
- Soviet leaders at least tentatively had accepted the possibility that American leaders were prepared to cooperate in establishing a relationship based on "peaceful coexistence;" and,
- The Soviet leadership was increasingly concerned with the rise of China in international diplomacy, and wished to offset developing relations between China and the United States.

In retrospect, some of these purported conclusions may have reflected a degree of mirror-imaging; but there can be no doubt that the emerging skepticism of the Soviet Union's technical elite about the feasibility of broad area defense, and the cynicism and resentment of military bureaucracies who stood to lose resources to the ABM effort, contributed to the reversal in Soviet attitudes toward seeking negotiated limits on ABMs in particular. Fear of U.S. technological superiority and industrial might also may have been factors: the Soviets knew that a determined United States could easily overwhelm them in an ABM race.

But the sequence of events in the historical record, cited earlier in this chapter, suggests that the most important incentive for Soviet interest in seeking negotiated constraints on ABM systems was the U.S. decision to deploy an ABM system designed primarily to protect U.S. silo-based ICBMs from a Soviet preemptive attack.

The primary objective of the U.S. ABM program at the beginning of the SALT talks was defined as the defense of ICBM bases rather than of the population. If carried forward, U.S. ABM deployments could have contributed substantially to the ability of these forces to survive, by shielding them from a Soviet preemptive attack designed to disarm the United States of its principal strategic weapons. Eliminating or severely constraining this U.S. program would facilitate the long-standing Soviet goal of holding these particular targets at risk. According to Thomas Wolfe, a RAND analyst who prepared an extensive study of the SALT negotiations, the ABM Treaty gave Soviet strategic planners "fresh reason for counting upon counterforce systems as the most effective means of carrying out the damage-limitation mission traditionally close to their hearts. . . . One might even speculate that the ABM Treaty [was] seen by at least some Soviet planners as a useful device for enhancing the counterforce potential of Soviet strategic systems, insofar as it placed strict limits on U.S. protection of launch sites and control centers, which would be a good deal easier to defend by ABM than cities."[49]

These were the immediate motives for Soviet interest in placing limits on U.S. ABM systems. Savel'yev and Detinov also cite three longer-term objectives that explain the Soviet decision to limit ballistic missile defenses.[50] These reasons illuminate not only the original motivations of the Soviets but also the emphatic commitment made by the Russian Federation to preserving the ABM Treaty.

The first objective noted by Savel'yev and Detinov was to "end uncertainty in the accelerating arms race." It seems clear that the Soviets wanted to head off a continuation of the ongoing arms competition with the United States. The Soviets may have wanted to shift resources from military to civilian purposes. Gerard Smith notes, "The United States undoubtedly was not alone in wanting to divert more of its resources to civilian needs rather than to additional strategic weaponry whose value was questionable. There must have been people in the Soviet leadership urging a different balance in meeting civilian and military needs."[51] Confidence in predicting the course of the arms competition was important to Soviet military planners operating on the basis of serial five-year plans, and allowed for a more effective allocation of resources.

The second objective was to "perfect the strategic balance"—that is, to register formal parity with the United States. Others agree with Savel'yev and Detinov on this point. Smith states, "A primary goal of the USSR was formal registration of strategic equality."[52] In fact, in reviewing the dynamic U.S.-Soviet strategic balance as it evolved throughout the 1960s and 1970s, it is clear that a brief moment of rough parity was achieved in 1969, after which the Soviet Union soon acquired superiority over the United States in many key indices of strategic nuclear power. Another author writes, "The most important reason for the Soviet agreement to begin SALT negotiations in 1969 was the Soviet Union's attainment of strategic nuclear parity with the United States."[53] For Soviet leaders, moreover, official U.S. recognition of the Soviet Union's political equality with the United States was just as important as the acknowledgement of formal military parity. The negotiations were a validation of their communist system, and underwrote their sense of influence in world affairs.

The third Soviet objective was to "attempt to keep some of the advantage that the Soviet leadership believed the nation had obtained in certain military areas," or to preserve the Soviet lead in offensive nuclear weapons, particularly large silo-based ICBMs. Soviet negotiators resolutely held out for an arms control agreement that protected their ABM deployment around Moscow and locked in their advantages in offensive weapons—namely the substantial Soviet lead in the numbers of deployed ICBMs and in total numbers of SLBMs and SSBNs. Soviet leaders may also have calculated that even in the absence of an agreement, diplomacy could be used to suppress any potential U.S. response to the Soviet Union's attainment of strategic nuclear superiority.

Savel'yev and Detinov make no mention of the ABM Treaty objective most often attributed to the Soviets by Western scholars: to codify mutual assured destruction. According to this oft-stated view, U.S. negotiators allegedly succeeded in convincing the Soviets of the inexorable logic of mutual assured destruction. Once convinced, the Soviets then signed the ABM Treaty, for much the same reasons as did the United States: to stabilize offense-dominant deterrence and to create a basis for further limits and reductions in strategic offensive arms. John B. Rhinelander, who served as legal advisor to the U.S. SALT I delegation, observed that Soviet agreement to Paragraph 2 of Article I of the ABM Treaty (which bans defense of the national territory or creating a base for such a defense) "embodies a political decision of the first magnitude. For the Soviet Union, it represents a significant shift in strategic doctrine by accepting, in a formal international agreement, that Soviet territory is and will remain defenseless against U.S. land-based and sea-based nuclear missiles."[54] McNamara's conviction that the Soviet Union either shared U.S. views of strategic stability through assured destruction, or could be convinced of their validity, is reflected in this perspective. Soviet acceptance of assured destruction was achieved through the persistent, and ultimately successful, schooling by American negotiators dedicated to "raising the Russian learning curve."

Soviet statements made throughout the SALT negotiations, however, indicated no sympathy for U.S. concepts of mutual societal vulnerability, much less any acceptance of the notion that promoting the vulnerability of *Soviet* offensive forces would somehow be beneficial. According to Wolfe, the Soviets "could not be moved to agree that *mutual* survivability of offensive forces would be good for the security of both parties."[55] Furthermore, Soviet strategic doctrine remained unchanged after the ABM Treaty was signed, thus discounting the idea of U.S.-Soviet "strategic convergence." More than five years after the ABM Treaty was concluded, the CIA published a rebuttal to many specific criticisms made by the so-called "B-Team" that had been convened in the late 1970s to prepare a competitive, alternative estimate of Soviet strategic intentions and capabilities.[56] But this CIA report did not dispute the B-Team's conclusion that no doctrinal convergence had taken place: "The Soviets have never accepted the concept of mutual assured destruction, with its connotation that some infinite level of force is sufficient for deterrence, although they recognize mutual deterrence as a present reality that will be very difficult to alter."[57] In short, there is no evidence that the Soviets ever came to share the American belief in the benefits of mutual assured destruction.[58] Wolfe concludes:

Although the ABM Treaty of 1972 might have marked the beginning of an altered Soviet outlook on the value of strategic defense and its relative importance in the offense-defense equation in the SALT era, no doctrinal revisions that would suggest such a waning of Soviet dedication to strategic defense had been forthcoming. Neither was downgrading of strategic defense apparent in the specific programs pursued by the Soviet Union after the ABM Treaty, particularly those having to do with improving the air defense and civil defense aspects of the USSR's strategic posture.[59]

CONCLUSIONS

Four observations can be derived from this review of the origins of the ABM Treaty. First, the United States and the Soviet Union traveled different roads to the negotiations that resulted in the ABM Treaty. The U.S. road was conditioned by the culture of "absolute vulnerability" that arose from postwar assessments of the political implications of atomic weapons; by its belief that any active defense against the threat of surprise nuclear attack was technically infeasible and politically destabilizing; and by the conviction that a condition of mutual assured destruction not only was inevitable but could be institutionalized for the sake of strategic stability. The U.S. road was largely paved by McNamara's policy prescriptions in the 1960s, which legitimized an offense-dominant approach to deterrence. The Soviet road to the Treaty was conditioned by a determination to avoid surprise attack by developing the ability to strike preemptively and disarm an enemy's nuclear forces; and by the fear that an opponent's ABM defense against offensive forces would frustrate this requirement. The Soviets were willing to accept strict limits on their own ABM system—which was postured to protect leadership assets rather than its population or retaliatory forces—in return for severe constraints on, or elimination of, the American Safeguard program, which was configured and optimized for defending U.S. ICBM silos. Nevertheless, the Soviets came to doubt the feasibility of nationwide defenses, and accepted the need for arms control limitations with the United States as a condition for access to Western aid and assistance.

Second, the Treaty itself was the product of a unique historical context. The United States and the Soviet Union were engaged in a global ideological confrontation, manifested in a strategic arms race that produced thousands of nuclear weapons, and this bipolar conflict dominated world politics, subsuming all regional conflicts. Nuclear weapons and the threat of surprise nuclear attack were the principal sources of insecurity. For the United States, the Treaty also was intended as a response, in part, to the declining domestic political fortunes of the Nixon administration, as well as to the growing political and budgetary demands of the Vietnam War. The Soviet Union recognized a chance to seize on these domestic distractions to engage the United States in establishing "peaceful coexistence." Facing severe resource constraints, the

Soviet Union had its own domestic reasons for seeking some moderation in the strategic arms competition with the United States.

Third, although some degree of common ground was certainly registered in the ABM Treaty, U.S. and Soviet objectives in signing the Treaty differed in substantial ways. The United States sought to codify and institutionalize a condition of mutual assured destruction, and to trade limits on its ABM program for the future promise of equal limitations on offensive nuclear arms. The Soviets, by contrast, never indicated any acceptance of MAD but sought to codify military parity and institutionalize political equality. They also wanted to stop expansion of U.S. ABM defense of ICBM silos, to facilitate holding these targets at risk.

Finally, U.S. objectives for signing the ABM Treaty have all been fulfilled, or have been rendered irrelevant by profound changes in the international strategic situation. The threat driving U.S. strategy and force acquisition considerations today is no longer surprise nuclear attack on an intercontinental scale, but the proliferation of weapons of mass destruction and their means of delivery to multiple states in regions scattered around the world. This is why the United States is now determined either to seek changes in the ABM Treaty or to abandon it altogether. Yet, for Russia, the objectives originally sought by Soviet leaders are still very much relevant, and may be even more so. Russia wants, as did its Soviet predecessor, to retain the international political equality with the United States represented by the ABM Treaty, and it is fearful that once released from its constraints, the United States will develop a missile shield that will only encourage and aggravate unilateralist American policies at the expense of Russian interests. This explains Russia's firm stance on retaining the Treaty unchanged. Bridging this gap without jeopardizing existing international strategic nuclear and nonproliferation arms control regimes will be a significant test of American diplomacy in the early twenty-first century.

NOTES

The views expressed in this chapter are the author's. Nothing herein should be construed as necessarily representing the views of the U.S. Department of State or any other U.S. government agency. The author gratefully acknowledges the following for comments and advice in preparing this chapter: Lt. Col. Glenn A. Trimmer, Benson D. Adams, David Nickels, and David Hoppler.

1. For background on these political battles, see Desmond Ball, *Politics and Force Levels: The Strategic Missile Program of the Kennedy Administration* (Berkeley: University of California Press, 1980).

2. See McNamara's account of this episode in Robert S. McNamara, *Blundering into Disaster: Surviving the First Century of the Nuclear Age* (New York: Pantheon Books, 1986), 57.

3. Jeanette Voas, *Soviet Attitudes towards Ballistic Missile Defence and the ABM Treaty* (London: International Institute for Strategic Studies, Adelphi Papers #255, Winter 1990), 25. See also Donald R. Baucom, *The Origins of SDI, 1944–1983* (Lawrence: University Press of Kansas, 1992), 27.

4. Paul Nitze, cited in Lawrence Freedman, *U.S. Intelligence and the Soviet Strategic Threat*, 2d ed. (Princeton: Princeton University Press, 1986), 89.

5. Ernest J. Yanarella, *The Missile Defense Controversy* (Lexington: University of Kentucky Press, 1977), 121–122; and Benson Adams, *Ballistic Missile Defense* (New York: American Elsevier, 1971), 165–173. For a detailed analysis of the bureaucratic rationale behind the Sentinel decision, see also Morton Halperin, *Bureaucratic Politics and Foreign Policy* (Washington, D.C.: Brookings Institution, 1974), especially 297–313.

6. "Address by Foreign Minister Gromyko to the Supreme Soviet, June 27, 1968," extracted in U.S. Arms Control and Disarmament Agency, *Documents on Disarmament 1968* (Washington, D.C.: U.S. Government Printing Office, 1969), 451–452.

7. "Remarks by President Johnson on the Signing of the Nonproliferation Treaty, July 1, 1968," *Documents on Disarmament 1968,* 460. For the Soviet government's reciprocal statement, see 466–470, esp. 467.

8. U.S. Arms Control and Disarmament Agency, *Arms Control and Disarmament Agreements: Texts and Histories of the Negotiations* (Washington, D.C.: U.S. Government Printing Office, 1990), 150–153.

9. "Statement by President Nixon on Missile Defense System, March 14, 1969," reprinted in *Documents on Disarmament 1969* (Washington, D.C.: U.S. Government Printing Office, 1969), 102–105. See also "News Conference Remarks by President Nixon on Ballistic Missile Defense System, March 14, 1969," extracted in ibid., 98–102. The statement is

also reprinted in Zbigniew Brzezinski, ed., *Promise or Peril: The Strategic Defense* Initiative (Washington, D.C.: Ethics and Public Policy Center, 1986), 26–30.

10. See President Nixon's comments to this effect, in "News Conference Remarks by President Nixon, June 19, 1969," extracted in *Documents on Disarmament 1969*, 255.

11. Statement of Secretary of Defense Melvin R. Laird before a joint session of the Senate Armed Services and Appropriations committees, February 20, 1970, in *Fiscal Year 1971 Defense Program and Budget* (Washington, D.C.: U.S. Government Printing Office, 1970), 39.

12. Ibid., 46.

13. Ibid., 50.

14. This survey of events draws on the detailed history given in Baucom, *The Origins of SDI*, 49–54. Ironically, the talks were held in Helsinki during the winter months and in Vienna during the summer months.

15. The following draws primarily on Henry Kissinger, *White House Years* (Boston: Little, Brown, 1979); Gerard Smith, *Doubletalk: The Story of SALT I* (Garden City, N.Y.: Doubleday, 1980); and John Newhouse, *Cold Dawn: The Story of SALT* (New York: Holt, Rinehart, and Winston, 1973).

16. Kissinger, *White House Years*, 149–150.

17. Ibid., 545; Newhouse, *Cold Dawn*, 179–185.

18. Kissinger, *White House Years*, 542.

19. Ibid., 813; Newhouse, *Cold Dawn*, 205–206; Smith, *Doubletalk*, 211.

20. Kissinger, *White House Years*, 819–820.

21. Bernard Brodie, ed., *The Absolute Weapon* (New York: Harcourt, Brace, 1946).

22. The origins of classical arms control theory are explored more fully in Kerry M. Kartchner, "The Objectives of Arms Control," in Jeffrey A. Larsen and Gregory J. Rattray, eds., *Arms Control Toward the 21st Century* (Boulder: Lynne Rienner, 1996), 19–34.

23. Military Posture Statement by Secretary of Defense McNamara to the Senate Armed Services Committee and the Department of Defense Subcommittee of the Senate Appropriations Committee [Extract], 25 Jan-

uary 1967, reprinted in *Documents on Disarmament 1967* (Washington, D.C.: U.S. Government Printing Office, 1968), 6.

24. For a thorough history of the rationale and evolution of McNamara's criteria of sufficiency, see Alain C. Enthoven and K. Wayne Smith, *How Much Is Enough? Shaping the Defense Program, 1961–1969* (New York: Harper & Row, 1971). See also William W. Kaufmann, *The McNamara Strategy* (New York: Harper and Row, 1964).

25. Excerpts from Congressional testimony by Secretary of Defense Robert McNamara on Strategic Forces, reprinted in Zbigniew Brzezinski, ed., *Promise or Peril: The Strategic Defense Initiative* (Washington, D.C.: Ethics and Public Policy Center, 1986), 23.

26. McNamara, *Documents on Disarmament,* 7.

27. A later study of McNamara's policies noted, "One of the key flaws of McNamara's outlook on strategic doctrine and ABM was its lack of any empirical concern for the real character of Soviet strategic thought." Ernest J. Yanarella, *The Missile Defense Controversy* (Lexington: University of Kentucky Press, 1977), 196.

28. McNamara, *Documents on Disarmament,* 9, ftn.7.

29. For example, see Herbert S. Dinerstein, *War and the Soviet Union* (New York: Praeger, 1959; revised ed., 1962).

30. Quoted in Benson Adams, *Ballistic Missile Defense* (New York: American Elsevier, 1971), 166.

31. McNamara, *Documents on Disarmament,* 3–4.

32. Herbert York and Jerome Wiesner, "National Security and the Test Ban," *Scientific American* (October 1964), reprinted in *Readings from Scientific American: Arms Control* (San Francisco: W. H. Freeman and Company, 1973), 129–139.

33. A description of this debate can be found in Adams, *Ballistic Missile Defense,* and in Yanarella, *The Missile Defense Controversy.*

34. See Abram Chayes and Jerome B. Wiesner, eds., *ABM: An Evaluation of the Decision to Deploy an Antiballistic Missile System* (New York: Harper & Row, 1969).

35. See Johan J. Holst and William Schneider, Jr., eds., *Why ABM? Policy Issues in the Missile Defense Controversy* (New York: Pergamon Press, 1969); and William R. Kintner, ed., *Safeguard: Why the ABM Makes Sense* (New York: Hawthorn Books, 1969).

52 Kerry M. Kartchner

36. J. P. Ruina, "U.S. and Soviet Strategic Arsenals," in Mason Willrich and John B. Rhinelander, eds., *SALT: The Moscow Agreements and Beyond* (New York: Free Press, 1974), 51.

37. Ruina, "U.S. and Soviet Strategic Arsenals."

38. NIE 11–4–77, "Soviet Strategic Objectives," declassified and reprinted in Donald P. Steury, ed., *Intentions and Capabilities: Estimates on Soviet Strategic Forces, 1950–1983* (CIA History Staff, Center for the Study of Intelligence, CIA, Washington, D.C., 1996), 393.

39. Voas, *Soviet Attitudes towards Ballistic Missile Defence and the ABM Treaty*, 25.

40. Gerard C. Smith, *Doubletalk: The Story of SALT I* (Lanham, Md.: University Press of America, 1985), 24.

41. Kissinger, *White House Years*, 538.

42. Richard Pipes, "Why the Soviet Union Thinks It Can Fight and Win a Nuclear War," *Commentary*, July 1977.

43. Dinerstein, *War and the Soviet Union*, 188.

44. Aleksandr G. Savel'yev and Nikolay N. Detinov, *The Big Five: Arms Control Decision-Making in the Soviet Union* (Westport, Conn.: Praeger, 1995), 2. The title of this book refers to the nickname for the Soviets' rough equivalent to the U.S. National Security Council, the highest defense policy making body.

45. The debate over ABM among Soviet military leaders was noted at the time by Western observers. See *Strategic Survey 1967* (London: Institute for Strategic Studies, 1968), 22.

46. Savel'yev and Detinov, *The Big Five*, 7.

47. Smith, *Doubletalk*, 31.

48. Marshall D. Shulman, "SALT and the Soviet Union," in Mason Willrich and John B. Rhinelander, eds., *SALT: The Moscow Agreements and Beyond* (New York: Free Press, 1974), 102.

49. Thomas W. Wolfe, *The SALT Experience* (Cambridge: Ballinger, 1979), 112.

50. Savel'yev and Detinov, *The Big Five*, 9.

51. Smith, *Doubletalk*, 33–34.

52. Ibid., 33.

53. Samuel B. Payne, Jr., *The Soviet Union and SALT* (Cambridge: MIT Press, 1980), 18.

54. John B. Rhinelander, "The SALT I Agreements," in Willrich and Rhinelander, eds., *SALT*, 127.

55. Wolfe, *The SALT Experience,* 107 (emphasis in original). Unable to persuade the Soviets to state for the record that mutual survivability of offensive forces would benefit both parties, the U.S. delegation was forced to place a *unilateral* statement on the record noting that "an objective of the follow-on negotiations should be to constrain and reduce on a long-term basis threats to the survivability of our respective strategic retaliatory forces." U.S. Arms Control and Disarmament Agency, *Arms Control and Disarmament Agreements,* 146.

56. Parts 1 and 3 of the B-Team's final report have been declassified and are reproduced in Steury, ed., *Intentions and Capabilities,* 365–390.

57. NIE 11–4–77, "Soviet Strategic Objectives," in Steury, ed., *Intentions and Capabilities,* 392–393.

58. Even today, Russian arguments in favor of retaining the ABM Treaty, and Russian statements denouncing the destabilizing effects of the proposed U.S. NMD program, *never* employ the terms "deterrence," or "mutual deterrence," or anything similar. In fact, it is difficult to find a contemporary Russian discussion of "deterrence" per se. Rather, contemporary Russian commentaries make frequent mention of the potentially debilitating effects of NMD on "strategic stability" and "global security," and strongly imply a visceral fear that NMD will exacerbate American adventurism and unilateralism, not that it will undermine any notional condition of mutual assured deterrence/destruction.

59. NIE 11–4–77, "Soviet Strategic Objectives," in Steury, ed., *Intentions and Capabilities,* 112–113, 127–128.

2

The Changing
Political-Military Environment

ROBERT JOSEPH

On 22 July 1999, President Clinton signed the National Missile Defense Act, which had been passed overwhelmingly by both houses of Congress. This law called for the United States to deploy effective national missile defenses (NMD) "as soon as is technologically possible." In signing the act, however, the President made clear that his administration had not yet made the decision to deploy missile defenses. In a carefully crafted statement released by the White House, the President emphasized that this decision would be made in the year 2000 and would be based on a number of factors, including an evaluation of the threat, the results of the development program, and progress in achieving arms control objectives. In particular, he noted the importance of "negotiating any amendments to the ABM Treaty that may be required to accommodate a possible NMD deployment."[1]

For NMD supporters, the National Missile Defense Act was a critical victory in a fifteen-year struggle, paving the way toward U.S. defense against the growing threat of long-range missiles in the hands of rogue states. President Clinton's reservations and qualifications were seen by most advocates as simply more of the same from an administration that had downgraded national missile defense programs and repeatedly lauded the ABM Treaty as the "cornerstone of strategic stability." Presi-

55

dent Clinton's willingness to sign the Act into law was attributed more to political expediency than to a commitment to take the necessary steps to protect the nation against the emerging rogue missile threat—a threat made concrete by the North Korean launch of the intercontinental-range Taepo Dong missile in August 1998. Nevertheless, although Clinton's remarks made evident that the ABM Treaty was still an obstacle, the momentum appeared to be with those who would deploy defenses. For NMD supporters, the political and military environment made imperative the deployment of strategic defenses.

For NMD opponents, the National Missile Defense Act was viewed as a challenge to what they held to be long-standing principles of strategic stability that had guided U.S.-Soviet and U.S.-Russian relations for almost thirty years. Most detractors argued that the emerging missile threat from rogue states or accidental launch was neither sufficiently urgent nor of a magnitude necessary to justify NMD deployment. Even for those opponents who expressed concern about this threat, the deployment of defenses would come at too high a price, not solely in terms of dollars but primarily in the anticipated disruption of relations with Russia, China, and U.S. allies. In other words, the reservations expressed by the President over the feasibility, costs, and arms control implications of missile defense deployments reflected the views of many NMD opponents. Opponents also appeared determined to block NMD deployments in the absence of amendments to the ABM Treaty—a Treaty considered a "sacred text" by the Clinton administration.[2] For NMD opponents, the political and military environment made imperative the preservation of the ABM Treaty, because the Treaty embodied the idea that defense of a nation's homeland against ballistic missiles would undermine international stability.

The positions of NMD supporters and opponents are derived from divergent views of the threat facing the United States and the best way to respond to this threat. This chapter describes the evolution of strategic thought regarding missile defense and the different policies adopted by past Republican and Democratic administrations to deal with the missile threat. It also examines the ballistic missile threat to the United States and the likely impact of NMD deployment on relations with Russia, China, and U.S. allies.

THE EVOLVING SECURITY SETTING: THE COLD-WAR YEARS

The 1972 ABM Treaty was signed between the United States and the Soviet Union at the height of the Cold War, when both parties were locked in a political, ideological, and military struggle. The threat to the United States from the Red Army in Central Europe and from Soviet nuclear-armed, long-range ballistic missiles that targeted U.S. territory was clear. The central goal of American security policy was to deter a Soviet attack against the United States and its allies.

Throughout the Cold War, offensive nuclear weapons were considered the basis of deterrence. In the early years, when the United States possessed a nuclear monopoly, a potential nuclear retaliation against Soviet cities following a Soviet attack on Western Europe was viewed as a credible deterrent. Because American territory was then invulnerable to attack from the Soviet Union, and because the United States could threaten nuclear destruction of the Soviet Union following an attack on U.S. allies, deterrence was seen as a viable way to obtain national security objectives.

Following the Soviet acquisition of nuclear weapons and intercontinental-range ballistic missiles, U.S. strategic force posture underwent a fundamental change. The requirement for secure second-strike capabilities led to the most substantial expansion of nuclear forces in U.S. history, including the establishment of the strategic triad of bombers, land-based missiles, and sea-based missiles. An equally pronounced change occurred in U.S. strategic thought. The new deterrence concepts of flexible response and graduated escalation, although placing more importance on conventional forces, still retained nuclear weapons at the core of deterrence. Most significantly, the original concept of massive retaliation—according to which the United States could threaten the Soviet Union while remaining safe from retaliation—gave way to the doctrine of mutual assured destruction (MAD). Proponents of this new doctrine, in and out of government, claimed that "stable" deterrence could now be based on the vulnerability of both sides to nuclear attack. If both sides understood that conflict could escalate to a central strategic exchange involving an unacceptable level of damage, neither side would initiate conflict. The result of this forbearance was crisis stability.

The ABM Treaty and the U.S.-Soviet Nuclear Balance

It was in this bipolar context that the ABM Treaty was designed. If both the United States and the Soviet Union were assured the ability to destroy each other, neither would be tempted to use nuclear weapons first in a crisis. This rationale was clearly reflected in the negotiating and ratification record surrounding the ABM Treaty; the prohibition of strategic defenses would ensure the "credibility" of offensive nuclear forces. In the MAD terms of the Treaty's protocol, the vulnerability of the parties' societies to nuclear annihilation would "lead to a decrease in the risk of outbreak of war involving nuclear weapons."

The language of Article I of the Treaty is explicit, committing each side "not to deploy ABM systems for a defense of its territory." By guaranteeing mutual vulnerability, the Treaty helped to assure stability in the Soviet-American strategic relationship. The Treaty negotiators did not provide an exception for what is today often referred to as a light territorial defense against third-country missile threats—threats that were not foreseen when the Treaty was signed.[3]

To ensure that the parties not "break out" from the Treaty or construct a foundation for a territorial defense, the Treaty places severe restrictions on radars (power, location, etc.), and forbids the development and testing of sea- and space-based ABM systems or components (as well as air- and land-mobile capabilities). Although theater missile defenses (TMD) are not explicitly proscribed by the ABM Treaty, the Treaty does prohibit the parties from giving non-ABM systems "capabilities to counter" strategic systems. Thus, although there are no formal limits on land- or sea-based TMD, these systems cannot be designed to defend against long-range missiles launched by any country at the United States.

Even before the negotiation of the ABM Treaty, U.S. programs to develop and deploy modest levels of strategic defenses, such as Sentinel and Safeguard, were attacked by missile defense critics on the grounds of technological feasibility and cost effectiveness, and as presenting a threat to arms-race and crisis stability. The national security debates of the 1960s and early 1970s reflected these criticisms. As a consequence, funding for missile defense programs was consistently reduced by Congress. The twelve ABM sites proposed by the Nixon administration before the ABM Treaty was concluded were whittled down in the budget process to two sites, a level that made little "strategic sense," in the words of Henry Kissinger.[4] In fact, the one ABM site fielded by the United States in the early 1970s to protect the Grand Forks ICBM force remained operational for only six months, because operating costs could not justify the limited defense coverage it provided. For the next decade, there were few serious challenges to MAD and the concept of deterrence based on offensive retaliation.

The Reagan Revolution

Not until President Reagan's announcement of the Strategic Defense Initiative (SDI) in March 1983 would the permanence of MAD and the desirability of the ABM Treaty come under sustained scrutiny. In his address to the nation, the President proposed as a long-term goal the development of a national missile defense that would render "nuclear weapons impotent and obsolete."[5] With such a defensive shield, Americans would not have to live with the threat of nuclear annihilation as the price of deterrence but would instead enjoy a deterrent based on protection from offensive missile threats.

The Reagan administration rejected MAD on both strategic and moral grounds, and sought to develop "highly reliable and effective" missile defenses to strengthen deterrence. As a first step in the deployment of increasingly robust defenses, the "phase one" objective was to field forces capable of intercepting a proportion of Soviet warheads sufficient to introduce substantial uncertainties in the calculations of Soviet planners. Introducing such uncertainties would enhance deterrence by undercutting incentives to attack the United States and its allies. In time, as technologies were developed to provide greater capabilities, the United States would deploy a more comprehensive homeland defense.

The Reagan administration saw the ABM Treaty as an obstacle to effective missile defenses because it inhibited research, development, testing, and deployment of the technologies and basing modes that had the highest payoff potential. Following an in-depth review of the negotiating record by the State Department's legal office, the administration announced that the United States had the right to develop and test space and mobile systems and components based on "other physical principles." Although strongly criticized by ABM Treaty supporters, this broad interpretation of the Treaty was defended by the Reagan administration and upheld as "legally correct." The overall efficacy of the Treaty also was questioned on the grounds that the Soviet Union was not complying with its terms. For years, Americans had been concerned that the Soviets had deployed a Treaty-prohibited ABM radar at Krasnoyarsk, a concern later validated by a Russian admission that the radar had been a blatant violation of the Treaty. During the Reagan years, however, the controversy over whether the Krasnoyarsk radar was a material breach of the ABM Treaty set off a heated debate about what would constitute a proportionate response to this Soviet arms control violation.

Although critics often charged that President Reagan failed to understand that defenses would not eliminate MAD because the Soviets would do everything in their power to penetrate any American defensive system, Reagan's opponents failed to realize that SDI was intended to transform the Soviet-American strategic relationship. In the Defense and Space talks, for instance, the Reagan administration sought Soviet agreement to move beyond the ABM Treaty regime to a defense-dominant relationship in which both sides would be unencumbered in deploying strategic defenses considered necessary for their own security. For its part, and contingent on implementation of START reductions in offensive nuclear forces, the United States also indicated a willingness to accept a multi-year transition period, during which time it would not withdraw from the ABM Treaty. As further encouragement to Moscow, Washington proposed confidence-building measures including "open laboratories" and information exchanges on research programs, and expressed an interest in exploring possibilities for a cooperative transition should defensive technologies prove feasible.

On the technology front, the Reagan administration, through the newly established Strategic Defense Initiative Organization, funded the aggressive pursuit of a number of strategic and theater missile defense capabilities. These comprised land-, sea-, and space-based sensor and interceptor programs that built on the revolution in computing and in other technologies that had occurred in the previous decade. For the longer term, more advanced technologies—for example, directed energy weapons such as lasers—also were explored.[6] By the end of Reagan's administration, the approaches considered most promising were space-based kinetic kill interceptors and space-based passive sensors. The SDI program also funded cooperative research and development efforts with allies, including the United Kingdom and Japan.

The Reagan administration did not just see SDI as a weapon that would allow the United States to beat the Soviet Union in an offense-defense arms race, as critics often charged. Instead, the administration believed that missile defenses offered a technical advance that opened up the possibility of creating a new strategic and political relationship between the superpowers. Reagan officials believed that MAD was not an inevitable by-product of superpower relations and that both Washington and Moscow could make the political decision to back away from Armageddon by creating a stable strategic balance based on robust defenses.

THE EVOLVING SECURITY SETTING: THE POST–COLD WAR YEARS

The end of the Cold War and, particularly, the demise of the Soviet Union in December 1991 ushered in a new era in security policy. No longer an implacable foe, Russia appeared to be searching for a place among Western nations by pursuing both democratic and free market reforms. As a consequence, the desire to build a strategic partnership replaced the adversarial distrust that had long defined the U.S.-Soviet relationship. It now seemed possible to transform Russian-American political relations and to eliminate the threat of MAD.

The G.H.W. Bush administration sought to capitalize on this profound change through arms control initiatives affecting offensive forces and through major changes in U.S. ABM programs. Both the United States and Russia took sweeping unilateral but reciprocal measures to reduce theater nuclear forces. Strategic force modernization programs were curtailed or abandoned. The START negotiations were re-energized and expanded. SDI programs and deployment architectures were reassessed and reoriented to the changed security environment in which a new and perhaps even more dangerous threat had begun to emerge—the threat of small hostile regimes armed with weapons of mass destruction and long-range ballistic missiles.

Global Protection Against Limited Strikes (GPALS)

Given the changes in the international political-military environment following the end of the Cold War, the Bush national security team put forth both an NMD plan and an arms control initiative. Following the Gulf War and the August 1991 attempted coup in the Soviet Union, Bush administration officials were most concerned about two developments. The first was the proliferation of ballistic missiles and nuclear, chemical, and biological weapons in the hands of leaders and regimes hostile to the United States. The second was the threat of an accidental or unauthorized launch, perhaps initiated by a breakaway military commander.

To deal with these limited threats, the Bush administration announced its intention to deploy GPALS—Global Protection Against Limited Strikes. Initially, the system was intended to consist of up to six ground-based sites with as many as 1,200 interceptors; a space-based sensor capability; and robust theater missile defenses. In the longer term, as the threat evolved, many looked to space-based interceptors as the key to defense against missile attack.[7]

In terms of arms control initiatives, during the summer and fall of 1992 the United States formally proposed fundamental changes to the ABM Treaty consistent with the GPALS concept. In the Ross-Mamedov High Level Group and in the Standing Consultative Commission, American representatives proposed eliminating restrictions on the development and testing of ABM systems. Officials also proposed eliminating restrictions on sensors. Disagreements in this area had for years dominated the contentious compliance debate. U.S. officials were convinced that no missile defense architecture that would permit even a limited territorial defense could be deployed without Treaty relief on sensors. They also proposed eliminating restrictions on the transfer of ABM systems and components to permit cooperative relationships on missile defenses with other countries, including Russia. Additionally, Americans called for the right to deploy additional ABM interceptor missiles beyond the one site allowed by the Treaty.[8]

The Bush administration's new position on NMD was presented to the Russians in a nonconfrontational, straightforward way. Officials made it clear that from the American viewpoint the growing threat of long-range missiles deployed by third parties compelled changes to the ABM Treaty.

The Russians also were told that the United States was willing to work with them on defenses but that, with or without them, the United States must protect itself from limited attacks. If modifications to the Treaty could be negotiated, then the Treaty could be retained. If not—and the message was direct—the United States would need to consider exercising its right to withdraw from the agreement, in accordance with the provisions of the ABM Treaty. American representatives also made clear that GPALS, with or without the ABM Treaty, would not threaten the offensive capability of the Russian force at START levels. The U.S. team stressed that with the end of the Cold War the United States and Russia should base their new relationship on common interests and cooperation, not on the suspicions that were the foundation of mutual assured destruction which had defined their relations as Cold War enemies.

The Russian reaction was telling. Their negotiators did not threaten or posture. They did not say yes or no; they mostly listened and asked questions to explore the U.S. proposals. At times it seemed as if the Russians were in fact seriously considering the U.S. proposal. President Yeltsin himself called for the joint development of a "Global Protection System" to protect "the world community" against ballistic missile attack.[9] Moreover, Russians apparently did not see American interest in GPALS and revising the ABM Treaty as reason to abandon arms control. While the United States was describing how changes to the ABM Treaty could enhance mutual security, the Russian and American negotiators concluded the START II agreement, providing for further reductions in strategic offensive capabilities, including the elimination of heavy multiple independently targeted reentry vehicle (MIRV) ICBMs, the core of the Russian nuclear force. Offensive force reductions, combined with preliminary discussions about the introduction of missile defenses, seemed to be laying the basis for a new Russian-American strategic relationship.

The Clinton Administration

In one of its most substantial departures from the Bush administration's security policy, the Clinton administration reversed course on national missile defense and the renegotiation of the ABM Treaty. In place of the Bush NMD program, the Clinton program focused on "technology demonstration and readiness" as a "hedge" against a potential future threat. In 1993, national missile defense programs were downgraded in priority, and funding was significantly reduced. Ongoing NMD programs, such as space-based sensors, were cut back; others, such as space-based interceptors, were killed. Funding for a ground-based interceptor and radar program was slashed and the third leg of the former SDI program—basic technology development—was severely scaled back.

The Clinton administration's reversal of the Bush position on the ABM Treaty was even more abrupt than its reorientation of Bush's NMD programs. Characterizing the Treaty as "the bedrock of strategic stability," the Clinton team undertook several measures to enhance the "viability and effectiveness" of the Treaty. They affirmed the "narrow" interpretation of the Treaty, making it more restrictive in the areas of permissible development and testing. They withdrew the proposed amendments that would have permitted GPALS deployment and the development and testing of space-based and sea-based systems. They negotiated a more restrictive agreement on ABM/TMD demarcation than had been sought by the Bush administration. They negotiated the "multilateralization" of the Treaty to include Belarus, Kazakstan, and Ukraine as signatories, making it more difficult to amend the Treaty in the future.[10] Unlike its predecessor, the Clinton administration saw the ABM Treaty not as a relic of a cold war that was now over but rather as the heart of its arms control policy.

Two factors explain the Clinton administration's policy on NMD and the ABM Treaty. The first was the benign view of the strategic missile threat to the United States held by the Clinton administration, at least until 1998. This assessment of the threat, especially that from rogue states, was later directly challenged by North Korean and Iranian programs that visibly demonstrated the need for defenses. The second factor was the concern that pushing for even light missile defenses would sour U.S. relations with Russia, preventing further progress on offensive nuclear reductions. This concern shaped U.S. policy on the ABM Treaty and the Clinton administration's approach to NMD deployments.

Assessing the New Missile Threat

The Persian Gulf War made evident how the international security environment was changing with the end of the Cold War. The threat that had defined the international setting for over forty years had been radically altered. At the time of Iraq's invasion of Kuwait, the Red Army was in a rapid and deep decline. The once formidable Soviet conventional force began disintegrating as it withdrew from East Germany and the other states of the defunct Warsaw Pact. The threat of a deliberate, large-scale attack on Western Europe receded with the coming to power of a reform-minded Russian government that sought common purpose with the West and that no longer commanded the conventional forces to mount a credible offensive. Given the changed political relationship, Russian nuclear forces, although still deployed in large numbers, were no longer perceived as an imminent threat. The greater concern in the West was for the safety and security of the Russian nuclear weapons infrastructure—a concern that led to the Cooperative Threat Reduction Program and other assistance to help prevent weapons from Russia's nuclear arsenal from ending up on the black market or in the hands of terrorists.

The decline of the Soviet threat, however, was accompanied by the rise of a new set of threats to the United States and its allies: a diverse group of small and unpredictable states armed with weapons of mass destruction and increasingly longer-range missiles. The central role of the ballistic missile in the arsenal of these states became evident during Desert Storm, when Iraq launched conventionally-armed Scud missiles at Israel and Saudi Arabia. One of the Scuds hit a U.S. military barracks in Saudi Arabia, resulting in one-quarter of all U.S. fatalities suffered in the conflict. Moreover, the investment of these states in nuclear, biological, and chemical weapons became very evident following Iraq's defeat.

In the aftermath of the Gulf conflict, international inspection teams revealed that Iraq had a significant nuclear, biological, and chemical (NBC) weapons program. Inspections authorized by the United Nations Special Commission (UNSCOM), as well as those of the International Atomic Energy Agency (IAEA) Action Team on Iraq, revealed that Saddam's NBC programs were far more comprehensive than had been esti-mated by U.S. intelligence agencies. In the words of one of the chief U.N. inspectors: "An immense military production establishment was found that was producing or striving to produce a broad range of chemical, biological, and nuclear weapons and missiles capable of de-livering them." Noting that this massive nuclear weapons effort had gone undetected in the face of international safeguards and other tra-ditional nonproliferation methods, he concluded that "the magnitude and advanced character" of Iraq's program "should stand as a monu-ment to the fallibility of on-site inspections and national intelligence when faced by a determined opponent."[11]

Just as the scope of Iraq's NBC capability was becoming clear, an-other state's efforts to acquire NBC and missile capabilities began to set off alarm bells in Washington. In 1992, following North Korean acces-sion to the Nuclear Non-Proliferation Treaty (NPT) and the collection of evidence by the IAEA during its initial inspections of the facilities at Yongbyon, suspicions grew that the North had already reprocessed plutonium from fuel rods for nuclear weapons. In early 1993, Py-ongyang ignited an almost two-year diplomatic crisis by refusing fur-ther on-site inspections—in violation of its NPT commitments—and by threatening to withdraw from the nonproliferation regime alto-gether. Although the immediate crisis would recede from the front pages of the world press following the signing of the Agreed Frame-work in the fall of 1994, concerns over North Korea's chemical and bio-logical weapons continue.

Even more visible was the expanding threat from North Korea's bal-listic missile program. In May 1993, Pyongyang conducted a flight test of its new No Dong missile over the Sea of Japan. Assessed to be capable of carrying unconventional warheads, and with a range greater than 1,000 kilometers, this missile was viewed at the time as only the first of several increasingly longer-range missiles being developed by North Korea for its own military and for sale to other states, including Iran.

With the Gulf War experience still fresh, the accelerated prolifera-tion of weapons of mass destruction and increasingly capable ballistic missiles vividly demonstrated the need for theater missile defenses to protect U.S. forces and allies. On this requirement, there was wide consensus across the U.S. defense community. The Clinton administration supported continued funding of theater missile defenses. It funded improvements to the Patriot anti-missile system (Patriot PAC-3), which was seen in action by millions on television during the Gulf War. It also funded the Army's more capable Theater High-Altitude Area Defense (THAAD) system and the development of a tactical missile defense system for U.S. Navy warships (Aegis/SM-2).[12]

By contrast, the immediacy of the long-range missile threat from rogue states was sharply disputed. For the Clinton team, the long-range threat was not considered urgent, although it was not excluded "sometime in the first decade of the next century." An unauthorized or accidental launch by Russia or China was assessed to be "unlikely," and the prospect of a deliberate attack by either of these states was judged to be "extremely low." These conclusions were reinforced by a 1995 National Intelligence Estimate (NIE) on "Emerging Missile Threats to North America during the Next Fifteen Years." The principal judgment of this assessment was that "no country, other than the major declared nuclear powers, will develop or otherwise acquire a ballistic missile in the next fifteen years that could threaten the contiguous 48 states or Canada."[13]

The conclusion of the 1995 NIE came under sharp criticism once it was leaked to the press. Critics pointed to two major failings. Intelligence analysts had not considered the threat posed by ballistic missiles to Hawaii and Alaska (the first two states to be within range of emerging missile threats), and they had treated the prospect of foreign assistance to proliferators as a "wild card" not to be considered in the central judgment (even though such assistance could accelerate both the rate of proliferation and the range and capability of missiles developed by other states). A number of prominent congressional leaders also noted the carefully construed language used in the report as well as the certainty with which it was stated, and charged that policy—not intelligence—drove the politically engineered conclusions. These concerns were further reinforced by the failure of the NIE's authors to state the critical assumptions on which their judgments were based, and by other "analytic shortcomings" that were later described in a General Accounting Office review.[14]

The Rumsfeld Commission and
the National Intelligence Council Estimate

In response to the 1995 NIE, Congress established a bipartisan commission to "assess the nature and magnitude of the existing and emerging
missile threat to the United States." Comprising experts with a broad
range of views and headed by former Secretary of Defense Donald
Rumsfeld, the Commission released its report in July 1998. This report,
containing the unanimous findings of the members, presented a much
different view of the emerging missile threat than that in the 1995 NIE.
The Commission concluded that "concerted efforts by a number of
overtly or potentially hostile nations to acquire ballistic missiles with biological or nuclear payloads pose a growing threat to the United States"
and that this threat is "broader, more mature and evolving more rapidly
than has been reported in estimates and reports by the Intelligence Community." Rumsfeld and his colleagues also warned that the Intelligence
Community's ability to provide timely and accurate estimates of ballistic
missile threats to the United States was eroding, and that under some
plausible scenarios, intelligence analysts might have little or no warning
before operational deployment of a ballistic missile force. The commission noted that extensive technical assistance from outside sources was
available to virtually any nation that wanted to develop ballistic missiles
and weapons of mass destruction. Perhaps most disturbing, the Commission estimated that countries such as North Korea and Iran could
threaten the United States within five years after deciding to acquire
long-range ballistic missiles, and that the United States might not be
aware that they had made such a decision until the missiles were being
deployed.[15]

In a dramatic validation of the findings of the Rumsfeld Commission,
North Korea captured global headlines with its launch of the long-range
Taepo Dong missile in August 1998. Once again, the U.S. intelligence
community was caught off guard. While Pyongyang announced to the
world that the launch was designed to place a satellite in orbit, the lesson for most American observers was clear: North Korea would soon
have the capability to strike American territory. Hawaii and Alaska were
coming into range of North Korean missiles that potentially could be
armed with chemical, biological, or nuclear weapons.

In the fall of 1999, the National Intelligence Council (NIC) released a report titled "Foreign Missile Development and Ballistic Missile Threat to the United States through 2015." The NIC report described the progress made in the previous eighteen months by states in Asia and the Middle East in developing long-range ballistic missiles. The report noted several alarming developments.

- North Korea's Taepo Dong-1 launch, that demonstrated its ability to deliver small payloads at intercontinental ranges (although the attempt to place a satellite in space failed, the launch revealed the North's acquisition of key staging and payload reentry technologies that are required for ICBMs).
- Iran's flight test of the Shahab-3 missile and Pakistan's flight test of the Ghauri missile (both are 1,300-kilometer-range missiles based on the North Korean No Dong).
- India's flight test of the Agni II missile, with a possible range of 2,000 km.
- China's flight test of the new mobile ICBM, the DF-31, with an expected range of about 8,000 km.

The report concluded that the proliferation of medium-range ballistic missiles "has created an immediate, serious, and growing threat to U.S. forces, interests, and allies, and has significantly altered the strategic balances in the Middle East and Asia."[16]

Assessing the emerging threat to American territory, the NIC suggested that during the next fifteen years North Korea "most likely" would acquire a small ICBM force, either by weaponizing the Taepo Dong-2 or by converting the Taepo Dong-1 space launch vehicle. The Taepo Dong-2 could carry "a several hundred kilogram payload (sufficient for early generation nuclear weapons) to the United States." Analysts also suggested that Iran probably would acquire an ICBM able to deliver a payload of several hundred kilograms "to many parts of the United States," and could test such a capability between 2005 and 2010. They also raised the possibility that Iraq could test an ICBM with sufficient range to strike the United States "in the last half of the next decade depending on the level of foreign assistance" Iraq received.

The report also considered the ballistic missile threat from Russia and China, noting that in 2015, Russia would retain as large a nuclear force "as its economy will allow but well short of START I or II limitations." On China, the authors stated that modernization would continue and that by 2015, Beijing would likely deploy "tens of missiles capable of targeting the United States." Analysts also noted that the Chinese strategic modernization program would produce both sea-based and land-mobile missiles with advanced warheads, based in part on U.S. technologies "gained through espionage."[17]

Together, the Rumsfeld Commission report, the Taepo Dong launch, and the revised NIC threat assessment led to a reevaluation of the ballistic missile threat facing the United States. The approval of the 1999 Missile Defense Act by overwhelming majorities in both the Senate and House, and the President's signing of the act into law, reflected this change. The Clinton administration now had to scramble to design a hasty response to a growing missile threat that it had downplayed for most of the 1990s. This response would attempt to balance concerns over the threat with concerns over the impact of even limited deployments of defenses on relations with Russia and the quest for further offensive arms control reductions.

THE POLICY IMPACT OF NMD DEPLOYMENTS

Unlike the Reagan and Bush administrations, which sought to change the political as well as the military basis of the Russian-American strategic relationship before deploying defenses, the Clinton administration never created an international political framework for the emergence of missile defenses. The result of this failure of diplomacy was strengthened opposition from Russia and China to U.S. missile defense proposals, as well as considerable unease among America's allies.

The Russian Reaction

Evidence of this failure to lay the political groundwork for the military and technical decision to deploy defenses can be seen in the Russian reaction to NMD. A number of U.S. and Russian officials have predicted dire consequences if the United States insists on amending the ABM Treaty or withdrawing from it. Several high-level members of the Duma have stated that any change to the ABM Treaty would result in Russia's withdrawal from the START II agreement and from any subsequently agreed reductions.[18] Others have suggested that the U.S. deployment of a national missile defense could lead to Russian abrogation of the 1987 Intermediate-range Nuclear Forces (INF) Treaty and the deployment of missiles prohibited under that accord. Although Russian President Vladimir Putin has been less strident on this issue than his predecessor, he also has appeared firm in his resistance to changing the ABM Treaty and has, at times, suggested that abandonment of the ABM Treaty would lead to a renewed nuclear arms race.

Russian assertions that dire consequences will flow from a U.S. deployment of even limited missile defenses, however, are inconsistent with Moscow's reaction to the Bush administration proposals in 1992 as well as Russia's approach to arms control and its own national security policies. Similar predictions were voiced in the contexts of NATO enlargement and air strikes on Iraq. Yet, in both of these examples, Russia acted on the basis of its interests, not its press statements. Russia's actions spoke louder than its words.

The same is true regarding arms control experience. When NATO decided to deploy intermediate-range nuclear forces in the early 1980s at the same time as it was negotiating the elimination of this entire class of nuclear weapons, the Soviet Union made stark threats to test the Alliance's resolve. Moscow promised to walk out of the negotiations when the first NATO missiles were fielded, and it made good on that threat in November 1983. But when it became clear that the Allies could not be shaken, the Soviet negotiators returned to the table, and the result was a total ban on these weapons.

The most recent example of Russia's pursuing its own arms control interests in the context of what Moscow refers to as "changing strategic realities" is perhaps the most instructive. When the breakup of the Soviet Union led Russia to conclude that the legal limits on deployed forces in its flank regions—limits established in the Conventional Armed Forces in Europe (CFE) Treaty—were no longer in its interest, its approach was straightforward: it insisted that the Treaty be changed. The United

States and the other parties accepted the Russian demand in the 1996 Flank Agreement. Since then, citing further changes in its security environment, Russia has insisted on additional changes to the CFE Treaty, and the West has accommodated these demands.

The principle is clear. Russia assesses the value of arms control agreements in the context of its defense requirements. When the security conditions change for Russia, it acts with determination to change the treaties. For the United States, the parallel to the ABM Treaty is evident. Although Moscow will not be pleased by U.S. attempts to modify the Treaty, it will most likely understand the U.S. position and probably will not act contrary to its own interests. Arms control negotiations to reduce nuclear stockpiles are important to Russia. To end the negotiations would end Moscow's best means for maintaining perceived parity in strategic forces—forces that remain the principal symbol of Russia's status as a major power.

Moreover, the future of offensive nuclear force reductions is less likely to be tied to formal arms control negotiations than to the realities of the post–Cold War world. According to almost all assessments, and independent of arms control outcomes, the Russians will be compelled by economics to go to much lower levels of offensive forces. Yet, even at the lowest force levels projected for Russia in the future, limited U.S. defenses would not undermine Russia's offensive capability. At the end of the day, if Moscow knows that U.S. defenses do not undermine its nuclear deterrent, it will be reassured that it has the force necessary to maintain its security.

The Chinese Reaction

The most vociferous opponent of U.S. missile defenses may well turn out to be the People's Republic of China, a country that has recently made threats to attack the United States with ballistic missiles.[19] Beijing repeatedly has asserted that U.S. deployment of theater missile defenses in Japan would upset the existing balance of forces, leading to a regional arms race. China has more directly threatened a strong response if Taiwan were provided assistance to build defenses, stating that such action would represent direct interference in China's internal affairs. According to Beijing, talk of such possible deployment, as well as of a U.S. national

missile defense, justifies China's own long-standing modernization programs. These include the development of mobile ICBMs, a new ballistic
missile submarine and sea-launched missile, MIRVs, and neutron (enhanced radiation) nuclear warheads.

China also has been a leading critic of U.S. efforts to explore potential
amendments to the ABM Treaty. Although Beijing seeks the public high
ground, describing the Treaty as "the cornerstone of global stability,"
the Treaty is most valuable to China as a *de facto* guarantor that Chinese
missiles can strike U.S. cities. China is free-riding on a Russian-American
arms control agreement that is no longer in the best interests of Washington and Moscow. Although it is not a party to the Treaty, China has
sought to create an international effort to block any amendments to the
Treaty. Working with Russia, China sponsored a 1999 UN resolution to
prohibit Treaty changes, and it has encouraged other governments also
to challenge any U.S. attempts to amend the Treaty.

Allied Reaction

The views of U.S. allies on national missile defenses and the ABM Treaty
are evolving. Two years ago, most would likely have argued that the political costs and risks would far outweigh the likely gains from deployment. Today, however, their views are very different. U.S. friends in
Asia, such as Japan and Taiwan—which experienced firsthand the over-
flight of the Korean Taepo Dong and of mainland Chinese missiles, respectively—are interested in exploring cooperative means to develop
and deploy ballistic missile defenses and are more reserved in their policy positions on the future of the ABM Treaty.

NATO allies continue to express concern about the possible Russian
reaction to ballistic missile defenses and about what is described as the
"decoupling" effects of a missile defense that would protect the United
States and not Europe. In other words, confidence in the U.S. security
guarantee would be undermined if American cities were less at risk of
attack than European cities.[20] This strained, counterintuitive argument
was quickly rejected by Clinton administration spokesmen, who stated
that U.S. credibility as an ally would be undermined if the United States
were vulnerable to blackmail by small states armed with weapons of

mass destruction and long-range missiles. The credibility of U.S. extended deterrence and threats to intervene in regional disputes would be strengthened if Americans were protected from regional missile threats.

British officials more recently have argued for the extension of U.S. missile defenses to cover European allies, especially if the Fylingdales radar, which is located in the United Kingdom, is to be upgraded to serve as an NMD sensor.[21] The French position also may have moderated. In February 2000, Defense Minister Alain Richard noted that Paris does not intend to be "absolutist or dogmatic" about U.S. missile defenses or the ABM Treaty.[22] Perhaps recognizing the domestic consensus in the United States on the need for a light national defense, American allies now appear increasingly reconciled to the prospect of U.S. deployment of missile defenses.

CONCLUSION

The Clinton administration's goal was to retain the central provisions of the ABM Treaty while seeking the right to deploy a defense against the near-term ballistic missile threat. With these dual objectives in mind, the administration sought Russian acceptance of its preferred architecture, which envisioned placing 100 ABM interceptors at a single site in Alaska, to be followed, perhaps, by a second land-based site.

This approach had a number of critical flaws. Strategically, the concept continues to base future U.S.-Russian relations on Cold War animosities, best symbolized by MAD and the ABM Treaty. In so doing, it perpetuates past distrust and suspicions that inhibit an improved relationship.

Even more significant, in an almost bizarre twist, the Clinton approach would have given Moscow a veto over future U.S. defense requirements. To get Moscow's approval of defense deployments, the Clinton administration proposed building a minimal defense that would be capable of defending against only a small number of North Korean missiles. When the number of missiles grew, or when North Korean designers added more capable countermeasures, a single site would be overwhelmed. Furthermore, because of the location of the proposed deployment site, there would be even less protection against missiles launched by Iran (a state that actively buys North Korean technology and missiles) and no protection against those who might attack U.S. allies. While the Clinton administration argued that if such threats were to emerge, the United States could again renegotiate further changes to the Treaty, few believed the latter to be a serious prospect.

In short, even if the Clinton administration had succeeded in achieving its stated objectives, the outcome would have been a dead-end defense. Moreover, as the components of the so-called "grand compromise" on strategic defenses and offenses emerged, it appeared that the Clinton team was willing to pay a high price for this outcome. Press reports suggested that in exchange for Russia's agreement to permit a single, land-based site in Alaska, the United States would reaffirm the Treaty's prohibitions on sea- and space-based missile defense capabilities. This would have foreclosed the pursuit of the potentially most attractive development options, and perhaps the only effective means to achieve boost and ascent phase intercepts to overcome sophisticated countermeasures that might be deployed in the years ahead.

Finally, moving from development to deployment, one must question the proposition that even very limited defenses could be fielded with only modest changes to the provisions of the Treaty. Article I embodies the purpose of the Treaty by committing each party "not to deploy ABM systems for a defense of the territory of its country and not to provide a base for such a defense." The words of Article I and their meaning are very clear; and if one applies plain and ordinary definitions, the language makes evident the need to confront the contradiction between today's imperative to defend America's population against ballistic missile attacks from rogue nations and the underlying strategic rationale of the Treaty.

NOTES

Ambassador Joseph wrote this chapter while on the faculty of the National Defense University. The views expressed are his own and do not necessarily reflect the position of the National Security Council or the U.S. government.

1. Statement by the President, Office of the Press Secretary, the White House, 23 July 1999.

2. See John D. Holum, Director, U.S. Arms Control and Disarmament Agency, address on national security negotiations, Wilton Park Conference, 25 April 1994.

3. Under the original terms of the Treaty, both parties were allowed two land-based sites (with up to 100 land-based interceptors at each) to defend the national capital and one ICBM field. In the logic of MAD, this "point defense" would contribute to the ability of the sides to retaliate in response to a first strike. (Under the 1974 Protocol to the Treaty, the sides agreed to reduce the number of permitted sites to one. Russia chose to deploy an ABM system around Moscow that probably was designed to protect against a small Chinese threat. The Russian site remains operational. The United States had for a short period an ABM site near Grand Forks, North Dakota, to defend one of the U.S. missile fields. Both the ABM interceptors and ICBM deployments near Grand Forks have been removed.)

4. Henry Kissinger, testimony before the Senate Foreign Relations Committee, Hearings on the ABM Treaty, 26 May 1999.

5. Reagan's SDI speech, March 1983, in *The Public Papers of the Presidents of the United States, Ronald Reagan* (Washington, D.C.: Government Printing Office, 1983), vol. 1.

6. Charles J. Infosino, *A Technical History of Ballistic Missile Defense from 1984–1994*, Department of Defense, Ballistic Missile Defense Organization, September 1995.

7. Michael O'Hanlon, "Star Wars Strikes Back: Can Missile Defense Work This Time?" *Foreign Affairs* 8, no. 6 (November 1999), 82.

8. Robert Joseph and Keith Payne, "Ballistic Missile Defense: The Need for a National Debate," *Strategic Forum* 37, (July 1995).

9. "Excerpts from Speeches by Leaders of Permanent Members of U.N. Council," *New York Times,* 1 February 1992, 5.

10. In the joint statement following the fourth ABM Treaty review in 1993, the parties stated their "commitment to the ABM Treaty" and the importance of "maintaining the viability of the Treaty in view of political and technological changes."

11. David Kay, "Denial and Deception Policies of WMD Proliferators: Iraq and Beyond," *Washington Quarterly* 18 (Winter 1995), 85.

12. Robert G. Bell, "Ballistic Missile Defense: An Administration Perspective," *Strategic Forum* 36 (July 1995), 3–4.

13. "Emerging Missile Threats to North America during the Next 15 Years," DCI National Intelligence Estimate, Department of Defense, President's Summary (November 1995), 1.

14. "Foreign Missile Threats: Analytic Soundness of Certain National Intelligence Estimates," General Accounting Office, GAO/NSIAD–96–225 National Intelligence Estimates B–274120 (August 1996).

15. Report of the Commission to Assess the Ballistic Missile Threat to the United States, House of Representatives, 104th Congress (July 1998), 2.

16. "Foreign Missile Developments and the Ballistic Missile Threat to the United States through 2015," DCI National Intelligence Estimate, Department of Defense, Executive Summary (September 1999), 3.

17. Ibid., 8.

18. Michael Gordon, "Putin Wins Vote in Parliament on Treaty to Cut Nuclear Arms," *New York Times,* 15 April 2000, 1. See also David Buchan and Stephen Fidler, "Star Wars Strikes Back," *Financial Times,* 6 October 1999, 22.

19. A recent commentary warning against U.S. support to Taiwan, published in the official Chinese military newspaper *Liberation Army Daily,* notes that China "is a country that has certain abilities of launching strategic counterattack and the capacity of launching a long-distance strike." Zhu Chengu, "Safeguarding the One-China Policy Is the Cornerstone of Peace in the Taiwan Strait—Splitting the Motherland by 'Taiwan Independence' Elements Is Bound to Provoke a War," *Liberation Army Daily,* in FBIS, 28 February 2000. Similar threats were made in 1995 by General Xiong Guangkai, the PLA's top intelligence official, who asserted that the United States would not be willing to trade Los Angeles for Taiwan. "China Threatens U.S. With Missile Strike," *Washington Times,* 29 February 2000, 1.

20. "Possible U.S. Missile Shield Alarms Europe," *Washington Post,* 6 November 1999, A1.

21. Michael Evans, "Britain Asks US to Widen Defense System," *London Times,* 31 January 2000.

22. Jim Hoagland, "Missile Defense Uncorked," *Washington Post,* 27 February 2000, B7.

3

The Changing
Technological Environment

DENNIS M. WARD

The debate over missile defense and the attendant questions about the future of the Anti-Ballistic Missile (ABM) Treaty have been driven largely by evolving perceptions of the ballistic missile threat to the United States and changes in U.S.-Russian relations following the end of the Cold War. But the increasing disconnect between the 1972 ABM Treaty and present-day security needs also arises from changes in the technology of ballistic missiles and the systems to counter them. Missile technology has proliferated, and many nations now have offensive ballistic missile capabilities that were not anticipated in the early 1970s. At the same time, technological advancements have created the potential for defensive capabilities that similarly could not be foreseen when the Treaty was signed in 1972. The result is a treaty that is increasingly out of step with technological realities. These discrepancies create conflicts between the Treaty's parties, over the interpretation of provisions that were drafted without today's technological realities in mind. New methods for accomplishing missile defense at both the theater and the strategic levels are increasingly constrained by the Treaty. This chapter examines the technological changes over the past thirty years that have created new interest in substantially revising the ABM Treaty.

DEVELOPMENTS IN OFFENSIVE FORCES

American policymakers' interest in both theater and national missile defenses is driven by their perceptions of new ballistic missile threats. The
threats stem from the proliferation of relatively unsophisticated missiles,
not from exotic technologies. Probably the most common theater ballistic
missile today is the Scud and its variants, developed by the Soviet Union,
which employ technology based on the German V-2 rocket of World War
II. When the ABM Treaty was signed in 1972, only the Soviet Union deployed Scud missiles.[1] Today, approximately twenty-two countries are
armed with these weapons. At least eleven other countries also possess
ballistic missiles with ranges greater than 100 kilometers.[2] But the transfer of relatively crude missile systems is only the first link in a chain of
events leading to the proliferation of missiles of greater range and technical sophistication. Many nations have used a combination of indigenous
ingenuity and outside assistance to create more capable weapons.

Rumsfeld Commission Findings

In 1998, Congress appointed the Commission to Assess the Ballistic Missile Threat to the United States to examine the reasons for the "new nonproliferation environment," in which access to the technology for ballistic
missiles and weapons of mass destruction is readily available. Donald
Rumsfeld, who became Secretary of Defense in the George W. Bush administration, chaired the commission. In its 1999 report, the commission
noted that in the aftermath of the Cold War some nations have been
working steadily to master ballistic missile technology, helped by Russia
and China. These states increasingly are trading technology and weapons
among themselves. Lax export controls in Western nations, including the
United States, as well as greater availability of technical information,
much of which formerly was classified, are putting previously out-of-
reach technology in the hands of aspiring missile powers. The proliferation of technological know-how and equipment (including computers
and test equipment) also aids in the development of ballistic missile capabilities.[3] The Commission concluded that ballistic missile proliferation
should be considered a permanent feature of the strategic landscape.

Among the most troubling developments were the increasing capabilities of North Korea and the transfer of missiles and missile technology to states that were potential adversaries of the United States.

North Korea

The missile program of the Democratic People's Republic of Korea (DPRK) provides a good illustration of the way old technology can be upgraded for the 21st century. Although the DPRK had tried to develop a missile capability based on Soviet surface-to-air missiles and unguided short-range missiles in the 1960s and early 1970s,[4] its ballistic missile development program did not begin in earnest until around 1975.[5] A deteriorating relationship with Moscow forced the DPRK to turn elsewhere for missile assistance. Egypt, with whom the DPRK had cooperated in the 1973 October War, obliged, supplying 65-kilometer-range Frog-7 missiles and launchers that North Korea reverse engineered within a few years. The main component of this nascent ballistic missile program, however, was a 600-kilometer-range missile jointly developed with the People's Republic of China (PRC) and designated the DF-61. The DF-61's range was important, because it would enable the DPRK to strike any target within the Republic of [South] Korea. Although the PRC cancelled the program for internal political reasons in 1978, that earlier cooperation provided important technological capabilities that North Korea put to use. The DPRK subsequently turned to the Scud to form the basis of its missile force.

The Soviet Union had transferred Scud-B missiles, with a range of 300 kilometers, to Egypt in 1973. Egypt sold them to North Korea in 1981.[6] By 1984, the DPRK, helped by Egyptian technicians, reverse engineered and flight tested the Scud Mod-A, essentially an indigenous copy of the Scud-B.[7] North Korean improvements to the original Russian design resulted in the Scud Mod-B, with slightly greater range than the original Scud. The DPRK began production of the Scud Mod-B in 1986.[8] The North Koreans began selling it to Iran in 1987, equipping Teheran with the arsenal needed for its 1988 "War of the Cities" with Iraq.[9]

North Korea's technological bootstrapping continued. It developed the 550-kilometer Scud-C by enlarging and lightening the Scud Mod-B. The Scud-C was first tested in 1990. Beginning in 1991, it was exported to Iran, along with the attendant production technology.[10] Although the Scud-C gave the DPRK the ability to reach all of South Korea, its range was insufficient to reach U.S. bases in Japan. DPRK officials apparently desired a new missile that could do precisely that, which would serve as the basis for an even longer-range missile. The effort to build this new missile, the No Dong, began in 1988. It featured a scaled-up Scud-C airframe and warhead along with a new engine and guidance system, which the DPRK developed with foreign (primarily Russian) assistance.[11] The 1,300-kilometer No Dong was first flight tested in 1993 and was operational shortly thereafter.[12]

The DPRK has since exported the No Dong. In April 1998 and April 1999, Pakistan tested its Ghauri missile, a No Dong purchased from the DPRK. Iran also has imported the No Dong, with deliveries beginning in 1994. Although Iran had participated in the No Dong development program from the beginning, it turned to Russia for assistance in improving the North Korean design. Iran's first test of its Shahab-3 missile occurred in 1998.

North Korea's long-term goal has been to acquire missiles capable of reaching the United States.[13] The No Dong put that goal within reach by providing the first stage of the DPRK's first intercontinental ballistic missile (ICBM), the Taepo Dong-1. Although many Western experts expected the Taepo Dong-1 to be a two-stage, medium-range ballistic missile (MRBM) with a range of up to 2,000 kilometers, the first launch of a Taepo Dong-1 in August 1998 revealed a three-stage missile capable of delivering small payloads to targets within a range of 6,000 kilometers.[14] The second stage was a Scud-C, and the third stage, a small solid-fuel rocket motor of unknown origin.[15] Although the first Taepo Dong-1 launch failed to place its small payload in orbit, the technical accomplishments it demonstrated shocked the military and intelligence communities in the United States.[16] The Taepo Dong-1 can deliver significant payloads to Alaska and Hawaii and small payloads to the western contiguous United States. Meanwhile, the DPRK is developing a more capable missile that could reach the entire United States with substantial payloads.[17] This new weapon is generally referred to as the Taepo Dong-2. This missile is expected to use a newly designed first stage, with a No Dong second stage. Such a configuration would enable the missile to deliver a 700- to 1,000-kilogram payload to a range of 6,700 kilometers. If equipped with a third stage similar to that used on the 1998 Taepo Dong-1 launch, it could deliver a 500- to 1,000-

kilogram payload within a range of 10,000 to 12,000 kilometers, thereby placing much of the United States at risk. U.S. intelligence authorities estimate that the Taepo Dong-2 could be flight tested at any time.[18]

Impact of North Korean Proliferation

Several features of the North Korean ballistic missile program have direct bearing on the evolution of missile defense technology. First, beginning with the Scud Mod-A, all DPRK missiles have been intended to carry weapons of mass destruction. The Scud variants are capable of delivering chemical and biological weapons, and the No Dong and Taepo Dong are probably capable of carrying a nuclear weapon.

Second, the DPRK has exported all of the ballistic missiles that it has produced. The Scud Mod-B was sold to Egypt, Iran, Syria, Vietnam, and the United Arab Emirates. The Scud Mod-C was sold to Egypt, Iran, and Syria. The No Dong has been provided to Pakistan and Iran. To date, there are no known transfers of the complete Taepo Dong-1, but because it is comprised of a No Dong and a Scud-C, both Pakistan and Iran already possess the Taepo Dong's main components. It might be only a matter of time and some outside assistance before Pakistan and Iran marry various components to create their own ICBMs.

Plentiful outside technical assistance for missile development is a third hallmark of the North Korean ballistic missile program. The DPRK has been both a recipient and a provider of technical assistance in the construction of ballistic missiles. Early cooperation with the Soviet Union gave way to cooperation with the PRC. Egypt subsequently entered the picture, providing hardware that the DPRK reverse engineered and then reexported to Egypt. Throughout the 1980s, the DPRK cooperated closely with Iran on the Scud-C. The DPRK also has shared ballistic missile technology with Libya.

Whether other countries will follow in North Korea's footsteps is unclear. Other nations have declared their intent or desire to obtain ICBMs. Some, like Iran, are making progress toward that goal.[19] But the North Korean model illustrates how the proliferation of offensive ballistic missile technology has drastically altered the geopolitical landscape since the ABM Treaty was signed in 1972. In the early 1970s, only the Soviet Union, among potential U.S. adversaries, was able to deliver missile payloads at intercontinental ranges. Today, the technology is increasingly available to nearly any nation that wishes to obtain a missile capability. The clear trend over the last several decades has been toward more missiles of longer range and greater accuracy.

DEVELOPMENTS IN DEFENSIVE TECHNOLOGY

The ABM Treaty restricts each party's right to deploy an anti-ballistic missile system, which is defined as a system to counter strategic ballistic missiles or their components in flight trajectory. In terms of the Treaty, an ABM system is composed of several elements: (1) interceptor missiles that are constructed and deployed for an ABM role, or of a type tested in an ABM mode; (2) launchers that are constructed and deployed for launching ABM interceptor missiles; and (3) radars that are constructed and deployed for an ABM role, or of a type tested in an ABM mode.[20] Thus, the ABM Treaty's restrictions are based on ABM systems that reflected the technology available in 1972: interceptor missiles, their launchers, and radars that tracked incoming missiles and guided the interceptors to their targets. Even though the Treaty delineates specifically what constitutes an ABM system, it fails to define the term "strategic ballistic missiles." This has proven an unfortunate omission, especially because the Treaty's central purpose is to limit the parties' ability to defend against a specific type of missile threat.

Anti-Ballistic Missile Technology circa 1972

Early U.S. and Soviet ABM systems were similar in design, although there were differences in the way each system operated.[21] In both the Soviet and the American systems, satellites equipped with infrared sensors were used to detect the hot exhaust of an adversary's ICBM, to alert command and control systems, and to provide officers on the ground with a rough calculation of the missile's trajectory. The first U.S. satellites for these purposes were put into orbit in 1970; the first Soviet systems were launched a few years later. Forward-deployed early warning radars were used to scan the sky in the direction of the attack and track the missiles once they came within range of the radar. ABM radars deployed in combination with interceptor missiles would wait for the missiles to enter their field of view. Once the ABM radar had tracked the missile long enough to compute an intercept point, an interceptor missile would be launched against the incoming warhead.

Both U.S. and Soviet anti-ballistic missile systems were command guided; that is, the interceptor missile's flight path was determined by commands transmitted from the ground through the ABM radar. The radar would track both the incoming ballistic missile and the outgoing interceptor, and command the interceptor to pitch or yaw as needed to bring it into the vicinity of the incoming target. The ABM radar also was used to discriminate among objects that might accompany an incoming warhead—rocket debris, decoy warheads, penetration aids, and even additional warheads—and to guide the interceptor missile to the desired target. Because the interceptor used a nuclear explosive to destroy the incoming warhead, great precision was not needed to make a successful interception. At the appropriate time, the interceptor's nuclear warhead was commanded to detonate, destroying the incoming warhead. The speeds at which the two missiles approached each other (about seven kilometers per second for a 10,000-km-range ICBM), relatively inaccurate interceptors, and the hardness of a ballistic missile's reentry vehicle made a nuclear-armed interceptor the only viable means for ensuring the destruction of the incoming nuclear weapon.

The missile defense systems on the drawing boards at the time the ABM Treaty was signed were essentially "point defenses"—capable of defending a relatively small region centered on the radar- and interceptor-deployment site, but limited by the day's technology from defending a larger area. Because the interceptor missile depended on guidance commands transmitted by the ABM radar, it was essentially tethered to that radar, and its operation was limited by the radar's range. The ABM radar was particularly crucial because it carried out the "battle management functions" required to sort out various targets and direct defensive missiles to their intercept points. The Treaty's numerous restrictions on the number, location, and operation of ABM radars, as well as on other radars that might be used for ABM purposes, suggest that radar technology created a fundamental constraint on ABM systems of the 1960s and early 1970s.[22]

National Missile Defense Technology circa 2000

Although the national missile defense systems now being contemplated are superficially similar to the systems deployed during the Cold War, new technologies are giving today's missile defenses new operational capabilities. A more capable interceptor employing a different kill mechanism (kinetic energy warheads rather than nuclear explosives), combined with advanced sensors, is creating a series of issues the ABM Treaty is not equipped to address.

Like its ancestor from the 1960s, the Safeguard system, the planned U.S. NMD system employs missiles, launchers, and radars to accomplish its mission. But the new system will be augmented by space-based sensors and early warning radars.[23] Intercepts will begin with launch detection by satellites employing infrared sensors that will track the boosting missiles until their rocket engines burn out. The initial satellite tracking data will be used to tell early warning radars where to expect to see the missiles enter their field of view. The early warning radars will form more accurate tracks of the inbound missiles, passing the data on to radars operating in the X-band (super high frequency). The X-band radars will track the incoming warhead and any objects accompanying it as they begin to descend toward their impact points. All the tracking data will be routed through a battle management, command, control, and communications system that will compute an intercept point and command the launch of one or more interceptor missiles.

Unlike command-guided interceptors, the NMD interceptor missile is capable of autonomous navigation to its intercept point. As the interceptor flies out to meet the incoming warhead, the battle management system regularly provides it with increasingly accurate reports of the target's trajectory. Using these in-flight target updates, the interceptor missile autonomously alters its course to meet the target. The interceptor also receives from the battle management system a target object map, or TOM, which is an image of how the incoming warhead and any accompanying objects are arrayed. The TOM is generated based on tracking data from the early warning and X-band radars and tells the interceptor missile what it should expect to see once it begins to engage the target.

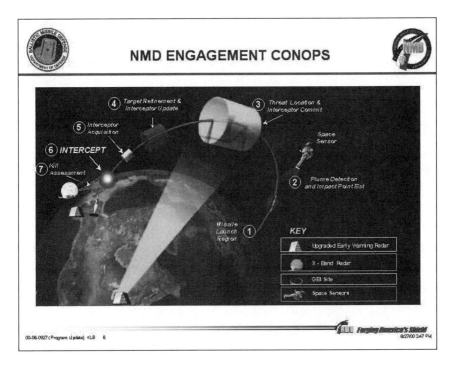

FIGURE 3.1   NMD Engagement CONOPS.
SOURCE: Ballistic Missile Defense Organization, program update slide, 27 June 2000, available on-line at http:/www.acq.osd.mil/bmdo/bmdolink/ images/conops.jpg

As the interceptor missile nears the intercept point, optical sensors on board the missile's kill vehicle scan the volume of space containing the approaching warhead and, using the TOM as a guide, make the initial efforts to pick out the warhead from among other objects or debris that are present. As the interceptor approaches its target, infrared sensors, capable of greater resolution and able to distinguish among objects of different temperature, take over for the optical sensors. The infrared sensors complete the identification of the warhead and guide the kill vehicle to a collision with it, destroying it with the enormous force generated when two masses totaling several hundred pounds collide at a combined speed of about ten kilometers per second.

Sensor Improvements

The current space-based launch detection system used by the United States for early warning of a missile launch, the Defense Support Program (DSP), is the same early warning system employed by the United States in 1972, although the satellites have been upgraded regularly over the years.[24] But DSP satellites will be replaced beginning in 2004, with a new system of missile warning satellites, the Space-Based Infrared System (SBIRS). SBIRS has two components. The SBIRS-High element will consist of launch detection satellites in geostationary and highly elliptical orbits. SBIRS-High satellites will replace the existing constellation of DSP satellites, and will greatly enhance U.S. launch detection capabilities. Whereas DSP satellites and their fixed sensors rotate slowly and their infrared sensors obtain data on a boosting missile's trajectory only a few times each minute, SBIRS-High satellites will have sensors that constantly view launch locations, providing continuous tracking of missiles in boost phase. SBIRS-High satellites will produce far more accurate estimates of a missile's trajectory than the DSP satellites they are replacing.

Like DSP, SBIRS-High will track missiles only until the point at which their rocket engines burn out and the missiles' trajectories become ballistic. But beginning in 2006, a new constellation of infrared satellites, SBIRS-Low, will be deployed in low earth orbit, where they will track the colder warheads and penetration aids through the mid-course phase of flight and the hot rocket exhaust during boost phase. The infrared sensors on SBIRS-Low will be both "scanning," viewing large areas of the earth's surface; and "staring," able to lock onto an object and track it through its flight path. Together these sensors will provide extremely precise data on the warhead's trajectory.

U.S. early warning radars also are being upgraded. The United States maintains early warning radars in Alaska, California, Massachusetts, England, and Greenland. These large phased-array radars operate at ultra high frequency (UHF) and can detect objects at longer ranges than X-band radars, but lack the degree of resolution needed for discrimination between warheads and other objects. As part of the U.S. NMD deployment, these radars will be upgraded with new data processing software and hardware that will greatly increase their ability to discriminate among warheads, decoys, and debris moving closely together through space.

The collection of improvements in sensor capabilities may seem incremental and unremarkable. But when combined with the improvements in interceptor missile technology, they actually have profound implications for the ABM Treaty, because they create a situation in which ABM radars no longer represent a major constraint on the conduct of strategic ballistic missile defense. The improved tracking provided by new generations of space-based sensors will provide far more accurate calculations of a missile's trajectory than were produced by battle management centers of the 1970s; this in turn will reduce the error associated with calculating interception points. The creation of onboard navigation capabilities means that the interceptor can guide itself to the intercept point without needing an ABM radar constantly to relay course directions and adjustments. If new data become available, the NMD system can exploit them by using an in-flight interceptor communications system to relay updated target information via radio to interceptors in flight. The discrimination data provided by early warning radars can paint a general picture of the target for the interceptor; advances in computer technology allow the interceptor itself to finish the job of picking out the missile warhead from a cloud of debris or decoys. U.S. NMD interceptors also are much faster than the interceptors that were used by earlier missile defense systems. With around twice the velocity of previous ABM missiles, they can protect much more territory than earlier missile defense systems.

What is remarkable about this new technology is that even a single site can provide at least some protection to the United States. An enhanced Capability 1 (C1) system—consisting of DSP or SBIRS-High satellites; upgraded early warning radars; an X-Band radar at Shemya, Alaska; a single interceptor site in central Alaska; and an in-flight communications system—can protect all fifty states from a limited attack originating in Northeast Asia or the Middle East.[25] A missile targeted at America's East Coast from the western reaches of the Middle East (e.g., Iran), however, would create a very challenging intercept problem for the system. A warhead approaching the United States from that direction would never enter into the radar coverage provided by the X-band ABM radar at Shemya. The intercept would be conducted solely on the basis of data received from satellites and early warning radars, and would be dependent on the ability of the interceptor missile to guide itself on its final approach to the intercept point.

Advances in sensor technology may eliminate the need for ground-based radars in future ABM systems. If the tracking data provided by the combination of SBIRS-High and -Low satellites proves to be of sufficient quality and resolution, the need for additional tracking by ground-based early warning radars would be eliminated, and reliable strategic missile defense could be performed using space-based sensors alone.

Political Rationale for BMD Improvements

Ironically, many of the technological advances incorporated into the NMD systems contemplated today are the result of efforts to develop missile defenses while staying within the bounds of the ABM Treaty. For years the Clinton administration maintained that there was no fundamental incompatibility between the ABM Treaty and national missile defense, despite the commitment each party undertook in Article I "not to deploy ABM systems for a defense of the territory of its country." The administration advanced the claim that Article I constituted a general prohibition that could not be violated unless one or more of the specific provisions contained in other articles of the ABM Treaty were violated. Thus, the Clinton administration tried to design an NMD system that could protect American territory from a single deployment site at Grand Forks, North Dakota, which had been the operating base for the missile defense system deployed by the United States under the terms of the ABM Treaty. This meant, of course, that interceptor missiles launched from Grand Forks had to be extremely fast in order to reach all parts of U.S. territory in time to complete an intercept. The idea that an NMD system might be deployed at Grand Forks also led to the need for upgraded early warning radars capable of performing early discrimination, because in some scenarios the single-site ABM radar simply would not be involved in an engagement. Ultimately, the laws of physics would not yield to the political need to try to live within the bounds of the ABM Treaty.[26] Eventually the Clinton administration admitted that sufficient coverage of the entire United States could not be accomplished from a single site at Grand Forks. Radar coverage of launches from North Korea required that an X-band

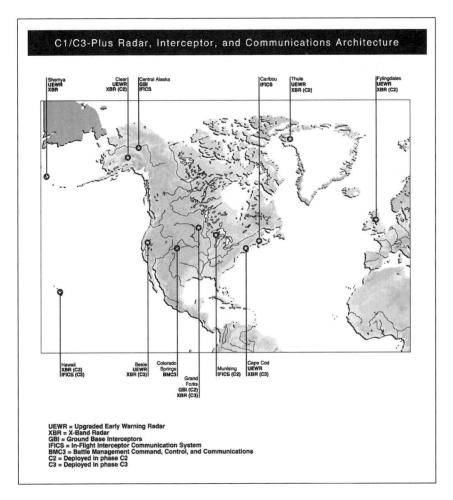

FIGURE 3.2   C1/C3-Plus Radar, Interceptor, and Communications
Architecture.
SOURCES: Ballistic Missile Defense Organization and David R. Tanks,
National Missile Defense: Policy Issues and Technology Capabilities
(Washington, DC: Institute for Foreign Policy Analysis, July 2000), p. x
available on-line at http://www.ifpa.org/pubs/nmd–bott.htm. Original
graphic created by Norman Tancioco.

radar be located far forward of the interceptor launch site, in violation of Article III of the treaty.[27]

Other Technologies

The Clinton administration confined its national missile defense development efforts to fixed, ground-based systems on the theory that such systems are more easily deemed compliant with the ABM Treaty. But development work done on various components of the planned missile defense systems might have conflicted with the Treaty. For example, the hit-to-kill technology now employed in the NMD system's ground-based interceptor warheads originally was intended for space-based interceptor missiles. Today's hit-to-kill warheads are direct descendants of the "Brilliant Pebbles" concepts introduced by the Strategic Defense Initiative of the 1980s. This technology is now being incorporated in warheads for surface-based missile defense. It also could be deployed in a space-based defense; but basing these hit-to-kill warheads in space would violate Article V of the ABM Treaty.

The Air Force's airborne laser (ABL) is designed to provide theater missile defense (TMD). But if it proves able to shoot down theater-range ballistic missiles, it also will be capable of shooting down strategic ballistic missiles. In fact, the strategic mission might even prove less challenging than theater defense. Long-range missiles burn longer and brighter than shorter-range missiles and thus make more inviting targets. The ABL also is demonstrating the feasibility of directed energy weapons on mobile platforms. These technological advances will have direct applicability in the space-based laser, which is now an experimental program.

Treaty Consequences

The missile defense programs currently underway pose numerous difficulties for the ABM Treaty. Even if Article I's fundamental prohibition on territorial defense and the treaty's restrictions on the location of the single permitted ABM site were lifted, the NMD system the United

States is on the verge of deploying creates serious conflicts with several other provisions of the ABM Treaty.

Since new technologies have eliminated the ABM radar as an essential component of ABM defense, an important question arises: what is substituting for the ABM radar? Some of the "battle management" functions previously performed by the ABM radar are taken up by the upgraded early warning radars. The planned system arguably violates Article VI(a)'s prohibition on giving non-ABM radars (in this case, the early warning radar) the capability to counter strategic ballistic missiles. If the two U.S. early warning radars that are deployed outside U.S. national territory are upgraded, they will violate Article IX's prohibition on the stationing of ABM components outside a party's national territory.[28] If functions previously conducted only by ABM radars are embodied in the tracking capability of the planned SBIRS satellites, this would arguably violate Article V's prohibition on space-based ABM components. Because these space-based sensors use infrared technology instead of radar, they arguably constitute an ABM component based on "other physical principles"; thus, their use would have to be negotiated among the parties. If interceptors are capable of conducting intercepts without an ABM radar, the Treaty's 1978 Agreed Statement leaves the question of their compliance to be decided by the Standing Consultative Commission (SCC).[29]

More exotic technologies on the horizon raise further questions. The ABL, for example, is both an air-based system and one based on other physical principles. As a TMD system, it is not "a system to counter strategic ballistic missiles or their elements in flight trajectory"; but it will unquestionably have the technical capability to serve in that role and thus could arguably violate Article VI(a). It could also constitute a violation of Article V, and if based overseas, of Article IX.

Thus, the technology employed in the NMD system now being tested—a system that the Clinton administration took great pains to make as treaty compliant as possible—and several other missile defenses now on the technological horizon create major conflicts with treaty provisions. These conflicts must be resolved if the United States is to deploy a national missile defense system and remain in compliance with the ABM Treaty. The possibility must be considered, however, that technological developments, to say nothing of growing interest in deploying national missile defense, can no longer be accommodated by

the existing ABM regime. John Rhinelander, who served as legal coun-
sel to the U.S. delegation that negotiated the ABM Treaty, testified to the
Senate in 1999:[30]

> [At the time of the ABM negotiations,] we felt we could look ahead
> about 10 years in terms of technology. But we couldn't look much
> beyond that. I thought personally that the ABM Treaty would be
> worked on through the Standing Consultative Commission; the
> treaty amended, interpreted, as you will, as technology changed, so
> you would have a live, viable, modern treaty to go with the technol-
> ogy as it was changed. That simply has not happened. Basically
> what you have is a treaty that is over 25 years old. Technology has
> evolved very significantly since then.

It is possible that these emerging issues concerning strategic defense
could be resolved through the normal operation of the SCC, which is em-
powered to negotiate modifications to the ABM Treaty to accommodate
the concerns produced by changes in technology or the strategic situation. But the SCC was never intended to serve as a forum to change the
ABM Treaty in fundamental ways, and historically it has had limited
success in doing so.

THEATER MISSILE DEFENSES

The proliferation of theater ballistic missiles has given rise to a class of
defensive systems that did not exist in 1972: theater missile defenses, or
TMD, intended to protect American troops overseas and U.S. allies. Because a variety of ballistic missile threats exists, several defensive systems have been developed in response to this proliferation. Relatively
heavy land-based systems are needed to provide broad protection for oc-
cupation forces in the interior of a theater of operations. Lighter, more
mobile land-based systems are needed to accompany ground forces as
they traverse territory. Sea-based systems are needed to protect troops
who must fight their way ashore in a theater of operations. The variety
of TMD systems stems from the fact that one type of system cannot meet
all the constraints imposed by various missions.

Most defense systems employ missiles, launchers, and radars to intercept ballistic missiles in the final (terminal) phase of the missile's flight trajectory. The probability that theater ballistic missiles will be equipped with nuclear, chemical, or biological warheads, however, makes terminal defenses a suboptimal way to stop a missile attack. For instance, a chemical warhead that is intercepted directly above its target might contaminate a large area with chemicals, making it nearly as effective as a warhead that is not intercepted at all. This kind of problem has fueled a drive toward more capable systems that can intercept warheads at extended ranges, or systems capable of conducting intercepts earlier in a ballistic missile's flight trajectory. Boost phase systems, for example, aim to intercept a missile very early in its flight, while its rocket engine is still burning. This approach has twin virtues: it destroys the incoming missile as far from its intended target as possible, and it increases the probability that, if destroyed, the missile will fall on the territory of the attacker—a possibility that could deter the launch of the missile in the first place.

Although the idea that defense against nonstrategic ballistic missiles would someday be possible was anticipated by the architects of the 1972 ABM Treaty, the negotiators did not incorporate any extensive limits on theater missile defenses into the Treaty.[31] Article VI(a) of the Treaty is the only provision that directly addresses defensive systems that are not ABM systems. Its proscriptions are general and were intended to preclude the use of (primarily Soviet) air defense systems to circumvent the Treaty's goal of constraining strategic defenses. Article VI(a) was not intended to set limits on TMD; the creation of highly capable TMD systems demonstrates the inadequacy of Article VI(a)'s vague provisions.

Land-Based Systems

The growing incompatibility between the ABM Treaty and theater missile defenses emerged following the Gulf War. During the war, the Patriot air defense system was hurriedly modified to enable it to intercept ballistic missiles, but this early defense system turned in a mixed performance. In response to the Iraqi use of Scuds against coalition targets and Patriot's weaknesses, the United States accelerated development of highly capable TMD systems. The first step undertaken was a program to improve the Patriot air defense system.

Patriot would form the lower tier of a layered theater ballistic missile defense.[32] Operating alone, it would be capable of defending relatively small areas against shorter-range ballistic missiles, such as the Scud. The upper tier was to be a new system designed exclusively for ballistic missile defense. This Theater High-Altitude Area Defense (THAAD) system was intended to defend large areas of territory against ballistic missiles with ranges of up to 3,000 kilometers. THAAD is a relatively large TMD system. It is not mobile in the sense that it can change locations quickly, but it can be transported to a theater of operations. It employs a powerful X-band phased array radar capable of tracking many targets simultaneously, and a 6-meter-long solid propellant missile equipped with a kill vehicle capable of operating both inside and outside the atmosphere. Its operation is conceptually similar to the Clinton administration's NMD system. Its radar scans the sky for incoming ballistic missiles and may be "cued"—told where to expect to see an incoming missile—by tracking data from DSP satellites. Cueing provides great operational advantages because it reduces the area that the onboard radar must search for an incoming target, thereby increasing THAAD's ability to detect targets at very long ranges. Once the target's trajectory is computed, an interceptor missile is launched and navigates to the intercept point, where it destroys the target by colliding with the incoming warhead.

THAAD's capabilities became a source of significant controversy within the United States. Article VI(a) prohibits giving non-ABM missiles, launchers, and radars "capabilities to counter strategic ballistic missiles." Questions emerged about whether THAAD could shoot down strategic ballistic missiles. The debate seemed to turn on exactly what was meant by the term "capabilities to counter" and exactly what constituted a "strategic ballistic missile." Neither of these terms is defined in the Treaty. The first Bush administration wrestled with the issue of what constituted "capabilities to counter" for TMD systems but failed to reach a conclusion before leaving office in 1993. The Clinton administration, as part of an effort to shore up the ABM Treaty, took a highly conservative view of the capabilities THAAD was permitted to have.

In 1993, the Clinton administration was directed by Congress to evaluate THAAD's compliance with the ABM Treaty. In response, the administration conducted a months-long analysis of THAAD's projected capabilities.[33] This evaluation took place as the administration was fashioning a comprehensive policy on ballistic missile defense. The evaluation of whether THAAD was compliant with the Treaty was based primarily on the capability of the radar to detect strategic ballistic missile warheads, and the ability of the interceptor to fly out to meet the warhead once an intercept point had been computed. Thus, two key characteristics of the system's performance—the radar's detection range and the speed of the interceptor—were the focus of the administration's efforts to assess THAAD's compliance with the ABM Treaty.

The analysis concluded that if high quality cueing data from DSP satellites were available, THAAD could detect an incoming warhead in time to allow an intercept. The Clinton administration concluded that until a clarification of the term "capabilities to counter" was negotiated, THAAD would have to be treated as though it were an ABM system and could not be tested. Ironically, only the Clinton administration and the arms control community in the United States argued that THAAD was not compliant with the ABM Treaty; Russian officials have never made such a claim.[34] In fact, the administration told Congress that despite its theoretical "capabilities to counter" strategic ballistic missiles, THAAD "could not be employed as an ABM system."[35] Nonetheless, the Clinton administration embarked on negotiations to determine a "demarcation" line between permitted and prohibited TMD capabilities, to allow THAAD to be designated fully compliant with the ABM Treaty.

It was not surprising that THAAD's performance would raise compliance issues, given this approach to assessing its capabilities. THAAD was intended to counter the most capable theater class missile existing in the early 1990s, China's CSS-2, with a range of around 3,000 kilometers. The least capable *strategic* ballistic missile subject to the 1972 SALT I Interim Offensive Agreement was the Soviet SSN-6, a submarine-launched missile with a range of approximately 3,000 kilometers. So between 1972 and the mid-1990s, the proliferation of ballistic missile technology created a near overlap between theater and strategic ballistic missiles. More-powerful radars were needed to detect such threats at greater distances, and advances in radar technology made such devices possible. Faster interceptor missiles were needed to intercept the incoming warheads at greater distances; again, advances in propellant technology and electronic miniaturization made such missiles possible. Thus, the proliferation of theater offensive capability, the defensive responses deemed necessary to meet that capability, and the technological advances that made such responses possible all combined to raise treaty conflicts and to produce an effect never intended by the agreement's negotiators: prohibiting defenses against tactical ballistic missiles.

Sea-Based Systems

The U.S. Navy also has pursued a two-tiered approach to theater ballistic missile defense in the wake of the Gulf War. The Navy's equivalent of the Patriot upgrade is the Navy Area Defense system. This is an evolutionary extension of the Navy's ship-based air defense capability, employing upgrades to the Aegis weapon system, radar, and missile to form the lower tier of naval missile defense. The system uses the Standard Missile Block IVA, a dual-capable interceptor missile that can attack aircraft or shorter-range ballistic missiles with its blast-fragmentation warhead.

The Navy Theater Wide system is a more capable, upper-tier, sea-based TMD system. Its technology and capabilities create potential conflicts with the ABM Treaty. In addition to further upgrades to the Aegis weapon system, the Theater Wide system will employ a much faster interceptor missile with a velocity likely to be between 4 and 4.5 kilometers per second, equipped with a kinetic kill vehicle capable of intercepts only outside the atmosphere. An interceptor missile of this velocity is considerably faster than ABM interceptors of the 1972 era, and potentially gives Navy Theater Wide significant "capabilities to counter" strategic ballistic missiles. Such was the concern of Congress when it directed the administration to evaluate Navy Theater Wide's compliance in 1994.

Since the system's flight testing was still years away, Navy Theater Wide's compliance evaluation also was by necessity a paper exercise, based on projected performance against strategic warheads. Unlike THAAD, however, Navy Theater Wide was declared not to have capabilities to counter strategic ballistic missiles. This judgment came as a surprise to many because the Navy's system had a faster interceptor than THAAD. The difference between the two systems' status stemmed from the lesser capability of the Aegis SPY-1 radar. The Navy maintained that an interceptor missile could not be launched from a ship until that ship's Aegis radar tracked the incoming missile. The detection range of the SPY-1, which was designed for air defense rather than missile defense, was insufficient to allow time to track a high-speed strategic missile, compute a trajectory, launch an interceptor, and intercept the incoming strategic warhead before it entered the atmosphere, where the Navy Theater Wide kill vehicle cannot operate. Thus, the Clinton administration claimed that the Navy Theater Wide program lacked a capability against strategic ballistic missiles, and it declared the system compliant with the ABM Treaty, provided the assumptions about its performance did not change significantly.

Since that initial determination, however, the Navy has continued to develop a Cooperative Engagement Capability, or CEC. The goal of the CEC is to combine or "fuse" tracking data from various sources into a single, composite track that can be used to fire a weapon from any ship that has access to the tracking data and is within range of the incoming warhead. For example, a missile launch from North Korea might be observed by ships off the Korean coast, by aircraft, and by satellites. Each sensor would track the missile's trajectory from a different perspective, and CEC would combine the data into a single estimate of the missile's trajectory. An Aegis ship with access to the fused tracking data would not need to wait until the missile entered its radar field. With tracking data of sufficiently high quality passed to it by other ships, it could launch an interceptor to meet the inbound missile at an appropriate place in its trajectory.

CEC already has been demonstrated to be an effective operational technique in hitting aircraft.[36] If this capability is employed in a ballistic missile defense, the implications for Navy Theater Wide, and its compliance with the ABM Treaty, are clear: a high-speed interceptor missile, coupled with the best tracking data available, produces not just an extremely capable TMD system but a system that could contribute to a national missile defense as well.

Boost Phase Intercept

The most prominent boost-phase system in development is the airborne laser (ABL), a Boeing 747 aircraft equipped with sensors and a megawatt-class chemical laser. Keying on a missile's hot exhaust, ABL's

infrared sensors autonomously detect and track ballistic missiles as they ascend with their engines burning. Once a track is achieved, the ABL's laser is aimed at the missile's engine and fired. If the laser is concentrated on a single spot for a sufficient time (on the order of a few seconds), it will burn a hole in the engine case, causing catastrophic destruction of the missile as it ruptures under the enormous pressure of the burning engine. The time required for the laser to burn through a missile, and hence the number of shots available from a single magazine of chemical laser fuel, depends on the distance to the target, the engine casing material, and the atmospheric conditions between the ABL and the target. The first attempt to shoot down a ballistic missile by ABL is scheduled for 2003. The system will have an initial operational capability in 2007.

The ABL is an example of a new weapon that the ABM Treaty did not anticipate. ABL is not an ABM system; that is, it is not "a system to counter strategic ballistic missiles or their elements in flight trajectory." Article VI(a) prohibits giving "capabilities to counter strategic ballistic missiles" not to non-ABM "systems" but to non-ABM "missiles, launchers, or radars." Because ABL contains none of these components, Article VI(a) does not appear to apply directly to the ABL. Likewise, Agreed Statement D calls for the negotiation of limits on ABM systems based on "other physical principles," but not TMD systems. Defenders of the ABM Treaty argue that a system's compliance status cannot be determined simply by the label attached to it and that the lack of a direct constraint on ABL is a loophole that was never intended by the Treaty's authors. But neither was it the intent of the Treaty's authors to restrict the parties' ability to defend themselves against theater ballistic missile attacks from third nations.

U.S. officials have considered other boost-phase TMD concepts, but little development work has been undertaken. One concept would equip unmanned aerial vehicles (UAVs) with infrared sensors and interceptor missiles. The UAVs would loiter in the vicinity of missile launch sites, detect launches with onboard sensors, and fire their interceptors at boosting missiles. In other concepts, the UAVs would receive their tracking data from links to networked sensors. These approaches to boost-phase intercept, however, raise issues with Article VI(a) and Article V's prohibition of air-based ABM systems.

DEMARCATION NEGOTIATIONS

Even as it was wrestling with the difficult compliance determinations for THAAD and Navy Theater Wide, the Clinton administration sought to resolve the ambiguity surrounding theater missile defenses through negotiations in the SCC. In November 1993, it initiated discussions in the SCC (with Russia, Belarus, Kazakstan, and Ukraine) on establishing a demarcation standard that would allow testing and deployment of advanced TMD systems without undermining the ABM Treaty's restrictions on strategic defense. The administration sought a clear standard that would update the Treaty in light of new technical advances.

The Clinton administration's initial demarcation proposal would have established a "demonstrated capability" standard, in which TMD systems were judged compliant provided they had not demonstrated capabilities to counter strategic ballistic missiles. Specifically, the administration proposed that TMD systems were compliant, provided they were not tested against target ballistic missiles traveling faster than 5 kilometers per second (km/s). The logic of this proposal rested on the fact that modern strategic ballistic missiles typically had velocities of 7 km/s, and the longest-range theater ballistic missiles (those of about 3,000 kilometers) reach a maximum velocity of 5 km/s. The proposal did not attempt to define a strategic ballistic missile but instead established a buffer zone between theater and strategic offensive missiles.

Russian officials accepted this logic with two caveats. First, they argued that the range of the target missile should also be restricted, to 3,500 kilometers; the U.S. accepted this proposal. But Russian officials also argued that a demonstrated capability standard was insufficient and would have to be accompanied by restrictions on a TMD system's inherent capability. They agreed that TMD systems using interceptor missiles with a maximum velocity at or below 3 km/s would not have capabilities to counter strategic missiles; but they argued that higher-velocity TMD interceptors should be banned. For the United States, such a demarcation line would have permitted THAAD, but not the planned Navy Theater Wide system or possible air-launched boost-phase systems with their anticipated interceptor velocities of more than 5 km/s. Citing Navy Theater Wide as an example, U.S. negotiators argued that interceptor velocity was only one factor influencing ABM capability and could not serve as the sole demarcation standard.

The negotiations continued for nearly four years, producing along the way a list of confidence-building measures, common understandings, "no plans" statements, and other measures intended to assuage concerns about the capabilities of planned TMD systems. At the conclusion of the negotiations in September 1997, two demarcation agreements were adopted. The First Agreed Statement acknowledged what the sides had agreed to from the outset of the negotiations: TMD systems with missile velocities at or below 3 km/s were compliant, provided they were tested only against theater ballistic missiles. The second demarcation "standard" was simply an agreement to disagree. It banned the testing of higher velocity TMD systems against target missiles exceeding 5 km/s in velocity and 3,500 kilometers in range; but adherence to these target missile restrictions alone did not make the system compliant. Each side would continue to make its own compliance determinations. The Second Agreed Statement of 1997 also expanded the ABM Treaty's restrictions on TMD systems by prohibiting the use of space-based interceptors for TMD purposes. In the course of the negotiations, the parties to the Treaty did not address the question of TMD systems based on other physical principles, such as lasers, despite Russian requests to do so.

Thus, the most recent attempt to update the ABM Treaty to reflect modern technical realities was largely unsuccessful. Despite four years of negotiations, agreement was reached only on issues about which there was no initial dispute. Moreover, events and the march of technology soon overtook a crucial part of the new agreement. In August 1998, North Korea tested its Taepo Dong-1 to a range of about 4,000 kilometers. The missile reached a velocity in excess of 5 km/s. Under the terms of the Second Agreed Statement, even if the United States were to buy a Taepo Dong-1 from North Korea, it could not legally test the Navy Theater Wide system against the missile.

The U.S. experience with demarcation negotiations does not bode well for future efforts to modernize the ABM Treaty. The inability of the parties to reach agreement on demarcation has guaranteed continuing friction between the United States and Russia over TMD systems. Knowing that the demarcation agreements are unlikely to win ratification, the Clinton administration never submitted them to the Senate.

In April 2000, the Russian Duma made entry into force of the START II Treaty (which was ratified by the United States in 1996) contingent on U.S. ratification of the 1997 demarcation agreements—an event that is unlikely to occur.

CONCLUSION

The technological advances of the last three decades have changed the nature of the ballistic missile threat and defense against ballistic missile attack. The ABM Treaty has not kept pace with these changes. Today's strategic ballistic missile defenses reflect the efforts by Treaty supporters to adhere as closely as possible to the Treaty's restrictions; yet these new systems cannot be made Treaty compliant with only a few minor changes to the ABM regime. The Treaty is even less capable of accommodating the more advanced capabilities that are on the horizon. The same is true for theater missile defense, which did not exist when the Treaty was signed in 1972. If the ABM Treaty is to remain viable, it must undergo a fundamental modernization that not only accommodates current technology but also creates new flexibility for timely adoption of new technologies, without painful and protracted negotiation. The imperatives of ballistic missile defense, as perceived by the United States, do not allow for an adaptive approach modeled on the demarcation experience. This might suggest that efforts to modify the Treaty to accommodate new technical realities are more likely to exacerbate potential conflicts than to resolve them.

NOTES

1. Scuds were deployed throughout the Warsaw Pact at this time but were under the control of Soviet forces.

2. Joseph Cirincione, prepared materials for testimony to the U.S. Senate, Committee on Governmental Affairs, Subcommittee on International Security, Proliferation, and Federal Services, Hearing on "The National Intelligence Estimate on the Ballistic Missile Threat to the United States," 9 February 2000.

3. Report of the Commission to Assess the Ballistic Missile Threat to the United States (the Rumsfeld Commission), Executive Summary, 17–19.

4. During this period, North Korea also received significant technical assistance from the People's Republic of China.

5. Joseph S. Bermudez, "A History of Ballistic Missile Development in the DPRK," Occasional Paper No. 2 (Monterey, Calif.: Center for Nonproliferation Studies, Monterey Institute of International Studies, 1999), 2.

6. "The Suppliers' Network," Center for Defense and International Security Studies (CDISS), available on line at http://www.cdiss.org/supply.htm.

7. "National Briefings: Iran," CDISS, available on line at http://www.cdiss.org/iran_b.htm.

8. "The Suppliers' Network."

9. "National Briefings: Iran."

10. Bermudez, "A History," 17.

11. The No Dong is also known by a number of other names, including Rodong, Scud Mod-D and Scud-D. See Bermudez, "A History," 20.

12. Bermudez, "A History," 22. As Bermudez notes, the No Dong probably entered low-rate production by January, 1991, even though its first flight test was more than two years away. This demonstrates a practice common in the missile programs of aspiring missile powers, by which operational deployment occurs with very little testing. While this practice incurs lower reliability and safety than U.S. standards would allow, most of the new missile powers have deemed these penalties acceptable. Intelligence officials have identified this "mirror-imaging"—the tendency to assume other states will use the same practices employed by the United States—as a reason for the failure of U.S. intelligence agencies to anticipate the pace of missile advances in aspiring powers. See Report of the Commission; and Robert Walpole, testimony to the U.S. Senate, Committee on Governmental Affairs, Subcommittee on International Security, Proliferation, and Federal Services, Hearing on "The National Intelligence Estimate on the Ballistic Missile Threat to the United States," 9 February 2000.

13. Bermudez, "A History," 14.

14. "Foreign Missile Developments and the Ballistic Missile Threat to the United States Through 2015," National Intelligence Council, Septem-

ber 1999, 9. The August 1998 Taepo Dong launch attempted (and failed) to put a small satellite into orbit. The apparent failure of the satellite was far less significant than the success of the rocket launch: As Robert Walpole, national intelligence officer for nuclear and strategic programs, pointed out, there is little useful distinction between a space launch vehicle and an intercontinental ballistic missile. The first, second, and third stages of the Taepo Dong had operated successfully, although the payload broke up and failed to reach orbit. See Bermudez, "A History," 30.

15. Robert D. Walpole, "North Korea's *Taepo Dong* Launch and Some Implications on the Ballistic Missile Threat to the United States," remarks to the Center for Strategic and International Studies, 8 December 1998, 2.

16. A 1995 national intelligence estimate downplayed the possibility of a "rogue states" ballistic missile threat to the United States before 2010. On 24 August 1998, Joint Chiefs Chairman Hugh Shelton gave Senator James Inhofe the Joint Chiefs' reaction to the Rumsfeld Commission report, which had challenged the intelligence community's assessment. Shelton wrote, "After carefully considering the portions of the report available to us, we remain confident that the Intelligence Community can provide the necessary warning of the indigenous development and deployment by a rogue state of an ICBM threat to the United States." One week later, North Korea launched its three-stage Taepo Dong-1. See Congressional Record—Senate, 9 September 1998, S10049.

17. Bermudez, "A History," 14.

18. "Foreign Missile Developments," 4.

19. Ibid., 10.

20. See Appendix A, "Treaty Between the United States of America and the Union of Soviet Socialist Republics on the Limitation of Anti-Ballistic Missile Systems (ABM Treaty)," Article II.

21. For a detailed description of the U.S. Safeguard system, see "ABM Research and Development at Bell Laboratories, Project History," Bell Laboratories, October 1975.

22. See Appendix A: ABM Treaty Articles II, III, V, VI(a), VI(b), and IX; Agreed Statements A, B, D, F, and G; Unilateral Statements B and D; and the 1978 Agreed Statement. Also see Appendix F: the 1985 Common Understanding.

23. For a description of the U.S. NMD system, see "National Missile Defense Program Architecture Fact Sheet," Ballistic Missile Defense Organization, available on line at http://www.acq.osd.mil/bmdo/bmdolink/pdf/jn9906.pdf (January 2000).

24. "Defense Support Program," TRW Corporation fact sheet, available on line at http://www.trw.com/seg/sats/DSP.htm.

25. A "limited" attack would involve a few warheads equipped with simple countermeasures.

26. North Korea is closer to parts of Alaska than is the permitted ABM site at Grand Forks. Given the time required to detect a launch, determine a trajectory and intercept point, and make the decision to launch a defensive missile, the interceptor is in a race it cannot win.

27. Article III requires that ABM radars and interceptors be contained in an area with a radius of 150 kilometers. The X-band ABM radar at Shemya, Alaska, will be located some 1,600 kilometers from the interceptor field at Ft. Greely, Alaska.

28. Giving a non-ABM missile, launcher, or radar "capabilities to counter"—proscribed by Article VI(a)—does not necessarily make that missile, launcher, or radar an ABM component as defined by Article II. But a test of an upgraded radar's intercept capability would constitute a test "in an ABM mode," thus meeting Article II's definition of an ABM radar.

29. The Standing Consultative Commission (SCC) is a permanent forum for the parties to the ABM Treaty, for the discussion of issues related to the Treaty—specifically, compliance issues. The SCC also provides a forum for the parties to modify the Treaty. The pace of negotiations, however, is glacial.

30. U.S. Senate, Committee on Governmental Affairs, Subcommittee on International Security, Proliferation, and Federal Services, Hearing on "The Future of the ABM Treaty," 28 April 1999, 15.

31. See testimony of Sidney Graybeal to the U.S. House of Representatives, National Security Committee, Research and Development Subcommittee, Hearing on the FY97 Defense Authorization for Ballistic Missile Defense, 26 March 1996.

32. Following the Gulf War, the Quick Response Program upgraded the Patriot's radar and provided it with a remote launch capability. Improvements to the battle management system and a new Guidance-En-

hanced Missile (GEM) provided the first PAC-3 capability. Additional radar and communications improvements, as well as an entirely new hit-to-kill missile, will complete the progression of Patriot from a 1970s surface-to-air-missile to a lower-tier theater ballistic missile defense system. See "Patriot Advanced Capability 3," Ballistic Missile Defense Organization Fact Sheet AQ–00–04, February 2000.

33. The analysis was based on paper designs, as THAAD's first flight test did not occur until 1995.

34. See the testimony of Dr. Kent Stansberry before the U.S. Senate Committee on Governmental Affairs, Subcommittee on International Security, Proliferation, and Federal Services, Hearing on "The Compliance Review Process and Missile Defense," S Hrg. 105-243, 21 July 1997, 29.

35. See testimony of Lt. General Malcolm O'Neill before the Senate Armed Services Committee, Hearing on FY95 Authorizations, 11 May 1994.

36. See "Summary of the Cruise Missile Defense ACTD Mountain Top Demonstration," Office of Naval Research, available on line at http://www.onr.navy.mil/sci_tech/special/zimet.htm (24 January 1997).

PART TWO

Defense, Arms Control, & Crisis Stability

4

Alternative Architectures and U.S. Politics

MICHAEL O'HANLON

The U.S. debate over national missile defense (NMD) appears likely to be resolved in favor of proponents of missile defenses. As a result, other debates that have lurked below the surface are becoming prominent. If the United States is going to deploy missile defenses, real decisions must be made about when to deploy a system, how large a missile defense capability to acquire, what types of technologies to incorporate into the missile defense system, and what type of revised treaty framework (if any) to attempt to negotiate with Moscow.

This chapter addresses some of the tough questions created by the debate over whether to deploy missile defenses and describes the domestic political forces that are likely to shape U.S. decisionmaking on the NMD issue. To do so, it employs the framework proposed by the editors of this volume. That framework delineates three broad categories of options for future ballistic missile defenses (BMD): one based on limited modifications to the Anti-Ballistic Missile (ABM) Treaty; one assuming moderate modifications that would allow virtually all systems now under development in larger numbers; and one envisioning an end to all treaty restrictions, and permitting unlimited future technological development. This chapter links one or more NMD systems to each of these categories and identifies the individuals or groups that have most actively promoted these systems.

The following analysis also considers choices to be made about the timing of deployments. Should they be quick, to provide the United States at least some possibility of protection within a few years? Or should they be made more patiently, to allow for normal weapons development schedules as well as more time to work out a revised ABM Treaty arrangement with Russia? If Treaty negotiations fail, should deployment allow time to mitigate the diplomatic and military repercussions of a U.S. decision to withdraw from the ABM Treaty outright?

This chapter's focus on systems that would violate the ABM Treaty in its current form is not intended to trivialize the relevance of the Treaty. Some missile defense proponents argue that the Treaty is already null and void, since one of the two original parties to the ABM Treaty, the Soviet Union, no longer exists. But that argument is too cavalier. Generalized to other areas, it would absolve Russia of the Soviet Union's other international responsibilities and treaty obligations—a development that would hardly be in the U.S. interest. The Bush administration may ultimately decide to withdraw from the ABM Treaty, but it will almost surely try very hard to amend it before going to such an extreme. In the end, the United States seems likely to deploy some sort of missile defenses even if Russia continues to object—but only after making sustained efforts to work out a negotiated deal, and even then, only in conjunction with other U.S. initiatives undertaken to assuage Moscow's security concerns. Unless the political groundwork is laid for these emerging missile defenses, NMD deployment could do more to increase nuclear danger than to reduce it.

APPROACHES REQUIRING LIMITED MODIFICATIONS TO THE ABM TREATY

Any NMD system would require a significant change to the 1972 ABM Treaty, since that treaty bans all national missile defense systems, allowing only localized, site-specific defenses. But the broader logic of the Treaty was to prevent defensive deployments that could destroy either the U.S. or Soviet second-strike retaliatory force and provoke an offense-defense arms race. The ABM Treaty was intended to ban strategically significant deployments that could prevent either side in the Cold War standoff from holding its opponent's society hostage. Missile defenses that are not strategically significant, at least in terms of the U.S.-Russian nuclear balance, might thus be grouped within a category of systems requiring only limited modifications to the Treaty, since they would be consistent with much of its original spirit. This section considers two systems of importance in the American debate over missile defenses that would require only limited modification of the ABM Treaty because they would not affect significantly the Russian-American strategic balance. The first system is the Clinton administration's planned national missile defense, particularly in its initial, more limited forms. The second system embodies a proposal for constructing a boost-phase defense by deploying fast ground-based, sea-based, or air-based interceptors near the potential launch points of countries that are judged to be threatening (e.g., North Korea, and perhaps Iran and Iraq).[1]

The Clinton National Missile Defense Program

The Clinton administration proposed a national missile defense system intended to intercept a modest number of warheads in outer space, with the goal of deploying an initial capability in Alaska by 2005. The complete system of 100 interceptors would have been deployed by 2007, assuming that a very optimistic development schedule could have been met. The threshold capability of 20 interceptors might be enough to shoot down perhaps five warheads. One hundred interceptors might shoot down dozens of warheads launched from nearby North Korea but only a few warheads launched from the more distant Middle East, since the Clinton system was not omnidirectional. The single Alaskan interceptor site would offer some protection for the entire country against intercontinental-range missiles approaching over the North Pole, especially from Asia. Its radar coverage and interceptor missiles, however, are placed in locations to provide maximum protection from missiles approaching the United States from over the North Pacific ocean.

Beginning in 1999 the Clinton administration allocated money in its future years defense program to deploy NMD. It added $6.6 billion to its defense plan for the years 2000 through 2005 to build missile defenses (for a total of $10.5 billion, including research and development costs).[2] Estimated total acquisition costs through 2005 eventually rose to $12.7 billion.[3] During spring 2000, the estimated life-cycle costs for the system were placed at approximately $20 billion (in constant 2000 dollars).[4] Even if costs increased by 50 percent over the latest estimates, as is normal for high-technology weaponry, they would hardly be enormous by comparison with other large-scale Pentagon aircraft, submarine, and ship acquisition programs.

The missile defenses proposed by President Clinton initially involved not only 100 very-high-speed interceptors but also a new "X-band" radar (with relatively high frequency and accuracy) and upgrades to various U.S. early-warning radars around the world. Improved radars were needed to detect incoming warheads and guide interceptors to them. This deployment plan was designated "C1" by the Pentagon.

An enhanced defense, termed "C2," would add three more X-band radars, interceptor missile upgrades, and an expanded communications infrastructure for the sharing of data among various sensors. It also might network the advanced space-based infrared surveillance (SBIRS-Low) satellite constellation to ground-based C1 radars. This sensor network would make C2 more effective against missile launches from the Middle East, which could emerge as a potential threat around 2010, and more capable against decoys and other countermeasures. It would be deployable by 2010 and would cost an additional $5 billion (not including the cost of the SBIRS-Low constellation, which would add another $10 billion to the total price tag).[5]

The C2 system would fall within some of the ABM Treaty guidelines, which allow as many as 100 long-range interceptors to be based at a single site. The ABM Treaty, however, does not permit a national territorial defense. The single interceptor base allowed by the Treaty is supposed to defend only the nation's capital or an intercontinental ballistic missile (ICBM) field. Thus, the ABM Treaty would need to be revised to permit deployment of the proposed C1 or C2 system.[6]

Are Development Schedules Realistic?   Was the Clinton administration plan sound? Hit-to-kill technology against an incoming reentry vehicle flying a clear trajectory now seems to be a reasonable technological basis for theater and national missile defenses

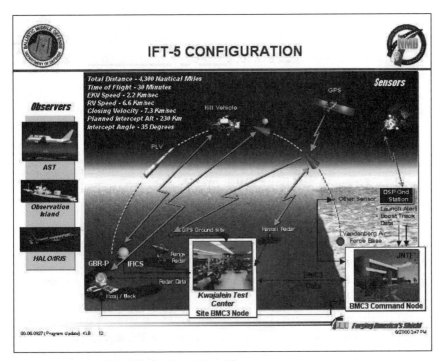

FIGURE 4.1   NMD Flight Test 5 Profile.
SOURCE: Ballistic Missile Defense Organization, program update slide, 27June 2000, available on-line at http:/www.acq.osd.mil/bmdo/ bmdolink/images/ift5prof.jpg

under development. Successful tests of Patriot PAC-3, Theater High-Altitude Area Defense (THAAD), and national missile defense systems were conducted in 1999, although critics charged that the 1999 NMD test was somewhat jury-rigged. An NMD test failure occurred in January 2000 when infrared sensors on the hit-to-kill vehicle lost the target just before anticipated intercept; another test failed in the summer of 2000 due to mechanical problems with the missile. But such problems are to be expected in high-technology development programs.[7] On the whole, missile defense technology appeared to be making important advances at century's end.

Critics might charge, however, that "hit-to-kill" technology programs have been rather hurried. Even the Ballistic Missile Defense Organization (BMDO) has acknowledged the apparent haste with which new technologies are being developed. In the words of Lieutenant General Ronald Kadish, director of BMDO, the program is being developed on a "high-risk schedule."[8] It is not clear why NMD should be deployed before shorter-range systems with much slower interceptors, like THAAD, can be fielded. Yet the Pentagon intended to do exactly that under the Clinton proposal.

Missile defenses do not have to work perfectly to produce desired outcomes. During Operation Desert Storm, imperfect missile defenses had a positive effect—if not militarily, then at least politically. Saddam Hussein fired about 90 Scud missiles at Israel and Saudi Arabia during the 1991 war, killing 28 U.S. soldiers, terrifying Israeli civilians, and nearly provoking an Israeli retaliatory strike that might have fractured the U.S.-led coalition. Yet the United States was able to persuade Israel not to retaliate, in part thanks to the deployment of American Patriot missiles to that country. Even though the early variant of the Patriot missile defense system, which had been designed primarily to shoot down airplanes, did not work well against Saddam's Scuds, it provided important political benefits.[9]

The experience with Patriot also reminds us that systems can be upgraded after they are deployed. Patriot's radar software now has the ability to distinguish between heavier and lighter objects so that it will no longer be fooled by the breakup of a missile's body during atmospheric reentry, as happened during Desert Storm, or by an enemy's use of simple decoys. Starting in 2001, the Pentagon is to deploy the next version of the Patriot with its new hit-to-kill interceptor missile. The interceptor has greater range, an onboard high-resolution radar and sophisticated computer processor, and 180 small thrusters for fine steering in the final phases of approach to the target (earlier Patriots had fins for steering, and employed blast-fragmentation warheads).[10] Experience with Patriot suggests that a national missile defense could be upgraded after being deployed, albeit at added cost, by improving its software, improving its sensors, or improving the interceptor missiles themselves. Indeed, the C2 system contemplated by the Clinton administration was designed to take advantage of future technologies.

A 1998 commission chaired by Secretary of Defense Donald Rumsfeld offered several reasons for deploying NMD promptly. It concluded unanimously that countries such as North Korea, Iran, and Iraq could quickly develop a missile threat against American territory. Criticizing the U.S. intelligence community (which had previously argued that Americans would have a decade or more of clear warning before most countries could acquire credible missile threats against the United States), the commission suggested that U.S. officials might now have little or no warning of this developing threat. That is because would-be proliferators could do much of their preliminary research in secret, conduct crash programs in missile testing, or buy missiles from abroad. The report also noted that proliferators could find other ways to threaten the United States—for example, with medium-range missiles launched from ships or from the territories of nearby countries.[11]

The sense of alarm created by the Rumsfeld Commission, however, could be counterproductive. Rushing a system through development may actually delay the point at which it becomes reliable. In addition, any U.S. missile defense program will have received so much attention by the time it is deployed that potential adversaries would surely know something about its test performance and operational capabilities. Indeed, another 1998 task force, this one led by retired General Larry Welch, argued that missile defense research programs were being pushed too rapidly, in what amounted to a "rush to failure."[12] General Hugh Shelton, Chairman of the Joint Chiefs of Staff, and Lieutenant General Kadish, director of BMDO, repeatedly have acknowledged that the NMD development schedule is very ambitious. The Clinton administration made plans to reach an initial decision on whether to deploy a national missile defense when only three of a total of nineteen integrated flight tests of the candidate system were completed, before the booster to be used in the system had been tested.[13] Even the total number of flight tests planned was modest for a major missile system. Although the last American ICBM to be deployed, the MX, was tested only nineteen times while under development, all other major strategic missile programs were tested at least twenty-five times. The Tomahawk cruise missile was tested seventy-four times; and the Patriot, perhaps the missile most comparable to the systems contemplated by the Clinton administration, was tested 114 times.[14]

The Decoy Question.   It is a challenge to any ballistic missile defense system to distinguish advanced countermeasures from actual warheads. This is not easy to do within the atmosphere; in the exoatmosphere, where BMD systems now under development will intercept incoming warheads, it is particularly difficult.[15] In outer space, air resistance cannot separate decoys from heavier warheads.[16] Even extremely light decoys would fly the same trajectory as true warheads, so speed could not be used to distinguish real missile warheads from fakes. To mimic the infrared heat signature of a warhead, thereby fooling sensors that measure temperature, decoys could be equipped with small heat generators. To fool radars or imaging infrared sensors, warheads and decoys alike could be placed inside radar-reflective balloons, which would make it impossible to see their interiors.[17] Such countermeasures would greatly limit the effectiveness not only of the missile defense system now under consideration by the United States but also of other exoatmospheric interceptors (including the Navy Theater Wide system used in a national missile defense mode).[18]

It is not, however, a trivial feat to develop decoy technology, nor is it easy to develop the technology to dispense decoys in space. After all, the superpowers did not construct multiple independently targeted reentry vehicle (MIRV) technology until they had deployed long-range ICBMs for more than a decade. (MIRV technology is more complex than decoy technology, but there are important parallels.) On the other hand, supporters of missile defenses who point to the difficulty that Britain had in developing ballistic missile countermeasures with its Chevaline system probably overstate the difficulty in developing decoys. The Chevaline system was designed to help warheads penetrate an endoatmospheric or terminal defense, and it is far more complex than what North Korea, Iran, Iraq, or some other country would need to defeat the planned U.S. exoatmospheric system. Nonetheless, realistic flight testing probably is required to make advanced decoys work. Thus, a state without the resources or diplomatic maneuvering room to conduct extensive flight testing might find it extremely difficult to deploy countermeasures.[19]

Countermeasures would be unnecessary for an attack that used bomblets filled with chemical or biological agents, because a single hit-to-kill interceptor could not destroy a cloud of tiny warheads moving through space. Such attacks would be less dangerous than those with nuclear warheads. Chemical weapons are intrinsically less lethal than nu-

clear or biological agents. Biological agents are most lethal when distrib-
uted over a wide area by a device like a crop duster. They also tend to be
most effective when the targeted country does not realize it has been attacked with biological agents until victims begin to show symptoms of
disease. Ballistic missiles are therefore a less than ideal means of delivering biological agents.[20]

In summary, a light nationwide defense using exoatmospheric interceptors could have serious limitations, but it might still be able to intercept the missile systems likely to be produced by North Korea or Iran in
the next decade. If China or Russia retaliated against a U.S. NMD deployment by transferring countermeasure technology to states developing an
ICBM capability (which the U.S. intelligence community fears they might
in fact do), then a BMD system would face additional challenges.[21]

Boost-Phase Endoatmospheric Interceptor Defense

To make it more difficult for an adversary to defeat America's missile defenses with fairly simple countermeasures, and to provide some defense
for regions outside of North America, the United States could develop
interceptor missiles for boost-phase defense. These would be fast-burn
rockets that would be fired immediately after an enemy launch was detected, catching up with the enemy ICBM while still in its boost phase
(that is, during the first few minutes of flight, while its rocket motor was
still ignited) within the atmosphere. At that point, the enemy ICBM—essentially a large gas tank—would be highly vulnerable and easy to detect, track, and hit. While in boost phase a missile would not yet have
had the chance to dispense decoys or countermeasures. Although a technologically advanced enemy could build fast-burn ICBMs to counter
such a defense system, these types of ICBMs would carry a smaller payload and be much harder to develop than missiles currently owned by
North Korea, Iraq, and Iran.[22]

Boost-phase interceptor systems could be deployed near the Korean
peninsula, in the Middle East, and near other potential trouble spots.
Given the nature of the threats, U.S.-Russian collaboration in constructing a boost-phase defense might be possible. Bases for boost-phase interceptors located on Russian territory would be particularly effective

against the North Korean threat. Turkey and countries in the Transcaucasus or Caspian regions would be desirable locations for boost-phase interceptors directed against threats from the Persian Gulf. Boost-phase defenses also could be based at sea.

The geographic limitations inherent in boost-phase defenses are both the system's greatest strength and its greatest weakness. Basing a defense on foreign territory would raise questions about its availability in wartime. In addition, land-based systems could become obsolete as old threats fade and new threats develop. But geography limits the reach of boost-phase defenses. Boost-phase interceptors targeted against one ICBM field could not be used to destroy missiles fired from other, more distant locations. This might make boost-phase defenses more acceptable to some leaders, because it could be demonstrated that it would be impossible to destroy missiles fired from their territory.

Boost-phase interceptor systems appear within technological reach on roughly the time horizon of the Clinton administration's planned C1 capability, and certainly as fast as the C2 system could be fielded. A boost-phase system would require a new interceptor of extremely high speed, but that could be built without radically new technology. Nor would a boost-phase defense require a sophisticated sensor network on a par with what the Clinton administration's program called for. Furthermore, such a system probably would not be as expensive as the currently envisioned NMD program.

This boost-phase defense concept also would require modifications to the ABM Treaty. But such modifications should not be very troubling to Moscow (or Beijing), since the defense would not work against missiles launched from the interior of Asia.[23] It would allow China and Russia to maintain their current deterrent forces, while allowing the United Sates to defend itself against so-called rogue states. Some analysts have estimated that the coverage zone of the defense would be about 1,000 kilometers beyond the location of the interceptor missile base. The interceptors would have only two to three minutes to make their intercepts, accelerating for about 100 seconds, and cruising at roughly 8 kilometers per second thereafter.[24] Missiles launched from central, western, and southern China or virtually anywhere in Russia would thus be beyond the range of interceptors based near the Korean peninsula, since they would have completed their boost phase before an interceptor fired after their launch

could reach them. Russian ICBMs based more than 1,000 kilometers below Russia's northern border would be invulnerable even if U.S. ships
with this boost-phase system were located in the Arctic Ocean.

APPROACHES ASSUMING MODEST
CHANGES TO THE ABM TREATY

This section considers more substantial changes to the ABM Treaty that
would allow deployment of virtually all systems now in development,
probably without quantitative or geographic constraints. The scenarios
considered here are at odds with the basic logic of the ABM Treaty, which
was premised on the idea that missile defenses should not be of such a
scale as to impinge significantly upon the strategic nuclear balance between the United States and Russia. The judgment that proposed systems
will undermine the Russian deterrent, however, is contingent on the relative effectiveness of missile defense technologies against the types of
countermeasures Russia could employ. If Russia can easily develop decoys and other devices to defeat U.S. missile defenses, then the latter may
present little or no threat to the effectiveness of the ABM Treaty.

But perhaps it would be acceptable to challenge the logic implicit in the
Treaty. On the one hand, the ABM Treaty was the product of a much different era. It resulted from the belief, widely held at the time, that the deployment of defenses would encourage an arms race without offering
meaningful benefits. On the other hand, even though the Cold War is over,
old arms race dynamics die hard. Both Russia and the United States maintain large and ready nuclear forces. Under these circumstances, deploying
NMD could rekindle Russian paranoia about strategic inferiority, possibly
halting offensive arms reductions and convincing Moscow to retain obsolete nuclear weapons systems. It could make Russia keep more forces on
alert, ready to launch on warning—with more ballistic missile submarines
at sea, for example, and perhaps a greater dispersal of tactical nuclear
weapons near Russia's borders with U.S. allies—at a time when Russian
equipment maintenance is shoddy. It also could threaten the Nunn-Lugar
Cooperative Threat Reduction program, with which the United States
helps Russia secure its poorly guarded nuclear arsenal. Thus, although
there is reason to think that the old ABM logic is no longer applicable,

there is also reason to worry about what could happen if the Treaty were abandoned altogether. Such considerations clearly will have to be weighed by policymakers considering Treaty revision or withdrawal.

In addition to the debate about the strategic consequences of abandoning the ABM regime, there are technical realities to consider. BMD systems relying on exoatmospheric interceptors probably will not be able to handle sophisticated decoys of the type that Russia or China could build. Technology, however, may provide a solution to the strategic dilemma posed above. By equipping their ICBM forces with sophisticated countermeasures, Russia and China may be able to defeat even robust U.S. missile defenses with a rather small second-strike deterrent force. By contrast, states that lack resources or sophisticated technology may not be able to deploy effective decoys—unless Russia or China provides them countermeasures.

This concern about possible export of countermeasure technology again underscores the importance of trying to work out a new strategic understanding with Moscow and Beijing prior to deploying defenses. Even if the United States cannot make them happy about NMD, it should do everything possible to be sure they do not retaliate against American missile deployments or efforts to modify the ABM Treaty.

An Expanded Form of the Current NMD System

The George W. Bush administration likely will choose to expand earlier U.S. plans for NMD. For example, the United States could deploy missile defense sites in both North Dakota and Alaska. If concerned about the sea-based ballistic missile threat, it also might add one or two defensive bases or special, dedicated ships along each coast, for a total of up to a half-dozen sites. A future administration could either continue to limit total interceptor numbers to 100, or expand them to 200 or more. Setting up two or more interceptor missile sites in this way is often described as the "C3" option. The Pentagon envisions possible deployment of a multiple-site system by 2011.[25] The C3 option, however, might cost as much as $10 billion more than the C2 option.[26]

The C3 option would be of such a scale and capability that it probably could not be viewed as strategically limited by Moscow. Given the poor state of Russia's nuclear forces and early-warning networks, only a very small fraction of its START II–constrained nuclear arsenal might survive a U.S. first strike, making even a small defense theoretically potent against it. It is possible that none of Russia's bombers, submarines, or mobile ICBMs in garrisons, and perhaps only 20 percent of its ICBMs, might survive a large-scale U.S. attack.[27] Under START II limits—which require that land-based missiles each have only one warhead—Russia could be left with fewer than 100 survivable warheads in a worst-case scenario. A highly capable U.S. defense with 200 interceptors might be able to destroy virtually all of a Russian second-strike force. These concerns could be amplified by a START III accord that further reduces offensive forces from START II levels.

To the extent Russian planners believe that they could not absolutely dismiss the possibility of a U.S. first strike—and military planners generally do not dismiss such possibilities—they might argue for violating START II limits or taking other steps in response to the U.S. NMD deployment. That might not matter to the United States as much as building a reliable defense against the emerging missile arsenals of other states. Russia's most logical response would simply be to develop countermeasures to defeat the defenses, a relatively benign development from a U.S. perspective. But if Russia had any doubt about the capability of those countermeasures, it would be difficult to describe the U.S. deployment of a 200-interceptor system as consistent with a limited revision of the ABM Treaty.

Navy Aegis Systems

The Navy Theater Wide defense system would use the Aegis radar deployed on about 60 U.S. Navy cruisers and destroyers to track enemy missiles, and a modified standard missile equipped with a hit-to-kill interceptor to destroy incoming warheads.

Of all the current U.S. theater missile defense (TMD) programs, the Navy Theater Wide system is the only one that has any potential role to play in a national or global missile defense system, thereby raising ABM Treaty compliance issues. The Treaty permits all theater missile defenses without restriction, but does not clearly define the demarcation point between theater and strategic missile defenses. In 1997, the United

States and Russia reached an accord that defined TMD as any system using interceptors that do not exceed speeds of 3 kilometers per second
and that are not tested against incoming warheads with speeds greater
than 5 kilometers per second or ranges greater than 3,500 kilometers.
This demarcation agreement is unlikely to be ratified by the U.S. Senate,
but it may nonetheless have some influence over policy. The Navy Theater Wide system, for instance, will not be tested against targets prohibited by the 1997 accord, even though its interceptor will eventually have
a maximum speed greater than 4 kilometers per second, making its status somewhat ambiguous. If Navy Theater Wide were linked to advanced sensors, its speed could be sufficient to give it some national missile defense capability.[28]

Seeing this NMD potential as a virtue, in 1999 a group convened by
the Heritage Foundation proposed using Aegis-equipped cruisers to
form a nationwide defense capability. It would, in their eyes, have offered a quick way to provide relatively "thick" nationwide defense in-
expensively. The Heritage group advocated buying about 650 interceptors to deploy on 22 cruisers (more than half of which would
presumably be in U.S. ports or coastal waters at any time, given normal
Navy ship rotation schedules). Other basing options included a barge
on the Great Lakes and a site in North Dakota. These interceptors would
be tested against long-range missile warheads to be sure they would
work against high-speed threats. Their radar systems would be linked
to large early-warning radars and satellites, including the SBIRS-Low
satellite system.[29]

BMDO estimated that the Aegis system suggested by the Heritage
Foundation would cost between $16 billion and $19 billion. That estimate includes the costs of dedicated ships (since defenses would be most
needed in wartime, a time when most Navy Aegis warships would be engaged in other missions) and upgraded missiles with enough range, ma-
neuverability, and nuclear hardness to provide reliable nationwide defense. Pentagon officials claimed that the planned Navy Theater Wide
missiles would not do the NMD job adequately.[30] Officials did concede,
however, that the Navy Theater Wide system might do a good job of
complementing a ground-based system by covering coastal areas better
than ground sites in Alaska or North Dakota could, and by providing
additional radars and interceptors.[31]

FUTURISTIC TECHNOLOGIES
WITHOUT TREATY CONSTRAINTS

Looking further into the future, one can imagine technologies other than ground-based interceptors. The two technologies of greatest interest are lasers and orbiting interceptors. Lasers could be airborne (if the location of a threat could be predicted and if it were a country of modest size), or space-based. Orbiting interceptors would be a derivative of the "Brilliant Pebbles" satellite weapons concept that figured prominently in the first Bush administration's Global Protection Against Limited Strikes (GPALS) system.

Other systems are within the reach of current technology. For example, to deal with the decoy threat, one could consider returning to the brute-force method of placing nuclear warheads atop exoatmospheric interceptor missiles. Exo-/endoatmospheric interceptor missiles also might be built that would leave the atmosphere to cover most of the distance they would need to fly, and then reenter the atmosphere to home in on a warhead as air resistance separates it from decoys. But these concepts have received little attention in the NMD debate.

Laser Technologies

Laser technologies that could be used to destroy missiles in their vulnerable boost phases remain in early development today.[32] There has been progress in these areas since the Strategic Defense Initiative of the early 1980s, but proponents expect greater advances in the near future.

The airborne laser program is intended to destroy missiles launched within a few hundred kilometers of the aircraft carrying the laser. The aircraft would be airborne and "on call" just outside enemy airspace at all times, since it would have to react within a very short period after launch of the missile. The Air Force plans to move the airborne laser into engineering and manufacturing development in 2004 and to have the system operating by 2009, with a total of seven aircraft and lasers (two of which could be airborne at any given time for extended periods), at a total cost of about $11 billion.

The aircraft would fly above cloud cover, at 40,000 feet. Each would contain enough chemical energy power for its laser to destroy 20 missiles, before the craft would have to land and refuel. The system is promising, but its development schedule is considered quite compressed; for example, the first airborne test firings of the laser are scheduled to occur only a few months before the first tests against actual targets, allowing little time for problem solving should anything go wrong. The program has not demonstrated the ability to track a target precisely enough to deliver a lethal dose of energy to the rocket. Nor have ground tests yet proven that the right kind of laser can even produce sufficient power to make the concept feasible. Ground tests have used a different type of laser than the one that ultimately would be needed in the weapon system.[33]

The space-based laser would provide more coverage than airborne systems. It would, however, require a substantial constellation of satellites to produce extensive coverage. The near-Earth part of outer space is enormous, and the Earth's curvature limits the area that a given satellite can cover at one time. More than thirty-five satellites might be needed to provide global coverage. The Pentagon hopes to build a demonstrator for this program (employing lasers with enough range to destroy targets up to 2,500 miles away within a few seconds) around 2010 and to be in a position to consider deployment by about 2020.[34] Speculating about the ultimate feasibility of this technology now is premature, but unless radical breakthroughs occur—as they must, to make the concept feasible—costs would be exorbitant. Each satellite would be huge (larger than the Hubble Space Telescope), extremely expensive to build, and very expensive to put into orbit. Using anything akin to current technologies, the total system cost would surely be well over $100 billion.[35]

GPALS

Some would advocate building a much larger national missile defense, such as former President George H. Bush's Global Protection Against Limited Strikes system. That design included 1,000 space-based "Brilliant Pebbles" and 750 ground-based interceptors at a total of six sites. Depending on how an enemy attacked, such a defense might be capable of shooting down 100 to 200 warheads, allowing no more than several warheads to get through. A system of this size would be needed, for instance, to defend against a launch by a rogue Russian commander, which might involve all the warheads on a submarine or within an ICBM field. A large system also would be needed to counter an expanded Chinese threat, should the United States decide to try to escape a mutual hostage relationship with Beijing.

GPALS would provide a second type of capability to complement ground-based missile defenses, providing redundancy as well as resilience against some types of countermeasures. It may be less futuristic than space-based lasers, but the problem of tracking and homing on reentry vehicles in space, as Brilliant Pebbles would have to do, is hardly trivial.

GPALS also would be very expensive. It would cost a minimum of $100 billion, given that weapons of such complexity can easily increase in cost by 50 percent or more during production.[36] Like the smaller and cheaper systems proposed by the Clinton administration, it too might be virtually useless against a missile force armed with sophisticated countermeasures. Brilliant Pebbles could be defeated by simple decoys and "anti-simulation" techniques that would make warheads resemble decoys.

THE DOMESTIC POLITICS OF MISSILE DEFENSES IN THE UNITED STATES

The options for a U.S. missile defense system vary in size, technological underpinnings, likely capabilities, arms control implications, and time horizons. They also vary in their political lineages and political support base within the United States. Understanding these dimensions of the BMD debate is important for gauging where U.S. NMD programs and deployments are headed. A decision to deploy would hardly be the end of the matter for the U.S. government and public.

To fully understand the politics of missile defense in the United States, one must first trace the development of the current consensus in favor of deploying some type of national missile defense quickly, and assess the strength of that consensus. Second, it has become increasingly important to identify the various schools of thought within the camps of missile defense proponents, and to estimate the relative strength and influence of each of these camps in the years ahead.

The Emergence of a Pro-NMD
Consensus in the United States

U.S. support for NMD over the past two decades dates from Ronald Reagan's 1983 Strategic Defense Initiative (SDI). The idea behind SDI is still popular, particularly among Republicans, and still is credited by many with helping to convince the Soviet Union that it could not win the global struggle with the West. Support for SDI eventually waned, but the concept received a boost during the 1991 Persian Gulf War when the emerging missile threat was graphically demonstrated. The Gulf War, however, primarily gave impetus to theater-defense efforts against shorter-range missiles such as the Iraqi Scud.

The Clinton administration's strategic defense plans date to the Republican takeover of Congress. As promised in their 1994 Contract with America, the Republican majority proceeded to write a defense authorization bill mandating a national missile defense by 2003. President Clinton vetoed the bill, but his administration then devised its "3+3" program to develop a system over three years, with a decision to be made in 2000 whether to deploy the system over the following three years. To make the program more realistic, the Pentagon's May 1997 Quadrennial Defense Review added $2.3 billion to the 3+3 program, doubling planned costs over the six-year period.[37]

Support for NMD grew in 1998. In that year, both Iran and North Korea surprised the U.S. intelligence community with missile tests that showed rapid progress in their respective missile programs. Iran tested the Shahab-3, with a range of some 1,300 kilometers, and continued to develop the Shahab-4, with an estimated range of at least 2,000 kilometers. North Korea tested the Taepo Dong-1, with a range of some 2,000 kilometers, and continued work on the Taepo Dong-2, with a range of 4,000 to 6,000 kilometers. (A range of 4,000 kilometers would put the Aleutian Islands within reach; a range of 6,000 kilometers would put most of Alaska and the small western islands of Hawaii at risk.) The Taepo Dong-2 might even be able to deliver a moderately large payload to the continental United States if North Korea were to succeed in adding a third stage to it, as it tried to do with the Taepo Dong-1 in 1998.[38]

After the Clinton administration submitted its missile defense budget in February 1999, which included money for eventual deployment, overwhelming majorities of both houses of Congress passed a bill declaring it the policy of the United States to deploy a national missile defense "as soon as technologically feasible." That seemingly made the U.S. position on missile defense clear and bipartisan—but with an important caveat. Amendments to the 1999 bill required that consideration be given to the budgetary and arms control implications of any such deployment.[39] Republican proponents of the bill considered these amendments secondary issues, but the President emphasized them when he signed the bill into law in July 1999, as had many Congressional arms control advocates when they voted for the legislation. One should not, therefore, read too much into the 1999 bill. The U.S. political winds are now blowing more strongly in favor of missile defenses; but just how strongly, is a function of which programs one is considering and of what Russia's reactions to each program may be.[40]

Schools of Thought Among
Missile Defense Supporters and Opponents

The above litany of proposals suggests three main camps of ballistic missile defense proponents: those favoring limited deployments (treaty compliant if possible—but in any case, measured, and designed to reassure Russia); those favoring more expansive efforts (but still bound by an arms control regime and the need to maintain positive U.S.-Russian relations);[41] and those relatively indifferent to any potential political effects of defenses on arms control or U.S.-Russian relations. At the risk of oversimplifying the matter, the first school appears most consistent with the Clinton/Gore approach, the second with former President Bush and moderate Republicans, and the third with many Republican conservatives, particularly those in Congress. President George W. Bush also can be placed in one of the latter two categories.

There is also a fourth group in Congress: missile defense opponents. Some are convinced that missile defenses will not work; others, that it cannot be consistent with good U.S.-Russian relations. A number may be willing to reconsider their positions someday, but most would put off that day of reckoning many years into the future.[42]

What is the likelihood that one of these groups will see its vision fulfilled? Answering this question requires conjecture; but several background points can help inform the speculation. First, technologically speaking, the Clinton administration would have been hard-pressed to have its NMD program ready for deployment by 2005. Most other national missile defense technologies will not be deployable before 2010. Even the Navy Theater Wide system, which is based on existing Aegis ships, will not be deployable before 2007.

Second, individuals' views on this subject differ, depending on their function and position in the government. Generally, Congress has been more willing to adopt strongly pro-BMD positions than have presidents. Even when George H. Bush promoted GPALS late in his presidency, he simultaneously gave high priority to negotiating START II—and profited from knowing that GPALS technology was not advanced enough to require him to consider violating the ABM Treaty or to try very hard to modify it in negotiations with Russia. He could have his cake (START II) and eat it too (laying out a vision for GPALS without having to take difficult steps to implement it). The present and future U.S. presidents will need to work with Russia on a range of security issues. Once he is out of office, a president's foreign policy record will be assessed partly as a function of what happened with Russia on his watch. These broader considerations, to say nothing of the state of the technology, argue in favor of a more tempered, patient approach to missile defenses than that preferred by many Republican pundits and members of Congress.

Third, there is an emerging twist to the traditional debate about strategic stability: the China angle. With a force of only about 20 ICBMs at present, China might not be able to overwhelm a C1 or C2 system through force of numbers alone. It would need countermeasures. The deployment of countermeasures, however, might not give the Chinese sufficient confidence in the effectiveness of their second-strike force, pushing them to consider a nuclear buildup in reply to U.S. defenses. Some Americans argue that these Chinese reactions should concern the United States. They suggest that Washington should limit its missile defenses so that the People's Republic of China (PRC) would know it could overwhelm those defenses, obviating the potential for an offense-defense arms competition or for even more destructive Chinese reactions, such as selling countermeasures to North Korea.

Those favoring the Clinton administration plans or boost-phase schemes for limited missile defenses will take solace in the knowledge that a modest Chinese nuclear buildup—at least, of the type the PRC now appears to have in the works—would be sufficient to restore a reliable deterrent to China (assuming that most of the PRC's missiles were relatively invulnerable to U.S. preemptive attack when placed on alert). The more conservative missile defense camps are generally so affronted by China's behavior of late, most notably in regard to Taiwan, that they would be little troubled by offending China in response. Remembering the comments of Chinese Lieutenant General Xiong Guangkai (a veiled threat to launch a nuclear attack on Los Angeles, should the United States take Taiwan's side in a China-Taiwan conflict), they would be quite content to deny China its deterrent.[43] Even if that proved impossible, they would not worry about a Chinese buildup leading to a "loose nukes" or command-and-control problem in the PRC (as might happen in beleaguered Russia), and so they would be willing to risk an offense-defense competition with the PRC. A threshold C1 or limited boost-phase system is unlikely to pose a fundamental threat to China's deterrent, so the first phase of U.S. BMD deployment would not confront the PRC issue as directly as subsequent phases. If Beijing takes particular umbrage at even a modest U.S. deployment, however, and threatens to proliferate countermeasures as a result, Washington may have no choice but to consider China's concerns about U.S. NMD.

CONCLUSION

Three conclusions can be drawn from this overview of the technical and domestic political forces shaping American decisions about deploying missile defenses. First, the domestic political situation in the United States seems to favor a limited national missile defense, akin to the Clinton administration's C1 or C2 capability of 100 interceptors at a single site. Deployment of the system would be completed by about 2010. Particularly since George W. Bush took office, U.S. policymakers are more likely to combine some form of the land-based C2 system with a modest boost-phase system targeted at North Korea or at another state that emerges as a pressing threat.[44]

Second, the U.S. Senate probably will not agree to limit the United States to this C2 capability by treaty, unless the new limits have only a short time horizon or are explicitly seen as an interim measure. A majority of the Senate might be happy with a C2-like arrangement for many years, and might be willing to accept a treaty allowing just that. But there will likely remain a sizeable minority insistent on greater U.S. flexibility. This minority might have enough votes to prevent ratification of any new arms control agreement that limits future U.S. choices about missile defense. Ironically, the chances of modifying the Treaty and having that modification ratified by the U.S. Senate might well be greater under a Republican president than they would have been had Al Gore won the presidency. Most opponents to such ratification would surely be Republican, and they might be more easily convinced to support ratification by a president of their own party than by a political opponent.

Third, it makes little sense to speculate further at this point. The fate of less advanced NMD technologies and more radical possible changes to the ABM Treaty will be decided only after many more years of research on NMD technologies and many more years of evolution in the U.S.-Russian relationship. What time will bring in each area cannot be easily forecast. We should therefore get used to the debate over ballistic missile defenses. It has been around a long time, and no final resolution is imminent.

NOTES

1. See Richard L. Garwin, "The Wrong Plan," *Bulletin of the Atomic Scientists,* vol. 56, no. 2, 36–41.

2. William S. Cohen, "FY 2000 Defense Budget: Briefing Slides," Department of Defense, February 1999.

3. Roberto Suro, "Missile Sensor Failed in Test's Final Seconds, Data Indicate," *Washington Post,* 20 January 2000, 4.

4. Geoffrey Forden, *Budgetary and Technical Implications of the Administration's Plan for National Missile Defense* (Washington, D.C.: Congressional Budget Office [CBO], April 2000), 10. The administration and CBO cost estimates differ by about $2 billion, or just over 10 percent.

5. Forden, *Budgetary and Technical Implications,* 5–17; "U.S. Limited National Missile Defense Program," briefing by the Honorable Walter B.

Slocombe, Under Secretary of Defense for Policy, Harvard-CSIS Ballistic Missile Defense Conference, Cambridge, Mass., 11 May 2000.

6. Testimony of the Honorable Walter B. Slocombe to the House Armed Services Committee, 13 October 1999.

7. Suro, "Missile Sensor Failed"; Bradley Graham, "U.S. Anti-Missile Test Is Latest in String of Successes," *Washington Post,* 4 October 1999, 1.

8. Statement of Lieutenant General Ronald T. Kadish, Director, Ballistic Missile Defense Organization, before the Senate Armed Services Committee, 28 February 2000, 6.

9. James Glanz, "Missile Defense Rides Again," *Science,* 16 April 1999, 418–419; Daniel G. Dupont, "In 1999, Patriot's Gulf War Performance vs. Iraqi SCUDs Still in Doubt: New Article Supports Postol-Lewis Analysis of Video Tapes," *Inside the Pentagon,* 24 June 1999, 5; Theodore A. Postol, "Correspondence: Patriot Experience in the Gulf War," *International Security,* vol. 17, no. 1, 225–240.

10. Bradley Graham, "Army Hit in New Mexico Test Said to Bode Well for Missile Defense," *Washington Post,* 16 March 1999, 7; Glanz, "Missile Defense Rides Again," 417.

11. Donald H. Rumsfeld et al., "Executive Summary of the Report of the Commission to Assess the Ballistic Missile Threat to the United States," pursuant to Public Law 201, House of Representatives, 104th Congress, Washington, D.C., 15 July 1998, 1–6, 11–13, available on line at http://www.house.gov/nsc/testimony/105thcongress.

12. "National Missile Defense Review Committee Report: Text of the 'Welch Report,'" *Arms Control Today,* November 1999, 14–20.

13. General Larry Welch et al., "Report of the Panel on Reducing Risk in Ballistic Missile Defense Flight Test Programs," (Washington, D.C.: Department of Defense, 27 February 1998), 7–27; Jeffrey A. Merkley, "Trident II Missile Test Program," staff Working Paper (Washington D.C.: CBO, February 1986), 7.

14. Kadish, Statement, 6; Forden, *Budgetary and Technical Implications,* 25.

15. George N. Lewis and Theodore A. Postol, "Future Challenges to Ballistic Missile Defense," *IEEE Spectrum* (September 1997), 60–68.

16. See Welch et al., "Report of the Panel," 56; see also Elaine M. Grossman, "Rumsfeld Commission Member Sticks to Guns on Opposing Defenses," *Inside the Pentagon,* 30 July 1998, 19–20.

17. David C. Wright, Testimony on the Technical Readiness of National Missile Defenses, before the U.S. Senate Committee on Foreign Re-

lations, 4 May 1999; Richard L. Garwin, Testimony on the Technical Readiness of National Missile Defenses, before the U.S. Senate Committee on Foreign Relations, 4 May 1999.

18. See Union of Concerned Scientists and MIT Security Studies Program, *Countermeasures* (April 2000).

19. Ibid., 145–148.

20. Defense Science Board 1998 Summer Study Task Force, *Joint Operations Superiority in the 21st Century* (Washington, D.C.: Department of Defense, 1998), 97–100; Office of Technology Assessment, *Proliferation of Weapons of Mass Destruction* (Washington, D.C., 1993), 52.

21. Bob Drogin and Tyler Marshall, "Missile Shield's Destabilizing Potential Cited," *Los Angeles Times,* 19 May 2000, 1.

22. Theodore A. Postol, "A Russian-US Boost-Phase Defense to Defend Russia and the US from Postulated Rogue-State ICBMs," briefing paper presented at Carnegie Endowment for International Peace, Washington, D.C., 12 October 1999.

23. Richard L. Garwin, "Effectiveness of Proposed National Missile Defense Against ICBMs from North Korea," 17 March 1999, available on line at http://www.fas.org/rlg/990317-nmd.htm (accessed 11 May 2001).

24. Richard Garwin, "Missile Defense Policy and Arms Control Issues," briefing paper, Council on Foreign Relations, New York, August 1999, available on line at http://www.fas.org/rlg.

25. Lieutenant General John Costello, Army Space and Missile Defense Command, "National and Theater Missile Defense," briefing slides presented at a meeting of the Association of the U.S. Army, Arlington, Va., 17 May 1999, available on line at http://www.smdc.army.mil.

26. Charles V. Peña and Barbara Conry, "National Missile Defense: Examining the Options," CATO Policy Analysis No. 337 (Washington, D.C.: Cato Institute, March 1999), 19.

27. See Congressional Budget Office, *The START Treaty and Beyond* (Washington, D.C.: CBO, 1991), 148.

28. See Theodore Postol, "Ballistic Missile Defenses and Deep Reductions," in Harold A. Feiveson, ed., *The Nuclear Turning Point* (Washington, D.C.: Brookings Institution, 1999), 86–89.

29. Ambassador Henry Cooper and the Heritage Foundation's Commission on Missile Defense, *Defending America: A Plan to Meet the Urgent Missile Threat* (Washington, D.C.: Heritage Foundation, 1999), 36–58.

30. Walter Pincus, "Estimate Skyrockets for Expanding Navy's Ship-Based Missile Defense," *Washington Post,* 5 March 1999, 4; Lieutenant General Lester Lyles, former Director, Ballistic Missile Defense Organiza-

tion, statement before the Subcommittee on Strategic Forces, Senate Committee on Armed Services, 24 February 1999, 11–14.

31. See Ballistic Missile Defense Organization, "Summary of Report to Congress on Utility of Sea-Based Assets to National Missile Defense" (Washington, D.C.: Department of Defense), 1 June 1999.

32. Kerry Gildea, "Theater Missile Defense Programs in Trouble, Top Pentagon Official Warns," *Aerospace Daily*, 25 May 1999; Geoffrey E. Forden, "The Airborne Laser," *IEEE Spectrum* (September 1997); John Donnelly, "Basis for Pentagon Approval of Airborne Laser 'Questionable'," *Defense Week*, 15 March 1999, 1.

33. Forden, "The Airborne Laser," 40–49; General Accounting Office, *Defense Acquisitions: DoD Efforts to Develop Laser Weapons for Theater Defense*, GAO/NSIAD–99–50 (March 1999), 4, 18–20, 24–29.

34. General Accounting Office, *Defense Acquisitions*, 5–6, 33–35; Frank Vizard, "Return to Star Wars," *Popular Science* (April 1999), 56–61; "Long Range Plan" (Colorado Springs, Colo.: United States Space Command, 1998), chapter 6, 14; Crockett L. Grabbe, "Physics of a Ballistic Missile Defense: The Chemical Laser Boost-phase Defense," *American Journal of Physics*, vol. 56, no. 1, 32–36.

35. Vizard, "Return to Star Wars," 59.

36. David Mosher and Michael O'Hanlon, *The START Treaty and Beyond* (Washington, D.C.: CBO, 1991), 69–70, 167–171.

37. Craig Cerniello, "QDR Supports Nuclear Status Quo, Adds Billions More to NMD Program," *Arms Control Today* (May 1997), 29.

38. George J. Tenet, Director, Central Intelligence Agency, testimony before the U.S. Senate Committee on Armed Services, 2 February 1999.

39. Floyd Spence, "Unveiling the Ballistic Missile Threat: The Ramifications of the Rumsfeld Report," *National Security Report*, vol. 2, issue 4; John Isaacs, "Missile Defense: It's Back," *Bulletin of the Atomic Scientists*, vol. 55, no. 4 (May/June 1999), 27–28; Joseph Cirincione, "The Persistence of the Missile Defense Illusion," paper presented to the Conference on Nuclear Disarmament, Safe Disposal of Nuclear Materials or New Weapons Development, Como, Italy, 2–4 July 1998.

40. "Cochran Announces Final Passage of National Missile Defense Bill," press release of Senator Thad Cochran, 21 May 1999.

41. According to polls about NATO expansion, relatively few Americans cited fear of Russia or other threats as a justification for Alliance expansion. A much larger number were concerned about expansion's potentially negative effects on U.S.-Russian relations. In light of this result, it is doubtful that most Americans would dismiss the significance of

NMD for U.S.-Russian relations. Most missile defense proponents will likely make at least a nod in Moscow's direction. See Steven Kull and I.M. Destler, *Misreading the Public: The Myth of a New Isolationism* (Washington, D.C.: Brookings Institution, 1999), 281–282.

42. See John Steinbruner, "National Missile Defense: Collision in Progress," *Arms Control Today*, vol. 29, no. 7, 3–6.

43. See Steven Lee Myers, "Chinese General's Visit Raises Only Limited Hopes," *New York Times*, 26 January 2000, A9.

44. For an endorsement of a boost-phase approach by prominent Democrats, see John Deutch, Harold Brown, and John P. White, "National Missile Defense: Is There Another Way?" *Foreign Policy* (Summer 2000).

5

Global Stability in a Changing Defense Environment

RICHARD J. HARKNETT

The Anti-Ballistic Missile (ABM) Treaty is as an important example of how arms control can help regulate security relations between states. The Treaty did not simply set ground rules for a particular weapons technology but instead helped create a specific strategic environment. The prohibition on missile defense technologies supported the condition of Mutual Assured Destruction (MAD) between the Soviet Union and the United States and created a set of expectations about how the superpowers would deter each other, approach crises, and modernize their nuclear forces. The ABM Treaty helped reduce Cold War concerns about crisis stability and the credibility of deterrence by eliminating an important obstacle to second-strike forces. U.S. deployment of a national missile defense (NMD) system is likely to create new security concerns among missile capable states. Anticipating the new strategic environment fostered by missile defenses is key to determining what type of arms control regime is needed to cope with these concerns.

Although institutional and legal constraints and the way policymakers perceive the intentions of others affect responses to other states, the military balance is the primary factor that shapes global strategic interactions. Policymakers place greater weight on capabilities because others' intentions are difficult to assess and can change quickly, and because institutions and international law are sometimes set aside in favor of national security calculations. Whether or not offense or defense appears dominant, or whether arsenals and doctrine are based on conventional or unconventional (nuclear, chemical, or biological) weapons also affects the strategic environment. When mutual offensive missile capabilities dominate security calculations, for example, policymakers generally prefer deterrence strategies to achieve security objectives. If defensive and offensive capabilities are combined, however, policymakers might come to see counterforce and preemptive strike doctrines as viable security strategies.

This chapter examines how various missile defense deployment plans will affect the future strategic setting. It explores how a revised ABM Treaty might help reduce crisis and arms race instability and concerns about the credibility of deterrence that could emerge in the aftermath of U.S. deployment of missile defenses. The analysis suggests that limited national missile defense would increase the ability of the United States to project power into regional trouble spots. Although more comprehensive missile defense systems, especially those deployed in the absence of a renegotiated ABM Treaty, could create arms race or crisis instability, limited defenses probably would create minimal instability in existing strategic relationships. All three forms of defensive systems might degrade crisis stability; but the impact of defenses varies depending on the level of missile capability possessed by potential U.S. opponents. Ultimately, the diplomatic path to deployment, reflected primarily in efforts to renegotiate the ABM Treaty, may have a greater impact on crisis and arms race stability than the specific capabilities of U.S. missile defenses.

To support these observations, the chapter first focuses on how national missile defenses might affect crisis stability; that is, will incentives to use offensive missile forces increase or decrease if the United States moves forward with plans to construct missile defenses? Second, the chapter explores how various U.S. missile deployments might affect arms race stability, extended deterrence, and the general diplomatic context of international relations. Third, it examines how defenses interact with the U.S. strategy of deterrence and explores the possibility that denial strategies might come to replace deterrence when dealing with states with limited missile arsenals.

CRISIS STABILITY AND
BALLISTIC MISSILE DEFENSE

Early in the 2000 American presidential race, the two leading candidates began to attack each other's foreign policy visions as being based on "Cold War thinking"—i.e., an out-of-date bias toward confrontation rather than cooperation. To be accused of thinking in Cold War terms was to be indicted for stale or even dangerous analysis. The Cold War, however, embodied a particular set of strategic conditions. The Soviet-American nuclear balance was characterized by relatively equal missile forces that could withstand a surprise attack and still inflict catastrophic levels of destruction in a retaliatory strike. In this strategic environment, the national security of each superpower depended on war avoidance. Because Soviets and Americans found themselves in this situation of MAD, their strategic relationship was said to be "crisis stable."

Despite political rhetoric, crisis stability is an analytically and pre-scriptively useful concept when it comes to assessing the interaction between offensive forces and defenses of unequal size and capability. Over the next twenty years, the United States could find itself faced with opponents that have limited offensive forces and no significant defenses. What is the effect on crisis stability when a state with significant offensive capabilities and missile defenses confronts several states with small and technologically limited offensive missile forces?

A crisis is a period of interaction between states when diplomacy is failing and hostilities appear imminent. Richard Ned Lebow notes that crises emerge when: (1) decisionmakers perceive that action taken or threatened by another international actor seriously handicaps national interests, bargaining reputation, or the leadership's ability to stay in power; (2) decisionmakers determine that any responsive action aside from surrender will raise a significant probability of armed conflict; and (3) decisionmakers on both sides perceive themselves to be working under time constraints.[1] Stability under these circumstances is achieved when opposing sides perceive little incentive for, or advantage from, initiating aggression. Thus, a stable crisis environment is one in which the stakes are high enough that a state considers them worth fighting for, and the perception is increasing that conflict is possible, but the incentive to make the first military move is low. Crisis stability also is enhanced if the incentive to escalate the destructiveness or scope of military attacks once a conflict breaks out is low. The consensus during the Cold War was that as long as MAD held (secure second-strike forces were possessed by both sides), crisis stability was solid and policies should not seek to undermine it.[2] A similar policy consensus might not emerge in the future, however, if new power projection capabilities and missile defenses offer an escape from MAD at the price of decreasing crisis stability.

U.S. missile defenses might reduce confidence in the ability of small arsenals to reach their targets, thereby creating added incentives for states with limited military capability to avoid conflict with the United States. Once a conflict looms on the horizon, however, U.S. missile defenses will tend to undermine crisis stability, if for no other reason than that they create incentives for the United States to launch preemptive counterforce attacks to diminish the opponent's offensive capabilities. The unresolved question is whether or not the United States can find a mix of missile defense deployments and diplomacy that can enhance its overall security.

Crisis Stability in the Absence of Missile Defenses

There is a clear interaction between crisis stability and U.S. policies of extended deterrence whereby the United States threatens to employ both conventional and nuclear forces to protect its allies. An opponent equipped with just a few missiles armed with nuclear, biological, or chemical warheads might calculate that it could undermine extended deterrence by threatening to hit American territory. In the absence of missile defenses, the U.S. response to this gambit probably would be to make clear that its escalation dominance would make any attack against U.S. territory or allies end in national suicide for the attacker.

Would the United States be reluctant to execute deterrent threats if it were faced with the possibility of retaliation? The answer to this question would depend on the credibility of the opponent's will and capability and the values placed at risk by a U.S. decision to act or not to act. Assuming that the United States would restrict its involvement if it were certain that it would suffer a nuclear, chemical, or biological attack against a U.S. city in return, the question really depends on the assessment of the opponent's will. If the United States did intervene on behalf of an ally (and thus was not deterred), why would a North Korea or an Iraq go ahead with a missile attack on the continental United States?

Three objectives might motivate an opponent to launch this type of attack: (1) to gain bargaining leverage for the negotiation of a cease-fire; (2) to escalate the conflict to reestablish intra-war deterrence; or (3) to inflict damage in a fatalistic act of aggression. If they actually were to execute these deterrent threats against countervalue (i.e., civilian) targets within the United States, weak states might find it more difficult to secure their objectives. For example, attacking the United States as an asymmetric response to U.S. intervention in a regional conflict would reduce an opponent's bargaining leverage, rather than increase it. Opponents armed with small missile arsenals cannot hope to defeat the United States. If small arsenal states were to use force to achieve some political objective, they would have to assume either that the United States would not respond at all or that a negotiated settlement could be reached after some minimal fighting. They would have to calculate that the United States would be willing to engage in limited warfare to obtain limited objectives. Limited warfare requires restraint both in tactics and in weapons used. Hitting an American city with a nuclear, chemical, or biological weapon would make it difficult for an American president to keep war limited. Indeed, this kind of attack constitutes a clear path to total war, one that would be fought primarily on the territory of the weaker challenger. A threat to retaliate against the United States with the intent to bolster wartime bargaining is best viewed as a bluff.

An attack against the United States also would eliminate any deterrent threat or leverage generated by the possibility of escalation. Indeed, if a small power began to place its long-range missiles on alert, it would simply invite a disarming American preemptive attack. A state with a limited arsenal probably would enjoy more leverage from the threat of escalation than from actually using its arsenal in an effort to achieve escalation dominance over the United States. Once again, use of weapons of mass destruction would prove counterproductive because such use would make it politically possible for American officials to unleash the full force of their arsenal.

The most plausible motivation for a weak state to launch a missile attack against an American city would be if its leaders feared that their regime faced imminent destruction and if they wished to inflict pain on the United States as they lost power or their lives. For many of the missile-capable regimes considered likely enemies of the United States, destruction of their communication or military infrastructure would be a serious concern, since the loss of political power would in reality amount to a death sentence for anyone associated with their regime.

For American officials, the possibility of irrational action by leaders who perceive that their survival is being put at risk during a regional conflict would have to be included in any calculation about how to conduct military operations. Although unlikely to prevent U.S. intervention, a missile threat involving weapons of mass destruction would force U.S. policymakers to devise a restrained response to regional aggression. U.S. officials would have to take steps not to place opponents in a position where they might consider using weapons of mass destruction because they believe that they have nothing left to lose. In this sense, a world without defenses prevents the United States from fully using its conventional military forces and opens a narrow opportunity for highly risk-acceptant leaders to achieve political objectives. American officials might be tempted to launch a preemptive strike to deprive regional opponents of their missile arsenals, and thus eliminate the possibility that the arsenal could be unleashed in a moment of desperation. But a preemptive counterforce attack could itself prompt opponents to make the irrational decision to use rather than lose their missile force. The possibility of this type of fatalistic aggression will constrain U.S. freedom of action in a crisis.

Preemption also could provoke an inadvertent or accidental launch as damaged command and control systems or panicked commanders respond to an attack. Preemption could be counterproductive unless U.S. officials were quite certain that *all* of their opponent's missiles could be destroyed.

On balance, in a world where vastly unequal offensive missile forces exist without defenses, there is more crisis instability than in a strategic setting of MAD. What would precipitate a missile attack on the United States is a narrow set of circumstances in which strategic calculations are influenced by desperation, not a rational consideration of the consequences of military action. U.S. military actions can influence the emergence of a creeping fatalism in enemy capitals, which could serve as a restraint on the conduct of U.S. operations against regimes armed with weapons of mass destruction and rudimentary missile forces. If both sides in a dispute possess missile arsenals—even though they differ greatly in size and capability—then the likelihood of attacks against countervalue targets on both sides of a conflict is reduced.[3]

Crisis Stability in a World with Limited Missile Defenses

The deployment of 100 interceptors in Alaska will have a varied impact on crisis stability, depending on the particular opponent the United States faces and the specific context of the military crisis. Unlike deterrence, which tends to focus on particular actions, defense is directed against specific capabilities in specific circumstances.

Pentagon officials estimate that four anti-ballistic missile interceptors would have to be allocated to destroy each incoming missile warhead. Assuming no decoys are deployed, about 20 interceptors should undermine the ability of opponents with only a couple of warheads to damage the United States with a missile assault. North Korea, Iran, and Iraq, as well as nuclear-capable Pakistan and India, probably could not deliver enough warheads at intercontinental distances to penetrate limited missile defenses during the early years of deployment.[4] The People's Republic of China might be able to overwhelm a 20-inteceptor force and it could easily increase the size of its force to penetrate a larger set of American defenses.

If the United States deploys a limited missile defense, U.S. leaders probably would be less concerned that intervention could result in a successful attack against American territory. This would strengthen extended deterrence. Crisis stability in confrontations with states with small arsenals could be undermined, however, because the United States would be able to escalate military operations with less risk. U.S. preemptive attacks against small missile arsenals would become a plausible way to reduce the small missile threat, making it easier for defenses to stop the very few weapons that escape destruction. The United States could still threaten to retaliate massively following any attack against American territory, thereby exploiting the bargaining leverage produced by its escalation dominance. States subjected to preemptive strikes against their small missile forces could still try to attack U.S. territory out of desperation, but American officials could reduce pressures to do so by forcing a quick military solution to the conflict or by making clear their limited aims in negotiations. In contrast, by bolstering the ability of

American forces to launch a preemptive attack, limited missile defense deployments could increase crisis stability by reducing the outbreak of crises. The leaders of small arsenal states would have an incentive to avoid giving the United States a pretext for preemption. Thus, while crisis stability would be undermined, limited NMD might make small states less likely to confront the United States or regional enemies.

Assuming no change in the Chinese nuclear force, critics of U.S. limited NMD would probably suggest that limited defenses would reduce crisis stability in Sino-American strategic relations. U.S. options for preemption, however, would be tempered by the great risk that a counterforce attack might not succeed completely and Chinese retaliation could overwhelm limited American defenses. The credible threat of Chinese conventional retaliation against American allies in Asia also could place an additional brake on U.S. preemptive options.

Against the only state possessing a similar nuclear arsenal, Russia, limited U.S. missile defenses would not affect the crisis stability produced by MAD. Even at proposed START III offensive force levels (1,500–2,500 warheads), small defensive deployments would not create incentives to preempt in a crisis. In the event of a nuclear exchange, Russia would likely target the NMD deployment sites and supporting infrastructure first, so that the United States could not establish escalation dominance in a post-attack situation. If limited missile defenses were deployed following a renegotiation of the ABM Treaty, such a system should have no discernible impact on the crisis stability inherent in the Russian-American strategic balance.

Crisis Stability and Moderate National Missile Defense

Moderate NMD would affect crisis stability in two ways. In conflicts with states with small arsenals, crisis stability would be undermined significantly, since the effects of retaliation against American territory after U.S. preemption would be greatly reduced.[5] Moderate NMD would provide U.S. decisionmakers with greater flexibility in crises, but the United States would also be more willing to intervene in regional conflicts and more capable of doing so. Again, this would create incentives for states equipped with small missile arsenals to avoid giving U.S. policymakers a pretext for intervention or for launching preemptive attacks, thereby reducing the likelihood of regional conflict. On balance, moderate defenses will decrease the likelihood of conflict while increasing the likelihood that the U.S. might launch preemptive counterforce attacks, which makes the escalation of a given conflict more likely.

If the United States deployed missile defenses with moderate capabilities, those defenses certainly would undermine the ability of the People's Republic of China to launch an attack against American territory. In a conflict in the Taiwan Strait, the Chinese could find themselves in a situation in which the military balance closely resembled past confrontations with the United States. American escalation dominance could again pose a strong deterrent to Chinese action.[6] In a twenty-first-century replay of a crisis in the Strait, moderate missile defenses, combined with capable theater missile defenses based on Taiwan, would create U.S. incentives both to launch a preemptive attack and to rely on conventional superiority alone to deter or blunt a Chinese attack. Moderate missile defenses would increase American flexibility and confidence in confrontations with China, although crisis stability could be weakened because American incentives to launch a preemptive attack would increase as a conflict in the Strait, for instance, worsened.

A moderately sized U.S. missile defense system also would have a negative effect on crisis stability in the Russia-American strategic relationship. Russia's ability to maintain a secure second-strike force would govern the extent of that impact. If the Russian nuclear missile force were to shrink significantly and its ability to modernize its submarine and bomber force declined, Russian planners might become concerned about suffering a disarming first strike in some crisis. U.S. deployment of missile systems with a moderate capability would likely create preemptive pressures that do not exist in today's Russian-American strategic balance.

Crisis Stability and Unregulated National Missile Defense

If the United States deploys highly robust defensive capabilities in the absence of an ABM regime, it would reduce crisis stability, increase American power projection, and enhance pre-crisis stability against

small arsenals and China. In this regard, there is little difference between moderate and unregulated deployments. Robust missile defenses
could undermine the crisis stability inherent in the Russian-American
strategic balance. Leaving aside the question of why the United States
might launch a nuclear attack against Russia, Russian planners would
confront a situation in which Americans could launch a nearly disarming blow against their strategic forces, especially if the air- and sea-
based legs of Russia's nuclear triad became unreliable. Russian planners probably would conclude that robust defenses would give the
United States bargaining leverage and escalation dominance in a future
crisis.

Crisis Stability, Nuclear Allies, and Arms Control Verification

During the Cold War, the United States faced two nuclear-capable missile states—the Soviet Union and the People's Republic of China—that
it essentially dealt with separately. In the twenty-first century, alliances between states armed with long-range missiles and weapons of
mass destruction could emerge quickly as a cost-effective response to
the deployment of missile defenses by the United States or other missile states.

A limited NMD system might be overwhelmed if several missile-armed
states were to establish a credible alliance and coordinate their attack
plans. If American confidence in U.S. defenses declines when faced with
a potential need to intercept twenty-five incoming warheads, then an alliance of several small-arsenal states may determine that goal is worth
pursuing as a means of reestablishing crisis stability. In isolation, each
state might be susceptible to a disarming first strike, but collectively
their arsenals might be able to survive attack and undertake a second
strike capable of penetrating U.S. defenses. An alliance not only could
reduce U.S. incentives to launch a preemptive attack, it also could decrease the credibility of American extended deterrence. If nuclear-mis-
sile alliances begin to form, however, they would complicate crisis interaction by introducing multiple decision centers. Questions would
emerge in all capitals involved, concerning the willingness of allies to

fulfill their treaty commitment to attack the United States. It would be unlikely that all members of the alliance would have equally powerful motivations to launch such an attack. Perceptions of the credibility of alliance commitments under these circumstances would greatly influence crisis stability.

Moderate or robust missile defenses would be resilient against even a credible alliance of states equipped with small missile arsenals and undermined only by alliances of states with large arsenals. By increasing the possibility of retaliation, alliances might enhance crisis stability; but reliance on allies (rather than self-reliance) raises issues of political credibility. A strategic environment of missile-equipped allies is less "crisis stable" than a world in which states rely on their own devices to guarantee their security; but it may be the only option available to most U.S. opponents, especially if the United States deploys more than limited missile defenses. Technology transfer and trade in missile components also are likely responses to U.S. defensive deployments. Although small-arsenal states might not be able to develop sophisticated decoys to undermine the reliability of limited NMD, more-sophisticated states might provide penetration technology to complicate American planning. Technological alliances—in contrast to formal defensive alliances—also are unlikely to raise political questions of reliability during crises. Technology alliances would allow states to enjoy the benefits of self-reliance with few of the drawbacks inherent in military cooperation when it comes to national defense.

There is a presumption among American missile defense proponents that the United States will deploy limited missile defenses in conjunction with a revised ABM Treaty. Russian confidence that limited defenses will indeed stay limited would likely require intrusive verification regimes. Even though such regimes tend to aid arms control, they might have a negative effect on crisis dynamics. How would the United States react to a Russian request for an on-site inspection during a brewing conflict with a third party allied with Moscow? Would it be prudent to give arms control inspectors access to the status of U.S. weapon systems that could be about to engage in nuclear combat? The verification–crisis stability interaction is likely to become more pronounced as U.S. officials confront the implications of the way arms control interacts with systems that are intended to fight and win, as opposed to deter, conflicts.

GLOBAL STABILITY AND MISSILE DEFENSE

Aside from the assessment of incentives and disincentives to be first to use military force, stability can be understood in terms of arms race pressures and the overall diplomatic tenor of international relations. This section explores the military and diplomatic reactions that states are likely to have to an American ballistic missile defense system. In terms of military capabilities, two outcomes are likely: arms racing (increasing production of missiles and weapons of mass destruction) or developing an asymmetric response (moving funding toward other delivery capabilities).

Limited National Missile Defense

According to American policymakers, limited NMD is directed at changing the U.S. strategic relationship with "countries of concern" (often referred to as rogue states) that raise the prospect of being undeterrable. Because these countries of concern often have extraordinarily limited resources, they simply could not contemplate building a large missile force without substantial outside help. Limited U.S. missile defenses would tend to reduce their incentives to funnel scarce resources toward missile technology. Instead, states with small missile arsenals would try to avoid a direct confrontation with American military capabilities. This would increase the search for alternative delivery strategies—for instance, terrorism. Limited U.S. missile defenses are unlikely to create an arms race, because most potential opponents lack the resources needed to engage in the race. Opponents of the United States are unlikely simply to give up when confronted with missile defenses, but will instead search for an asymmetric response that somehow holds U.S. targets at risk.

For China and Russia, limited U.S. defenses will pose some challenge. The likeliest Chinese response will be to accelerate China's planned strategic modernization and thus bolster the credibility of its nuclear deterrent. If China were faced with limited U.S. defenses, an increase in offensive arms would not have to be very extensive to reestablish China's confidence in its force. Beijing might act more quickly if U.S. NMD were somehow linked to theater missile defense (TMD) deployments to Taiwan or elsewhere in Asia. China's expansion of its nuclear force could fuel an arms race in South Asia, if the primary rationale for India's nuclear arsenal is New Delhi's perception of external threats.[7] By contrast, Russia might take no action in response to limited U.S. deployment, especially if that deployment took place within some revision of the ABM Treaty. If an arms control regime exists that constrains future U.S. deployments, Moscow might be willing to tolerate limited U.S. defenses. Russia probably would not feel a need to direct resources toward expansion of its nuclear force.

U.S. deployment of limited missile defenses, if accompanied by revision of the ABM Treaty, therefore appears unlikely to produce a shock capable of upsetting the tenor of international relations or inciting a return to strategic arms racing.

Moderate and Unregulated National Missile Defense

U.S. deployment of moderate or highly capable defenses would have a significant impact on international relations, especially if it took place through unilateral American action. Highly capable U.S. missile defense deployments would decrease arms race stability in East Asia, because China probably would feel compelled to accelerate its strategic modernization to compensate for U.S. national defenses and to respond to imminent integration of U.S. TMD and NMD. Capable missile defenses could change the strategic environment across the Taiwan Strait. The Chinese might perceive that the window of opportunity to settle the Taiwan issue was closing fast, if they lost confidence in their ability to hold Taiwan or U.S. forces at risk. The PRC may calculate that once TMD is deployed, Taiwan's independence would become a *fait accompli*. U.S. deployment of a moderate national missile defense could add preventive war calculations to a Chinese decision to accelerate its nuclear force modernization, creating a dangerous mix of strategic incentives.

If moderate deployment takes place over Russian objections, Russian leaders would feel strong incentives to respond somehow to U.S. defensive deployments, although their strategic force modernization would ultimately be constrained by their economic weakness. Russia might simply come to terms with the perception that the United States is becoming increasingly less vulnerable to a Russian second strike; but this seems unlikely in a state that still aspires to great power status. More likely, Russia might respond to American missile deployments by forming alliances with other missile states. States with small missile arsenals might find an alliance with Russia attractive, but Moscow would get little more than nuisance value from this kind of partnership. A Sino-Russian alliance might have some strategic benefit from Moscow's perspective and would be the most threatening combination of allies from an American perspective, although there are a number of obstacles to a nuclear partnership that locks together the fate of both states. But if leaders in Moscow and Beijing believe that the United States is motivated by revisionist or expansionist intentions, then their motives for balancing against the United States might be strong enough to overcome the obstacles to alliance.

The amount of instability created by U.S. deployments of significant defenses also might hinge on the reaction of America's allies. To the extent that American statecraft can convince allies that U.S. missile defenses will support extended deterrence without upsetting the Russian-American strategic balance or destroying the international arms control regime, the prospect of allied accommodation will increase. American allies, however, tend to place great weight on the existing arms control framework inherited from the Cold War, and they remain wary of defensive capabilities that threaten to change a familiar strategic landscape. Significant U.S. NMD deployments, especially if accompanied by acrimony in the arms control arena, could cause allies to drift toward greater independence in security policy. Euro-Atlantic security ties might weaken, but they will not break. European governments, constrained by limited resources available for defense spending, will not be able to "go it alone," especially as the distinction between TMD and NMD becomes increasingly blurred.

DETERRENCE AND THE LOGIC OF MISSILE DEFENSE

The debate over missile defense emerged in the context of the Cold War nuclear confrontation between the United States and the Soviet Union, making missile defense synonymous with defense against nuclear attack. As a result, much of the debate over national missile defense overlooks the fact that defenses are directed against a delivery system, not a specific warhead. This is an important observation, because the strategic effect of missile defenses changes depending on whether a nuclear, chemical, biological, or conventional warhead is used by the attacking force. Missile defenses also will have a different strategic impact depending on whether they are intended to bolster deterrence or to deny opponents the ability to strike the United States with long-range missiles.

Consider the following scenarios. During a confrontation in the Middle East, a U.S. president is told that a missile has been launched from Iraq. American missile defenses go into action but fail to intercept a conventional warhead, which causes minor damage to the naval base at Norfolk, Virginia, an important logistics hub supporting U.S. forces fighting in Iraq. What sort of U.S. retaliation would be appropriate under these circumstances? What retaliation would be appropriate if it was a nuclear warhead that detonated over Norfolk, completely destroying the base? What sort of action should the National Command Authorities take if the engagement was successful, intercepting what appears to be a nuclear warhead high over the Atlantic Ocean? Despite the success or failure of missile defenses in each of these scenarios, deterrence has failed. Does that failure of deterrence matter?

The answer to this question depends on the type of warhead used in the attack and the type of strategy adopted by the country deploying defenses. If the strategic objective is to undertake a defense by denying opponents the ability to damage the United States, then retaliation might not be called for if the defenses are successful or if opponents only manage to penetrate American defenses with a few conventional warheads causing minimal damage. The denial strategy is typically envisioned by proponents of national missile defenses, who often discuss scenarios in which defenses destroy most, if not all, incoming warheads. Nothing much is said about what occurs following the initial exchange between an opponent's offensive missiles and U.S. defenses. But denial strategies used to describe the strategic impact of defenses are realistic only if the defensive systems are highly reliable and the damage projected to occur is minimal. These conditions are met, however, only when facing conventionally armed opponents, whereas missile defenses are apparently intended to stop missiles tipped with nuclear, biological, or chemical warheads. Even if defenses work extraordinarily well, the detonation of a single nuclear, biological, or chemical warhead over a major U.S. city would produce significant loss of life. Even if they possess robust missile defenses, American leaders would likely want to dissuade adversaries from attempting an attack in the first place, by issuing strong threats of retaliation. Missile defenses, and the denial strategies often used to justify their deployment, are probably best viewed as a supplement, not a replacement, to deterrence.

Despite the deployment of defenses, U.S. policy should continue to affect the decision calculus of opponents as long as three conditions exist: (1) the United States is facing opponents armed with weapons of mass destruction and long-range missiles; (2) defenses are not perfect; and (3) the risk of significant damage to urban areas exists. As long as these conditions continue, opponents will have to be dissuaded from launching an attack, and thus deterrence will remain the strategic starting point when thinking about missile defenses. If the dominant strategy is deterrence, defensive capabilities can play a supportive role by reducing the contestable nature of retaliatory costs. In other words, defenses can guarantee the survivability of second-strike forces, eliminating the possibility that opponents can escape cataclysmic damage if they use weapons of mass destruction first in a crisis. The opposite holds true as well. Defense can undermine deterrence if threatened costs come to be viewed as more open to manipulation, and if their reduction to acceptable levels becomes possible. If a deterrer's ability to exact a cost on an attacker is heavily dependent on the deterring country's ability to blunt an opponent's offensive force, then deterrence becomes a contest between offensive and defensive forces—a contest that is more likely to result in arms race and crisis instability.

Contesting the Will to Respond

If faced with an opponent armed with even a rudimentary nuclear, biological, or chemical weapon capability, a country would want the strongest possible deterrent threat in place, given the risk of enormous damage posed by just a few of these unconventional weapons. Extraordinarily risk-acceptant opponents might question U.S. willingness to use nuclear weapons to respond to a highly limited attack involving weapons of mass destruction. But U.S. restraint would evaporate following an attack on American territory. More problematic would be a successful missile intercept that made it impossible to identify the type of warhead that was destroyed in flight. In terms of resolve to carry out deterrent responses after a successful intercept, it might be politically impossible to justify launching a nuclear retaliatory strike, especially since it would appear that nuclear war had just been avoided. For a small-arsenal state, a missile armed with a conventional warhead (or no warhead at all) might serve as a proverbial "shot across the bow," forcing U.S. policymakers to reassess their war aims and to seek a negotiated settlement of a conflict. Once missile defenses are deployed, it would thus appear necessary to change the nature of U.S. deterrent threats. The deterrent threat must be against the *launching* of a missile attack rather than the impact of the warhead.[8] Any perceived lessening of willingness to respond to missile launch, as opposed to the detonation of a warhead, could provide small-arsenal states with bargaining leverage in wartime.

Missile defenses also can affect deterrence by strengthening the credibility of extended deterrence and the overall willingness of U.S. policymakers to intervene in regional conflicts. Debated intensely during the Cold War, concerns about the credibility of extended deterrence were reflected in open-ended questions posed about the willingness of the United States, for example, to risk the destruction of New York to deter attacks on Paris. By reducing the risks of retaliation against the United States, missile defenses should increase the credibility of extended deterrence. Yet, American allies now appear worried that missile defenses will again decouple them from Washington, by increasing the strategic and political flexibility enjoyed by the United States. From the allied perspective, missile defenses might make the United States more willing to run strategic risks, leaving its allies as the logical targets for retaliation. Missile defenses thus seem to produce a strange paradox when it comes to extended deterrence from an allied perspective. Defenses reduce concerns about the credibility of extended deterrence while creating the perception that conflicts might become more likely.

CONCLUSION: THE POLICY IMPLICATIONS OF NATIONAL MISSILE DEFENSE

U.S. deployment of missile defenses requires only a modest change in American strategic doctrine, but it does raise the prospect of altering American strategic behavior. Even deployment of highly capable missile defenses does not displace deterrence as the basis of U.S. national security policy, if for no other reason than that opponents can still deliver weapons of mass destruction to American territory, using unconventional methods such as terrorism. Retaliatory threats to shape the behavior and security calculations of America's opponents remain the foundation of national security policy in a world of defense, although the likelihood will increase that U.S. policymakers might consider launching preemptive strikes against opponents' small missile arsenals during crises.

The question is whether deterrence, the arms race, and crisis stability will be undermined by the various types of missile defenses that are now considered technically feasible by U.S. officials. The answer is mixed. Extended deterrence is strengthened, because missile defenses will bolster the credibility of deterrent threats. Limited missile defenses enhance America's capability to project power into the regions most likely to require U.S. military intervention in the next twenty years. But this increase in the ability to project force comes at the price of increased crisis instability as the combination of defense and precision-guided conventional weapons provides the United States with preemptive capabilities against nascent missile forces.[9] Limited defenses, however, are unlikely to lead to systemic arms race and crisis instability—an outcome more likely to occur if the U.S. deploys highly capable defenses in the absence of a revised ABM Treaty.

How will missile defenses fit into American grand strategy? During the Cold War, the need to contain the threat posed by the Soviet Union was clear. Today, the United States has no peer competitor, and its foreign and defense policies are based on this favorable international distribution of political and economic power. The emerging strategic question now confronting the United States is how to preserve its overwhelming strategic advantage. To the extent that superpower status in the twenty-first century is defined by an ability to project military power and economic and political influence beyond one's border, emerging missile arsenals tend to undermine America's dominant position on the world stage. There is a strong incentive for the United States to counter emerging challenges to its ability to dominate the global conventional battlefield. The development of missile defenses is best seen as a response to a threat, albeit a weak one, to limit U.S. force projection capabilities.

By enhancing U.S. extended deterrence threats and the ability to intervene in regional conflicts, deployment of limited missile defenses enhances America's great power status over the short term. But the arms race and crisis instability unleashed by highly capable defenses deployed in the absence of a revised ABM Treaty would probably undermine America's strategic position over the long term. The deterrent effect of small missile arsenals on America's ability to intervene in regional disputes may be overstated. The United States will be able to intervene even in the absence of missile defenses, but it will have to do so with limited war aims and careful crisis management. Regardless of which missile defense is actually deployed, the ability of the United States to renegotiate the ABM Treaty and to sustain the international arms control regime following missile defense deployments will serve as an important indicator of the emerging diplomatic environment. NMD deployments must be accompanied by adept diplomacy to move U.S. allies, and Russia and China, toward a world of defense, unless American policymakers assume that states will simply acquiesce to America's deployment of highly capable defenses—an assumption not supported by history. The movement toward a world of defense creates the risk of arms race and crisis instability but produces a marginal gain in U.S. ability to extend deterrence, intervene in regional conflicts, and protect its territory from missile attack. As with most policy questions, the difficult task here will be to identify the balance between status quo and change that best secures U.S. interests.

NOTES

1. Adapted from Richard Ned Lebow, *Between Peace and War: The Nature of International Crises* (Baltimore: Johns Hopkins University Press, 1981), 7–12.

2. The political psychology wing of deterrence theory tended to question the stability of MAD as well. The two most oft-cited critiques are Richard Ned Lebow, *Nuclear Crisis Management: A Dangerous Illusion* (Ithaca: Cornell University Press, 1987); and Robert Jervis, Janice Gross Stein, and Richard Ned Lebow, *Psychology and Deterrence* (Baltimore: Johns Hopkins University Press, 1985). A good overview is Gilbert Win-

ham, ed., *New Issues in International Crisis Management* (Boulder: Westview Press, 1988).

3. The Bush administration's handling of the Persian Gulf crisis may be instructive. Before the allied bombing began in January 1991, a number of signals were sent to Saddam Hussein that the conduct of the war would remain limited unless he used unconventional weapons. The letter sent from President Bush to the Iraqi leader was carefully crafted, arguing that the interests of Iraq as a nation would be harmed if Iraq did not back down. But the letter made the specific link to Saddam Hussein himself and his interests when discussing weapons of mass destruction. Bush wrote: "The United States will not tolerate the use of chemical or biological weapons. . . . You will be held directly responsible for terrorist actions against any member of the coalition. The American people would demand the strongest possible response. You and your country will pay a terrible price if you order unconscionable acts of this sort." There was an implicit limitation, however, built into this letter: do not cross these lines, and the war will remain limited. By January 1991, a limited war had become the least problematic outcome for both sides. See Richard J. Harknett, *Lenses of Analysis: A Visual Framework for the Study of International Relations* (New York: W.W. Norton, forthcoming).

4. The use of decoys would reduce confidence levels. According to documents released in the spring of 2000 regarding American negotiations on revising the ABM Treaty, the first-phase deployment of limited NMD would only have radar capacity to track some "dozen" warheads. See the *New York Times*, 28 April 2000, "ABM Proposal: Ready To Work With Russia," available on line at http://www.nytimes.com/library/world/global/042800arms-text.html.

5. This assumes that small arsenal states have not increased the risk to the United States through other means. This seems possible and likely, but a more detailed explanation is beyond the scope of this book.

6. This view is presented more fully in Richard J. Harknett and Brian King, "Eisenhower and the Nuclear Sword," presented at the Midwest Political Science Association, in Chicago, Illinois (April 1995).

7. The expansion of Chinese nuclear forces also could create incentives for greater policy coordination, if not alignment, between India and the United States. For an explanation of the logic behind this claim, see Richard J. Harknett and Jeff VanDenBerg, "Alignment Theory and Interrelated Threats," *Security Studies* 6, no. 3:113–154. For a survey of competing views on Indian motivations for testing a nuclear device, see Sumit Ganguly, "Explaining Indian Nuclear Policy," *Current History* 98, no. 632:438–441.

8. This type of deterrent posture opens the door for a new arms control regime to help manage missile testing. States would have to construct a system to distinguish between launches that were tests and those that were attacks, otherwise how would one know that the missile that fell into the sea off the North Korean coast was not a failed attempt to attack the United States? This is a good example of the rationale for new arms control initiatives even if missile defenses are deployed and the ABM Treaty is abandoned.

9. The strength of the link between NMD and the information technology revolution in military affairs now under examination by the U.S. military will have an impact on global balancing. See Richard J. Harknett and the JCISS Study Group, "The Risks of a Networked Military," *Orbis* (Winter 1999/2000):127–143.

6

The Future of Arms Control

JULIAN SCHOFIELD

Although ballistic missile defense (BMD) may address the immediate security concerns of America and its allies, it is provocative to other major powers, and it undermines efforts to promote nonproliferation and arms race stability.[1] Nuclear weapon and ballistic missile proliferation, combined with the rise of several powerful actors on the world stage, make the adoption of a single bilateral arms control treaty, however, an unpromising way to control future missile defenses.[2] Over the next twenty years, U.S. security might best be served by national missile defense (NMD) and theater missile defenses (TMD) that comply with several bilateral arms control arrangements, embedded within a multilateral arms control regime that prevents states from adopting dangerous or destabilizing defensive systems.[3] U.S. interests also might be well served if NMD deployment were combined with selective disengagement from regional disputes.

This chapter unfolds in five stages. First, it describes U.S. arms control policy. Second, it explains why bilateral arms control arrangements are increasingly irrelevant in the aftermath of the Cold War. Third, the chapter analyzes the benefits of disengagement from international politics. Fourth, it describes the interactive logic of arms control and balance-of-power politics. The chapter concludes by enumerating several factors that U.S. officials should consider when thinking about the future of defensive arms control.

159

U.S. ARMS CONTROL POLICY

U.S. arms control policy has two goals: to preserve arms race and crisis stability, thereby reducing the risks of war, and to help preserve the security and freedom of action of the United States and its allies. The three strategies for achieving these goals involve maintaining minimal deterrence with Russia, undertaking limited disarmament initiatives, and slowing the proliferation of nuclear weapons and associated delivery systems.[4]

The 1972 ABM Treaty contributes to these U.S. arms control goals in several ways. It enhances crisis stability by minimizing the preemptive incentive for war. The Treaty prevents signatories from erecting a defensive barrier that would reduce confidence in second-strike forces, thereby preserving deterrence relationships at relatively modest force levels. During the Cold War, the Treaty slowed the arms race, thereby minimizing windows of opportunity and fear that could have worsened a simmering conflict. Today, the Treaty still eliminates the threat of a costly and destabilizing competition between defensive systems and offensive countermeasures, which would poison U.S.-Russian relations. By helping preserve the dominance of offensive forces, the ABM Treaty enhances the credibility of U.S. extended deterrence, which in turn slows the proliferation of weapons of mass destruction (WMD) to America's allies and adversaries.

The ABM Treaty is under pressure for revision as the emergence of new technology creates renewed political interest in ballistic missile defenses. Recent nuclear tests by India and Pakistan, and progress in North Korea's and Iran's missile programs, have added urgency to the warnings issued by the 1998 Rumsfeld Commission about the vulnerability of the United States to missile attack.[5] But the underlying problem with efforts to revise the Treaty is that these efforts address today's security concerns, not the future security environment in which contemplated defenses will operate. The fact that America will soon possess the most extensive missile defense system in the world while continuing to be a central player in a global arms control regime makes the United States a target of nations seeking to change the status quo. Given the growing number of states with either a *de facto* or a *de jure* interest in missile defenses and arms control, it will be increasingly difficult for U.S. policymakers to balance these competing interests as U.S. missile defenses become operational.

THE LOGIC OF ARMS CONTROL

Arms control enhances security by devising rules and restrictions on defense postures whose regularity generates the expectations of future benefit necessary to sustain international cooperation on limiting arms.[6] The feasibility of arms control agreements is affected by the *calculation problem:* the difficulty in balancing different interests and the increased cost of system management as the number of participants increases. The current ABM Treaty maximizes predictability by minimizing the number of participants—the United States, Russia, Kazakhstan, Belarus, and Ukraine—thereby facilitating Treaty negotiations.[7] Even though bilateral agreements permit the greatest issue depth, they are easier to negotiate than multilateral agreements, because fewer competing interests generally are at stake.

The ABM Treaty will remain in force as long as the perceived benefit of Russian-American cooperation outweighs the risk that third parties will exploit the two countries' mutual restraint. The impact of a state as unimportant and militarily weak as North Korea on U.S. incentives to build missile defenses, however, indicates that the threshold for disrupting this cooperation is relatively low. Normally, common threats would provide an incentive for collaboration; but Russia has expressed little interest in constraining its former Cold War allies.[8] Abandoning the ABM Treaty would be an extreme response to the North Korean challenge. But attempting to incorporate third party threats into a revised Treaty will create significant negotiating challenges, because emerging arsenals do not pose symmetrical threats. Similarly, a truly multilateral ABM Treaty would be difficult to negotiate, especially given that states are extremely sensitive to their ranking (particularly at times when the prospect of an arms race or a war looms large). Under these circumstances, an agreement would fix the relative distribution of benefits derived from cooperation, thereby affecting the incentives for different actors to cooperate.[9] Other analysts suggest that a multilateral ABM Treaty would be particularly useful as a strategy to engage and socialize potential challengers such as China or Iran to the prevailing international order.[10]

Any effort to negotiate a universal ABM Treaty would encounter several obstacles. For instance, a universal treaty might undermine U.S. ability to apply the sanctions necessary to maintain a global regime for limiting defenses.[11] Another problem would be satisfying the interests of states that have no intention of deploying missile defenses. A tiered agreement modeled on the Nuclear Non-Proliferation Treaty might create different constraints and responsibilities for states, according to whether they possessed or lacked defenses. A tiered agreement, however, would only be sustainable if those seeking to acquire missile defenses could be restrained, which implies that technology transfer and development need to be cartelized. To overcome these competing incentives, an optimal configuration for a revised ABM Treaty might consist of a universal agreement with a restricted scope, coupled with select bilateral arrangements between key powers. Alternatively, a revised Treaty could be a tiered agreement, with the privileged upper tier using this to replace more detailed bilateral agreements.

ARMS CONTROL AND THE BALANCE OF POWER

The balance of power describes the tendency of states to balance against emerging threats, thereby preserving their independence.[12] A secondary effect of the balance of power is that officials contemplating war must take into account potential interference or exploitation by third-party states.[13] Arms control, however, can interfere with some of the more positive effects produced by balance-of-power politics. Arms control agreements can lock states into fixed relations that are at best slow to adjust to the uneven growth in economic and military power among states. Arms control also can inhibit a leader's ability to balance against emerging threats. National leaders might be slow to rearm in the face of an emerging threat if rearmament would threaten existing arms control agreements. Bilateral agreements can freeze a given distribution of power without considering how changes in the strength of third parties can affect the desirability of the original agreement.[14]

Even as arms control agreements can restrain states through formal agreements, so can balance-of-power politics restrain state behavior. State officials, for instance, must weigh uncertainty about other states' reactions to their initiatives, especially in multipolar systems where several powerful states enjoy greater freedom of action than in a bipolar setting.[15] Because uncertainty about third-party behavior will increase as a multipolar international system gradually emerges from the bipolarity of the Cold War, balance-of-power politics is more likely to dissuade states from initiating warfare in an emerging multipolar situation.[16] Already there are signs that states are responding to an emerging multipolarity in strategic relationships. Russia's new national security policy of 10 January 2000, for example, assumes a global multipolarity, which is an indication of Russia's susceptibility to third-party (Chinese) threats.[17] Simultaneously, the emergence of several great powers and important regional actors will make it increasingly difficult to update the existing ABM Treaty. The issue depth embodied in the current agreement would handicap multilateral negotiation. Overall, the pressures created by balance-of-power politics in a multipolar world are more likely to constrain arsenals than any effort to formalize and constrain strategic relationships using a multilateral ABM regime.

Revision of the ABM Treaty depends in large part on the configuration of the international system. The distraction of U.S. rivals by third-party states is less effective than a negotiated ABM Treaty in enhancing U.S. security in a bipolar environment, and more effective at enhancing U.S. security in a multipolar setting. Therefore, as multipolarity emerges, the United States must permit greater diffusion of missile defense benefits and responsibility to its regional allies so that they can begin to participate more vigorously in balance-of-power politics. The diffusion of BMD technology also would reduce the central role played by the United States as a supplier of extended deterrence and theater missile defenses. When several states have an independent missile defense capability, nations contemplating aggression would perceive reduced incentives to target the United States as the strategic hub which links America and its powerful allies to regional disputes.

Today's strategies for deploying national missile defense and revising the ABM Treaty must advance some conception of the future security environment, because systems and treaties will not reach full operation until decades hence. If international relations are becoming multipolar, which is at least as likely a prospect as the persistence of American primacy well into the twenty-first century, current thinking about arms control agreements that limit defenses must take into account balance-of-power politics in a multipolar setting. U.S. security strategy should come to rely increasingly on the balance of power to create regional third-party threats that will engage insatiable adversaries. This strategy might then be complemented by comprehensive bilateral ABM Treaties with satiable rivals, and a thin multilateral ABM Treaty, with manageable negotiating costs, to constrain developments that would be considered more or less universally undesirable (for example, placing nuclear-armed missile interceptors into orbit).

THE ABM TREATY AND U.S. NATIONAL SECURITY

The ABM Treaty fosters U.S. national security in several ways. The treaty promotes arms race stability, thereby reducing the likelihood that an unrestrained arms competition can instigate a spiral of hostility leading to war. The agreement also promotes crisis stability, especially by preventing particularly threatening types of defensive systems. It slows the proliferation of weapons of mass destruction and missile systems.

Arms Race Stability

An arms race is an action-reaction process in which two states are engaged in a weapons buildup.[18] As this arms competition intensifies, adversaries both create and act on the (mis)perception that some significant military advantage, often referred to as a window of opportunity, is about to be achieved by one side in the arms race. These windows of opportunity are dangerous because they create incentives for arms-racing parties to launch a preemptive or preventive war, especially if one of the competitors is approaching exhaustion.[19] It is unlikely that a prospective American BMD system would generate significant incentives for small states such as Iran, Iraq, Libya, North Korea, and possibly Syria, to launch a preventive war to stop the deployment of missile defenses. Such defenses, however, might provoke an arms race with Russia or China. John Holum, senior advisor for arms control to President Clinton and the Secretary of State, has noted, "We don't want NMD to give China incentives to go beyond the ongoing strategic modernization program they had planned before NMD became an issue."[20] At a minimum, the prospect of U.S. missile defenses is likely to imperil the further reduction in Russian and American strategic offensive forces envisioned for the next Strategic Arms Reduction Treaty (START III).

The ABM Treaty reduces the prospects for an arms race between Russia and the United States by reducing the intensity of the action-reaction process—specifically, the deployment spiral of nuclear missiles, missile defenses, and countermeasures. It reduces the mutual costs of deterrence, permitting a strategic balance at reduced force levels without a concomitant reduction in security. This aspect of the ABM Treaty applies primarily to the Russian-American strategic relationship, since smaller states lack the resources to engage in a sustained arms competition with a global superpower.[21] The stabilizing effects of the ABM Treaty, however, already may have expanded beyond Russian-American relations. Chinese strategists, for example, may have sized their strategic arsenal on the assumption that significant missile defenses would not reduce the effectiveness of their modest retaliatory force.

Crisis Stability

The ABM Treaty enhances the security of the United States and Russia by eliminating weapons whose performance characteristics may be conducive to war.[22] The ABM Treaty helps create deterrent postures that do not encourage surprise attacks, first strikes, decapitation attacks, preemption, offensive advantages, or the deployment of vulnerable "use-it-or-lose-it" systems. The ABM Treaty enhances crisis stability between the United States and Russia by preserving the *status quo* vulnerability of their countervalue targets to retaliatory second strikes. Neither side has an incentive to resort to nuclear first use in a crisis. Preserving crisis stability is particularly important if minimum deterrence strategies are to guide future force reductions in the arsenals of these former Cold War rivals.[23] There is considerable fear within the Russian military that missile defenses could be used to limit the damage caused by their retaliatory second-strike forces. The possibility of U.S. NMD and significant modification of the ABM Treaty has prompted Russian calls for a return to a hair-trigger alert status for their strategic forces and for redeployment of multiple independently targetable reentry vehicles (MIRVs) on their vulnerable fixed-silo intercontinental ballistic missiles (ICBMs), which are banned under START II. These developments would detract from crisis stability.[24]

If weapons that provide some first strike advantages against one opponent cannot be used simultaneously to hold third parties at bay, then their destabilizing effects are less pronounced. This is why preemptive wars, designed to take advantage of first-strike weapons, are so rare.[25] But if NMD rendered preemption or war possible, it could actually lead to greater conflict. It is the fear of nuclear retaliation that underpins restraint between nuclear-armed antagonists.[26]

By contrast, stability (certain nuclear retaliation) creates opportunities for instability (conventional conflict) because leaders could engage in hostilities without the fear of placing their nation at complete risk—a situation known as the "stability-instability paradox."[27] If the ABM Treaty permitted comprehensive missile defenses that would reduce the threat of escalation, it might increase the possibility that disputes could become militarized. Alternatively, missile defenses could increase the amount of damage a state ultimately suffers in a second strike because its opponents might launch enormous numbers of weapons to assure penetration of its defenses. The amount of damage suffered in such attacks primarily would be a function of the effectiveness of defenses and not the size of the attacking force. Massive attacks launched for penetration could eliminate the opportunity for the bargaining or diplomacy necessary to keep wars limited.

Slowing the Proliferation of Weapons of Mass Destruction

Although there is no clear link between the proliferation of weapons of mass destruction and the outbreak of war, defenses probably will have some effect on the spread of chemical, biological, and nuclear weapons. Some observers suggest that at a minimum there is a moral hazard: U.S. leaders may decline to pursue nonproliferation aggressively, knowing that the consequences to the United States are lessened by missile defenses.[28] Others suggest that missile defenses would create global proliferation incentives, leading to a relative decline in the power of the system hegemon and the existing nonproliferation regime.[29]

Universal nonproliferation agreements are the primary arms control measure for limiting the spread of nuclear, chemical, and biological weapons. But given the tendency for military technology to diffuse throughout the world, no nonproliferation regime can ever do much more than slow the spread of military technology. Moreover, the balance of power at best plays a limited role in retarding proliferation; in fact, efforts to maintain military parity could be a source of proliferation pressure. Thus, a prospective ABM Treaty aimed at halting the proliferation of national missile defenses (e.g., one reinforcing the restrictions imposed by Article IX of the current Treaty, which limits transfer of missile defense technology to third parties) would suffer from many of the problems associated with the 1967 Non-Proliferation Treaty. A bilateral agreement that restricted the transfer of technology would leave the parties to the Treaty at a disadvantage in relation to other states. A multilateral suppliers' agreement could at best have a temporary effect on the rate of proliferation. Eventually, "dual-use" technologies would spread across the globe, especially because missile defenses do not rely on a key component or raw material. The great powers would find a universal agreement difficult to enforce, and a nonuniversal agreement would appear illegitimate to the majority of "have-not" states.

Extended nuclear deterrence slows nuclear proliferation among U.S. allies. By guaranteeing the nuclear security of Germany and Japan, the United States eliminates the possibility that regional arms races will be generated by these states' efforts to guarantee their own security unilaterally.[30] U.S. missile defenses could increase U.S. allies' perception of the credibility of extended deterrence, because defenses reduce the potential for opponents to deter American intervention by threatening the United States directly with retaliation. BMD also would reduce competitors' incentives to obtain nuclear arms and their most militarily useful means of delivery—long-range missiles.[31] From the American perspective, furthermore, U.S. national missile defense would undermine other states' incentives to align with emerging great powers.

National missile defense would transform extended deterrence.[32] Whereas extended deterrence ultimately has rested on U.S. strategic forces, many of the missile defense systems contemplated by the United States rely on forward operating bases. Considerable political hurdles and Treaty restrictions, however, would have to be overcome to base BMD components on allied territory. Moreover, military logic would dictate that any NMD system should protect sensors and radars integral to the overall functioning of the system. Defense of U.S. territory requires upgrades in sensors located in Canada, Greenland, and the United Kingdom. These sensors should be protected by some combination of NMD or TMD.

Boost-phase defenses, which are advocated by some critics of the Clinton administration's missile defense programs, would depend entirely on forward-based sensors and interceptors. But these bases could be under direct threat themselves from either military attack or domestic opposition. If the United States places reliance on boost-phase endoatmospheric interceptors, it might have to consider deploying them at sites in Turkey, Taiwan, Okinawa (Japan), South Korea, Kuwait, Cyprus, and Masirah Island (Oman).[33] The United States would have to be prepared to defend these bases. The combination of forward bases—which make U.S. allies the logical targets of any effort to penetrate U.S. missile defenses—with U.S. national defenses, may reduce allied confidence in extended deterrence. NMD could even increase allied interest in developing an autonomous retaliatory capability. According to Henry Kissinger, "Our European allies will interpret an anti-missile program as decoupling the defense of Europe from America, because the United States might be perceived as withdrawing into a Fortress America."[34] Recalling the Strategic Defense Initiative (SDI) debate of the 1980s, which became normatively associated with strategic instability and nuclear war among some allied electorates, the United States must remain sensitive to the possible emergence of grassroots opposition to forward-based sensors or interceptors. Alternatively, American dependence on these forward bases (especially those associated with boost-phase defenses) may cause the United States to be drawn into regional conflicts that do not serve its interests, especially if the sensors serve the dual purpose of local air defense.[35]

Given the complexity of missile defense systems, their proliferation probably would be accompanied by the political alignment of small states with major powers, which would be sources of defense technologies and weapon systems. Missile defense technology therefore is likely to spread first to states hostile to the United States rather than to U.S. allies, increasing the costs of U.S. intervention in regional conflicts.

PROSPECTS FOR A REVISED ABM TREATY

The effects of minor, moderate, or extreme revisions of the ABM Treaty depend to a large extent on the compatibility of the Treaty with the balance of power. Efforts to revise the Treaty thus should be evaluated in terms of the international situation that will exist in about two decades (the time it will take to test and deploy a significant BMD capability). Given the expectation that the proliferation of nuclear weapons and missile delivery systems will continue—since without this proliferation there would be no need for missile defenses against "rogue" states—one could expect that a multipolar international system will be emerging by 2020. One also would expect that by 2020 several other states would have ambitious missile defense programs under development. By contrast, the C1 system contemplated by the Clinton administration would be deployed in an international setting more similar to today's situation. In other words, the strategic context in which missile defenses must operate—and not just the technical characteristics of contemplated systems—must inform efforts to revise the ABM Treaty.

Minor Revision (2010)

A revised ABM Treaty to accommodate the Clinton administration's planned C1 threshold system would be put to the test as early as the year 2010. Within that period, the United States would remain the world's dominant economic and military power. By 2010, U.S. conventional units might find it increasingly difficult to project force against more sophisticated adversaries possessing better conventional defenses or asymmetric countermeasures (i.e., weapons of mass destruction). Nuclear and missile proliferation would continue; but despite Chinese strategic modernization, no state would engage the United States (or Russia for that matter) in a nuclear arms race. Precluding the creation of an exceptionally effective alliance as a counterbalance to American power (e.g., an alliance of Russia and China, or possibly Russia and India), the United States will remain the dominant player on the international scene. There will be no significant new threats to U.S. security.

Continuity therefore would be the chief goal of any revision of the ABM Treaty to permit a U.S. missile defense system. The Treaty would have to include only the current signatories (the United States, Russia, Ukraine, Kazakhstan, and Belarus). Russian and American officials might even consider revising the Treaty as a bilateral agreement. Treaty revision also should focus on eliminating any arms-race or crisis instability introduced by U.S. NMD deployments. A revised Treaty should provide ample reassurance to the Russians that their second-strike retaliatory force is not put at risk by U.S. missile defenses. Reinforcing arms-race stability could be a real challenge for a revised Treaty, however, if the START process leads to further offensive arms reductions or if U.S. officials decide to deploy more capable defenses. A revised ABM Treaty also might constrain deployment nodes or technologies that create the potential for building highly capable defenses rapidly (such as space-based or sea-based systems or nuclear-armed interceptors).

However, even if only minor revisions are contemplated, the United States might well seek to expand the purpose of the Treaty. Russians and Americans could incorporate new confidence-building measures into a revised Treaty. At a minimum, these initiatives would renew national confidence in deterrent forces; at a maximum, they could foster further reductions in offensive systems and the possible integration of Russian and American missile defenses. Efforts to use missile defenses to bolster nonproliferation objectives could be added to the negotiating agenda. Russian and American policymakers need to agree about how strong defenses will have to be to discourage proliferation. U.S. policymakers also might think about giving the Russians a voice in the export of American missile technology, in return for a Russian pledge not to sell countermeasure technology without U.S. approval.

Moderate Revision (2015)

To accommodate more-ambitious ballistic missile defense systems, such as the Bush administration's preferred C3-plus deployments combined with an advanced version of the Navy Theater Wide system and an array of space-based and land-based sensors, more significant modification of the

ABM Treaty will have to occur. These moderate Treaty revisions and more ambitious defenses would both come into play around 2015–2020. Although the system would offer significant protection against an accidental attack involving a few dozen warheads, it probably would not stop a Russian or Chinese second strike involving several hundred warheads.[36]

Predicting the nature of world politics in 2015 is more challenging. The proliferation of nuclear weapons, associated delivery systems, and increasingly capable conventional weapons will have continued at a moderate pace, turning several states into significant regional powers.[37] China and Russia will have begun to deploy their own missile defense systems. Regional powers will have begun to deploy countermeasures to defeat missile defenses. Several states also will have deployed missile defenses that have a significant effect on specific, enduring rivalries. By 2015 the United States will have transferred missile defense technology to key allies in Europe, the Middle East, and Asia, and these states will have programs underway to deploy defensive systems designed to respond to regional threats. Although the United States will retain a degree of economic and military primacy in world politics, the rise of Chinese power, Russia's revival, and the emergence of several significant regional powers could constrain U.S. freedom of action. By 2020, balance-of-power politics, associated with multipolarity, might be emerging in international relations.

Under these circumstances, U.S. policymakers might choose among three approaches to modifying the ABM Treaty. One option would be to create a regime to limit missile defenses, based on a series of bilateral agreements. A revised bilateral agreement with Russia could be undertaken to reduce concerns about the breakout potential embodied in U.S. systems as well as to decrease the prospects of arms-race and crisis instability between the world's two major nuclear powers.[38] U.S. officials also might consider signing bilateral ABM agreements with China or with various regional powers (e.g., India or Iran). Problems are likely to occur in these bilateral talks, however, as states assess the impact of agreements on regional rivalries. Equity issues might become acute in these negotiations as U.S. officials attempt to constrain some arsenals while tolerating the deployment of more effective defenses by some states. U.S. officials also might find themselves involved in efforts to prevent offensive-defensive arms races between India and China, India and Pakistan, or Israel and Iran.[39]

A major drawback inherent in bilateral agreements is that they make treaty signatories vulnerable to exploitation by third parties. India and Pakistan might agree to restrict missile defenses, for instance, only to discover that China is willing to exploit their bilateral agreement to deny India a second-strike capability against the People's Republic. U.S. officials also might find bilateral agreements a poor means of influencing global trends in the development of missile defenses. Instead of bilateral agreements, they might choose a second option: a universal variant of the ABM Treaty that could promote international norms against certain types of missile defenses (e.g., nuclear-armed interceptors) that threaten third parties or offer enormous breakout potential. A universal ABM Treaty also might include an agreement to post warnings of both offensive and defensive missile test launches so as to reduce the possibility that testing might lead to escalation. A universal ABM agreement would have to be more limited in scope than a bilateral arrangement, for the simple reason that it would be extraordinarily difficult to reach a political agreement among multiple parties over the definitions of crisis-stable and equitable distributions of defensive capability. Minimizing the depth of the agreement would help maximize international involvement in the Treaty.

A third option that combines more depth with only slightly less coverage than a universal agreement is a tiered, multilateral arrangement that applies restrictions in a discriminatory fashion. For example, states with significant missile defenses—e.g., Russia, China, the United States, and Japan—would tie their defense deployments to mutually agreed upon levels, whereas other states' deployments would be restricted so that they did not interfere with the stability of mutual nuclear deterrence among the great powers. If smaller powers agreed to these conditions, the great powers might abandon preemptive or preventive war strategies and capabilities against ballistic missile threats and instead rely on an international body to punish states that do not abide by the tiered agreement.[40] A tiered ABM Treaty could be made more legitimate by placing renewed emphasis on Article XI of the existing Treaty, which commits the signatories to a negotiated reduction in offensive arms. The tiered variant also might curb the proliferation of missile defense technology, strengthen the Missile Technology Control Regime, and share formal linkages with the Nuclear Non-Proliferation Treaty.

The End of the ABM Treaty (2020+)

The decision to abandon the ABM Treaty will depend to a large extent on whether or not Americans believe they can obtain favorable security outcomes without direct management of the international system. Americans might come to believe, for example, that their wealth and technological prowess would allow them to outpace any potential competitor in an offensive-defensive arms race. Alternatively, U.S. officials might come to believe that the deployment of BMD, regional rivalries, proliferation of weapons of mass destruction and associated delivery systems, and selective U.S. disengagement from peripheral areas provide sufficient security in the absence of an ABM Treaty.

As proliferation continues and states develop more significant military capabilities, it might be possible for a highly capable U.S. military simply to stand aside as regional rivals expend increasing resources in arms races or open warfare. Indeed, if U.S. policymakers chose to rely on a balance-of-power system rather than make efforts to manage international developments via an arms control regime, proliferation might even be viewed in a positive way.[41] Increased nuclear proliferation would provide alternative regional threats to states that are currently worrisome to U.S. leaders. This same logic also would seem to apply to threats created by emerging great power competitors. The United States could deflect threats by encouraging uncertainty about third-party interventions in ostensibly bilateral disputes.

Unilateral abandonment of the ABM Treaty, either through abrogation or withdrawal as allowed by the Treaty, would generate much ill will in the international community. The demise of the ABM Treaty likely would provoke limited Russian rearmament and retaliatory proliferation of countermeasures technology. Other states, such as China and Iran, might begin to share sensitive technology once they had a common interest in penetrating U.S. defenses. Of course, if U.S. missile defenses appeared highly effective, further strengthening U.S. strategic primacy, then the anti-American rhetoric and actions prompted by the end of the ABM Treaty would eventually fade as friend and foe alike came to terms with the *fait accompli*.

An important consideration, therefore, is whether the United States is affected less by third-party behavior than other major actors in the international system.[42] Today, the United States is a target of states seeking to upset the status quo, because it provides an important management function in world politics. The United States, for example, provides extended deterrence, which helps reduce demand-side pressures that could fuel the proliferation of nuclear, chemical, and biological weapons. By 2020, however, the number of states that could mount a credible threat against the United States while still holding regional rivals at bay will be quite few. In the absence of the ABM Treaty, it might become clear that other states had benefited greatly from the arms-race and crisis stability produced by the general absence of missile defenses in strategic arsenals. Regional rivalries could become heated, counterintuitively increasing the relative power and security enjoyed by the United States.

CONCLUSION

The next few years probably will provide a window of opportunity for revising the ABM Treaty. Russian-American relations are still warm enough to develop a normative basis for a future Treaty and to conduct productive talks about the future of the deterrence relationship between the two former adversaries. The benefits of keeping policy options open through noncommitment will, however, quickly dissipate by the time more-advanced missile defense systems become operational. If multipolarity does continue to develop in the next few decades, it will become increasingly clear that a single missile defense agreement cannot satisfy competing political visions, technologies, and military doctrines. Superficial agreements to abstain from universally unwanted technologies or behaviors are of course possible under these conditions, but they will not do much to increase the security of the states involved.

Policymakers and scholars alike should realize that no matter how well intentioned they may be, their arms control efforts will fail if they do not take into account the conditions in which future agreements must operate. Today's debate about revision of the ABM Treaty is mired in concerns about current threats posed by marginal states or the latest twists in negotiating tactics. What is generally missing is a vision of how U.S. policymakers hope to use arms control and national missile defense to shape the future international security environment. This is unfortunate, because most missile defense systems contemplated today will not be operational for decades to come; and unless accurate estimates of the future security context are used in revising the ABM Treaty, any new Treaty will be ineffective and short-lived.

NOTES

1. See John D. Holum, "The President's NMD Decision and U.S. Foreign Policy," Conference on the International Reactions to U.S. National and Missile Defense Deployments, Stanford University, 3 March 2000, 1–2.

2. On the inevitability of multipolarity, see Christopher Layne, "The Unipolar Illusion: Why New Great Powers Will Rise," *International Security* 17 (4), 5–49; Kenneth Waltz, "The Emerging Structure of International Politics," *International Security* 18 (2), 44–79; for a criticism of this assumption, see Paul Schroeder, "Historical Reality vs. Neo-realist Theory," *International Relations* 19, 108–148; Ethan B. Kapstein, "Does Unipolarity Have a Future?" in Ethan B. Kapstein and Michael Mastanduno, eds., *Unipolar Politics: Realism and State Strategies After the Cold War* (New York: Columbia University Press, 1999), 464–490. Colin Gray argues that a return to nuclear confrontation will most likely occur within a bipolar context characterized by greater balancing than during the Cold War (see Colin Gray, *The Second Nuclear Age* [Boulder: Lynne Rienner, 1999], 25).

3. Samuel Huntington, "The Lonely Superpower," *Foreign Affairs* 78 (2), 35–49; Michael Patrick Tkacik, "Nuclear Deterrence, Arms Control, and Multipolarity: An Argument for Incremental Policy Change," *Armed Forces & Society* 22 (3), 357–377.

4. William S. Cohen, Secretary of Defense, *Annual Report to the President and the Congress* (Washington, D.C.: Department of Defense, 2000), 73.

5. Ibid.

6. Hedley Bull, *The Control of the Arms Race: Disarmament and Arms Control in the Missile Age* (London: Weidenfeld & Nicolson, 1961), 30; Thomas C. Schelling and Morton Halperin, *Strategy and Arms Control* (New York: Twentieth Century Fund, 1961), 77. See also Kerry Kartchner, "The Objectives of Arms Control," in Jeffrey A. Larsen and Gregory Rattray, eds., *Arms Control Towards the 21st Century* (Boulder: Lynne Ri-

enner, 1996), 19–34; and Robert Axelrod and Robert O. Keohane, "Achieving Cooperation under Anarchy: Strategies and Institutions," in David Baldwin, ed., *Neorealism and Neoliberalism: The Contemporary Debate* (New York: Columbia University Press, 1993), 91–92.

7. The ABM Treaty has been multilateral since the fourth ABM Review in 1993. See Mancur Olson, *The Logic of Collective Action: Public Goods and the Theory of Groups* (Cambridge: Harvard University Press, 1971).

8. Holum, "The President's NMD Decision," 5.

9. Charles Lipson, "International Cooperation in Security and Economic Affairs," *World Politics* 37 (1984), 1–23; Duncan Snidal, "Relative Gains and the Pattern of International Cooperation," in Baldwin, *Neorealism and Neoliberalism*, 171; Trevor Taylor, "The Arms Control Process: The International Context," in Larsen and Rattray, eds., *Arms Control*, 35–54.

10. On the prospects of multilateralism, see Joseph Pilat, "Arms Control, Verification, and Transparency," in Larsen and Rattray, eds., *Arms Control*, 84–88.

11. For arms control and hegemony, see James Ferguson, "The Changing Arms Control Agenda: New Meanings, New Players," *Arms Control* 12 (1991), 191–210. For an exploration of the problems with a universal ABM treaty, see Sidney Graybeal and Patricia McFate, "Strategic Defensive Arms Control," in Larsen and Rattray, eds., *Arms Control*, 134.

12. Stephen Walt, *The Origins of Alliances* (Ithaca: Cornell University Press, 1987), 18n, 21–22; Ernst B. Haas, "The Balance of Power," *World Politics* 5 (1953), 442–477.

13. Geoffrey Blainey, *The Causes of War*, 3d edition (New York: Free Press, 1988), 58. For empirical evidence of this effect, see Scott Sigmund Gartner and Randolph M. Siverson, "War Expansion and War Outcome," *Journal of Conflict Resolution* 40 (March 1996), 4–15.

14. Michael J. Mazarr and Richard K. Betts, "Correspondence—A Farewell to Arms Control?" *International Security* 17 (1993), 188–200; Robert Gilpin, *War and Change in World Politics* (Cambridge: Cambridge University Press, 1981), 94; Robert Powell, "Stability and the Distribution of Power," *World Politics* 48 (1996), 239–267. For criticism of this conception of international relations by other realists, see Kenneth N. Waltz, "The Stability of a Bipolar World," *Dædalus* (1964), 881–909; Randall L. Schweller, "Bandwagoning for Profit," *International Security* 19 (1994), 72–107.

15. Karl Deutsch and J. David Singer, "Multipolar Power Systems and International Security," in James N. Rosenau, ed., *International Politics*

and Foreign Policy (New York: Free Press, 1969). This perspective contrasts with that of Kenneth Waltz, who argues that bipolarity is the most stable system (see Kenneth Waltz, "Stability of a Bipolar World," 881–909). The stability Waltz describes may be better explained by the presence of nuclear weapons than as a function of the dynamics of the international system (see Kenneth Waltz, *Theory of International Politics* [Reading, Mass.: Addison-Wesley, 1979]).

16. Deutsch and Singer, "Multipolar Power Systems," 315; Bruce Bueno de Mesquita, "Measuring Systemic Polarity," *Journal of Conflict Resolution* 19 (1975), 90.

17. Philip C. Bleek, "Russia Adopts New Security Concept; Appears to Lower Nuclear Threshold," *Arms Control Today*, January/February 2000. For context, see Jennifer G. Mathers, *The Russian Nuclear Shield from Stalin to Yeltsin* (London: Macmillan, 2000).

18. Robert Jervis, "Cooperation Under the Security Dilemma," *World Politics* 30 (January 1978), 167–214; George W. Downs, "Arms Races and War," in Philip Tetlock, ed., *Behavior, Society and Nuclear War* (New York: Oxford University Press, 1989), 90; R. Leng, "When Will They Ever Learn: Coercive Bargaining in Recurrent Crises," *Journal of Conflict Resolution* 27 (1983), 379–419.

19. James D. Morrow, "A Twist of Truth: A Reexamination of the Effects of Arms Races on the Occurrence of War," *Journal of Conflict Resolution* 33 (1989), 500–529.

20. Holum, "The President's NMD Decision," 9.

21. David Denoon, *Ballistic Missile Defense in the Post–Cold War Era* (Boulder: Westview, 1995), 6–7.

22. Jack S. Levy, "The Offensive/Defensive Balance of Military Technology: A Theoretical and Historical Analysis," *International Studies Quarterly* 28 (1984), 219–238.

23. George Quester, "The Continuing Debate on Minimal Deterrence," in T. V. Paul, Richard Harknett, and James Wirtz, eds., *The Absolute Weapon Revisited—Nuclear Arms and the Emerging International Order* (Ann Arbor: University of Michigan Press, 1998), 167–188.

24. Holum, "The President's NMD Decision," 5.

25. Dan Reiter, "Exploding the Powder Keg Myth: Preemptive Wars Almost Never Happen," *International Security* 20 (2), 5–34; Robert Jervis, "Arms Control, Stability, and Causes of War," *Political Science Quarterly* 108 (1993), 252.

26. Jervis, "Arms Control," 248; Colin Gray, "Arms Control Does Not Control Arms," *Orbis* 37 (1993), 335.

27. Glenn Snyder, "The Balance of Power and the Balance of Terror," in Paul Seabury, *Balance of Power* (San Francisco: Chandler Publishing Company, 1965), 185–186; Robert Jervis, *The Meaning of the Nuclear Revolution: Statecraft and the Prospect of Armageddon* (Ithaca: Cornell University Press, 1989), 19.

28. Holum, "The President's NMD Decision," 7.

29. Peter R. Lavoy, "The Strategic Consequences of Nuclear Proliferation: A Review Essay," *Strategic Studies* 4 (1995), 695–753; Scott Sagan and Kenneth Waltz, *The Spread of Nuclear Weapons: A Debate* (New York: W. W. Norton, 1995).

30. Most key U.S. allies either abstained or voted in support of the United States in a U.N. General Assembly resolution to uphold the ABM Treaty (5 November 1999 Press Release GA/DIS/3161). Canada is likely to support any U.S. NMD initiative. See James Ferguson, "Forum Report: Canada and Ballistic Missile Defence," 26–27 November 1998, available on line at http://www.umanitoba.ca/centres/defence/forum.htm; and David Rudd, Jim Hanson, and Jessica Blitt, eds., *Canada and Missile Defence* (Toronto: Canadian Institute of Strategic Studies, 2000). Japan, Germany, and Italy are involved in regional BMD systems with the United States (Satodhi Morimoto, "TMD and Japan's Security," December 1999, presented at the 1999 Asia-Pacific Security Forum Conference, "The Dynamics of Asia-Pacific Security: A Fin-de-Siècle Assessment," 17–18 December 1999, Taipei, Taiwan; Cohen, *Annual Report to the President*, 75). Australia is supportive of an ABM Treaty revision consistent with U.S. security (see "Australia-U.S. Ministerial Consultations Joint Communiqué," 3 November 1999, available on line at http://www.usis-australia.gov).

31. Gilles Andréani, "The Disarray of US Non-Proliferation Policy," *Survival* 41 (4), 50. For the criticism that NMD will deter nuclear proliferation, see George Lewis, Lisbeth Gronlund, and David Wright, "National Missile Defense: An Indefensible System," *Foreign Policy*, Winter 1999–2000, 129.

32. Benjamin Valentino, "Allies No More: Small Nuclear Powers and Opponents of Ballistic Missile Defenses in the Post–Cold War Era," *Security Studies* 7 (2), 215–234.

33. For an elaboration, see Michael O'Hanlon's chapter in this volume; Richard L. Garwin, "Effectiveness of Proposed National Missile Defense Against ICBMs from North Korea," 17 March 1999, available on line at http://www.fas.org/rlg (accessed 14 May 2001).

34. Henry Kissinger, "The Next President's First Obligation," *Washington Post*, 9 February 2000.

35. Cohen, *Annual Report to the President*, 74.

36. Russian negotiators claim that Russia's SS-27 ICBMs can penetrate any NMD built in the near future. See Holum, "The President's NMD Decision," 4. One estimate puts the Chinese ICBM arsenal at only a few dozen by 2015 (Bob Walpole, *Foreign Missile Developments and the Ballistic Missile Threat to the United States Through 2015* [Washington, D.C.: National Intelligence Council, September 1999], 5).

37. Department of Defense, DCI National Intelligence Estimate, "Foreign Missile Developments and the Ballistic Missile Threat to the United States Through 2015," Executive Summary, September 1999.

38. Banning Garrett and Bonnie Glaser, "Chinese Perspectives on Nuclear Arms Control," *International Security* 20, 3 (Winter 1995/1996), 43–78.

39. See Paul Bracken, *Fire in the East: The Rise of Asian Military Power and the Second Nuclear Age* (New York: HarperCollins, 1999), 66–70; Stephen Cambone, "The United States and Theatre Missile Defence in North-East Asia," *Survival* 30, 3 (Autumn 1997), 66–84; Michael Eisenstadt, "Living with a Nuclear Iran?" *Survival* 41, 3 (Autumn 1999), 124–148.

40. Ivo H. Daalder, James M. Goldgeier, and James M. Lindsay, "Deploying NMD: Not Whether, But How," *Survival* 42, 1 (Spring 2000), 11.

41. Kenneth Waltz, *The Spread of Nuclear Weapons: More May Be Better* (London: International Institute for Strategic Studies, 1981).

42. See Christopher Layne, "From Preponderance to Offshore Balancing," *International Security* 22, 1 (Summer 1997), 86–124.

PART THREE

Regional Responses to National Missile Defense

7

China

BRADLEY ROBERTS

Chinese leaders were taken by surprise by the July 1998 agreement between the Clinton administration and the Republican-led Congress to move to deploy a national missile defense (NMD). To be sure, China had worried about the prospect of such a defense ever since President Ronald Reagan's 1983 "Star Wars" speech. And the prospect of the deployment of theater missile defenses to the territory of U.S. friends and allies in East Asia had generated rising concern in Beijing through the mid-1990s. But policymakers in Beijing apparently did not anticipate the impact of the Rumsfeld Commission report and North Korea's launch of its Taepo Dong-2 missile on U.S. NMD policy.

The People's Republic of China (PRC) responded to renewed U.S. interest in NMD by working to prevent any change to the status quo as embodied in the Anti-Ballistic Missile (ABM) Treaty. In the following months China's disarmament ambassador, Sha Zukang, called for multilateralizing the ABM Treaty so that China could have a say in its fate.[1]

China and Russia also issued a joint communiqué stating that "to preserve and strengthen the ABM treaty is of critical importance," arguing that the treaty is "the cornerstone for maintaining strategic stability" and that undermining it would result in an arms race and "place additional obstacles to the disarmament process."[2] China and Russia co-sponsored a resolution of the 54th United Nations General Assembly on "preservation of and compliance with the ABM Treaty," which China deemed "a collective appeal by the international community to the United States."[3] Additionally, Ambassador Sha threatened "disastrous consequences" if the ABM Treaty were to be amended or abolished, a theme echoed at the Conference on Disarmament in Geneva and at the review conference of the Nuclear Non-Proliferation Treaty in New York in spring 2000.[4] As an adjunct to their support of the ABM Treaty, China's leaders also decided to spend an additional $9.7 billion "to boost China's second strike capabilities in response to any nuclear attack."[5]

If Beijing was caught by surprise by the National Missile Defense Act, Washington also was surprised by China's reaction. China had received little attention in the U.S. debate on NMD. That debate had been dominated instead by two other concerns: countering the proliferation of long-range missiles, and protecting strategic stability with Russia. Until China's vociferous complaints, virtually no thought had been given in Washington to China's interests and potential reactions. Now, concern about China's potential reactions to NMD could loom large in the assessment of the impact that NMD would have on the strategic environment and arms control. As John Holum argued in March 2000, China is in some ways "the toughest case": "The objective facts are that China today has a small strategic force, and that the North Koreans live in the same neighborhood; thus even a limited NMD system aimed at the North Korean threat could also significantly erode China's deterrent capability against the United States," Holum wrote.[6]

China has undertaken an extensive strategic modernization program in recent years.[7] This effort, long predating the U.S. NMD decision, will provide China with the capabilities to overcome the "damage" done to its deterrent by U.S. NMD. U.S. analysts project a Chinese buildup tied to NMD. As one group has argued, China is "likely to respond to a U.S. NMD system by deploying more of its own ICBMs and by developing more sophisticated countermeasures, both developments that are likely in any event as China continues to modernize its armed forces."[8]

Is this assessment and prediction valid? Will Beijing take steps to protect its deterrent? How should Washington respond to those steps? This chapter begins by describing the context in which China's reactions to NMD are taking shape. China's response to NMD is likely to range beyond the strictly military-technical into the political-military realm. The chapter explores Chinese thinking on a variety of issues, with the hope of better understanding the strategic perspective informing China's policy decisions. It focuses especially on how the perception of the United States as a "rogue hegemon" affects China's interests. This task is difficult, because strong rhetoric plays such a significant role in Chinese politics, and because policymaking in a one-party state is a closed process. The survey of opinions and arguments included here should not be taken at face value, but it does provide important clues to Chinese strategic perspectives. The chapter then explores the possible impact of alternative U.S. choices vis-à-vis NMD and the ABM Treaty. Different choices in Washington will lead to different choices in Beijing. The chapter then considers the implications of China's choices for the United States. Assuming that China's reactions include a buildup of its offensive nuclear forces, how might the U.S.-PRC relationship be transformed? Can the United States live with such a buildup? Should it?

CHINA'S DOMESTIC CONTEXT

Understanding how China might react to NMD and ABM developments requires an understanding of its ongoing modernization program, the debate about the United States and the requirements of Chinese security in the post–Cold War era, the changing leadership dynamic in Beijing, and the Taiwan conflict.

Strategic Modernization

China is midstream in a long-running effort to develop, produce, and deploy follow-on strategic systems. Today its forces consist primarily of short-range ballistic missiles tipped with conventional warheads and medium-range ballistic missiles tipped with either conventional or nuclear warheads. Intercontinental ballistic missiles (ICBMs) with nuclear weapons are a relatively small fraction of its overall missile force. China has been making modest improvements to the range, mobility, and accuracy of these systems as well as improvements in their capacity to penetrate defenses by means of countermeasures and sheer numbers.[9]

Where this modernization program is headed remains an open question, at least for outside observers. The 1999 U.S. National Intelligence Estimate (NIE) on the ballistic missile threat concluded that "by 2015, China is likely to have tens of missiles capable of targeting the United States, including a few tens of more survivable land- and sea-based mobile missiles with smaller nuclear warheads."[10] The Cox committee, which investigated allegations of Chinese espionage in the U.S. nuclear weapons complex, concluded that China is capable of an "aggressive deployment of upwards of 1,000 thermonuclear warheads on ICBMs by 2015."[11] There is no publicly available evidence indicating that China has defined the key parameters of its future force: whether the intercontinental component will remain relatively small in the overall mix; whether new systems will be deployed, with multiple warhead capabilities; or whether nuclear warheads will be deployed on theater systems.

This modernization program had its genesis in a number of concerns. First is the fact that systems deployed two or three decades ago are reaching the end of their serviceable lives. Second is the availability of new technology and expertise from Russia, and the wealth to acquire them, made possible by a prosperous economy. Third are concerns about the effectiveness of missile forces, arising from the vulnerability of silo-based missiles to preemption and their limited ability to penetrate defenses.

Modernization also has been driven by the shift in focus from Russia to the United States in Chinese military planning. With the end of the Cold War, China's leaders worry less about invasion from the north and west. But more than ever they worry about the possibility of confrontation with the United States over Taiwan.

In summer 1999, China successfully tested for the first time a new long-range ballistic missile, the DF-31, whose development began roughly two decades ago with an eye toward the need to penetrate the thick defenses shielding Moscow from attack. According to a February 2000 U.S. National Intelligence Estimate, the DF-31 will be targeted primarily at Russia and Asia as it enters into service in the near future.[12] But the DF-31 does not fully resolve the strategic problem now before China. Although it has a range sufficient to reach Moscow and coastal cities in the western United States, it cannot hit other parts of the United States. The 2000 NIE notes further that China is expected to test a longer-range mobile ICBM in the next several years, as well as a new submarine-launched ballistic missile, both of which will be capable of reaching any target in the United States.

For Beijing, then, the challenge of penetrating an adversary's ballistic missile defense is a familiar problem. It apparently has constructed a force capable of meeting its objectives vis-à-vis Moscow's defenses. This suggests that it also can construct a force capable of penetrating limited U.S. missile defenses. As many have argued, U.S. NMD probably will lead to a buildup of China's intercontinental nuclear force, aimed at restoring the status quo ante: to ensure that China can still deliver to U.S. targets roughly the same number of warheads that might now be possible in the absence of such defenses.[13] China also is well on the way to deploying a force of 600 to 800 short-range missiles capable of striking targets in Taiwan and the strait, potentially overwhelming even a stout theater missile defense.

This strategic modernization program is unfolding at a time of significant debate in China about nuclear doctrine. From the very start of its nuclear program in the 1950s, China has adhered to a doctrine of minimum deterrence (in Western parlance), aimed at protecting it from coercion by the other nuclear powers and gaining a place in the nuclear club. It also has embraced a doctrine of no first use. But a debate has emerged, led by proponents of a shift to a more robust nuclear doctrine offering some limited war-fighting options, which Western experts describe as limited deterrence.[14] Moreover, a debate about the possible contributions of nuclear weapons to China's national security has emerged in response to Russia's recommitment to nuclear weapons and nuclear first use as well as to nuclear testing in South Asia and the possibility of nuclear confrontation with India.

Chinese concerns about the effectiveness of existing forces are only magnified by these developments around the PRC's periphery. Having listened to repeated Russian statements on the implications of U.S. withdrawal from the ABM Treaty, some Chinese experts expect Russia to undertake a modernization of its own defenses, emphasizing its short- and intermediate-range nuclear forces. Such a move would be of great concern to China. Those experts suspect that Russia would try to recoup the costs of such steps by selling advanced missile defense technology to India, further complicating China's planning and targeting environment.

When they also consider the possibility that U.S. theater missile defenses will be deployed in East Asia, China's experts conclude that U.S. withdrawal from the ABM Treaty will set in motion a chain of events that will undermine two decades of efforts to improve the effectiveness of Chinese forces. They worry about the loss of coercive leverage. This suggests the possibility of a trajectory for China's future force that has not yet been considered in the United States: a buildup to hedge against a broader set of requirements than those dictated by the U.S.-PRC relationship alone.

China's modernization program long predates NMD and will presumably extend decades into the future. China's force will grow larger and more capable, whatever the United States does. This point was made by Clinton administration officials in the NMD debate: "Whether or not we proceed with national missile defense, China's nuclear forces would expand in a way that would make this system less threatening to China."[15] Washington should not let Beijing blame it for every new deployment. But it also is true that NMD is likely to affect the future trajectory of the Chinese modernization effort.

The long time-horizons that inform China's investment policies and strategic posture provide insight into Chinese leaders' understanding of NMD. The Clinton administration proposed to construct a thin defense aimed at the so-called C1 threat. But Chinese experts find it impossible to believe that the United States would stop there. If indeed the United States is responding to the proliferation of missiles to small regional states and believes that this trend will continue, they argue, then by Washington's own logic it will not stop at C1. Indeed, the deployment of a second set of 100 interceptors was part of the Clinton administration's plan. Moreover, China's leaders can find a great deal of evidence in the U.S. political debate to suggest that thin defenses are merely a prelude to thicker defenses. And whatever reassurances they may have heard from Clinton administration representatives, they view the Bush administration as even less likely to stop at a "thin" defense. Moreover, the Chinese have heard a steady stream of expert opinion from Moscow reiterating the long-held view that the United States will never stop in the effort to construct a maximally effective defense once it heads down that path. This is another reason for thinking that China may well look beyond how to respond to just a limited deployment of missile defenses.

U.S. Hegemony, Global Trends, and NMD

China's concerns about NMD have as much to do with U.S. intentions as with U.S. capabilities. As Shen Dingli of Fudan University has argued, China "remains strongly suspicious of the U.S. intentions in terms of NMD development."[16] Chinese experts pose two key questions: Does Washington intend to use NMD to harm China's interests? Can China count on balance-of-power politics to help check whatever malevolent intentions Washington may have?

Following the collapse of the Soviet Union, the United States has emerged as China's most important military planning problem, given the unresolved dispute over Taiwan. But the United States also has emerged as the country that can best help China modernize. Managing the bilateral relationship with Washington is thus one of Beijing's central challenges.

Beijing apparently had high hopes for this bilateral relationship in the early 1990s, and sought a commitment from Washington to pursue joint development of "a constructive strategic partnership." Its enthusiasm for the relationship with Washington was magnified by its own domestic economic growth and its tentative emergence into the global economy. In the second half of the 1990s, enthusiasm gave way to disappointment when Washington seemed incapable of meeting Beijing's expectations. Some in Beijing have blamed this U.S. failure on the fact that Washington's China policy is regularly taken hostage by one or another political faction for some short-term domestic political gain. Others have perceived a more nefarious explanation. They see the United States as bent on preventing China's emergence as a major power in the decades ahead. They believe the United States is committed to the encirclement and containment of China, a view they support with selective arguments about revisions to the U.S. defense guidelines with Japan, about U.S. support for leaders in Taipei, and about U.S. military activities in Central Asia. This perception is enhanced by resentment over the way the United States uses force to accomplish its foreign policy goals and by what many Chinese view as Washington's refusal to subject its use of force in places like Yugoslavia and Iraq to due process at the United Nations Security Council. Some argue that the United States is the great danger on the world scene today, as the world's only superpower besotted by its own predominance. They view the United States as a rogue hegemon. They mock

American fears of a rising China becoming a revanchist power, arguing that America is the truly anti–status quo power. They support this argument with the assessment that Washington consistently acts to put itself above the very laws it helped to write, by using military force to compromise the sovereignty of others, and by putting its national values ahead of both the national sovereignty of others and international stability.

Chinese analysts cannot believe that the United States does not have a master plan to contain China. This reflects their own innate sense of China's natural place in the world. But it also reflects their understanding that China is the only country that could challenge U.S. preeminence in East Asia. The bombing of China's embassy in Belgrade in May 1999 helped consolidate this view. For many Chinese, the bombing was a definitive event affecting their view of the United States, just as the Tienanmen Square crackdown was definitive in shaping American views of China.[17] In Chinese eyes, the bombing was aimed at humbling Beijing and at reminding the world of China's inferior power position vis-à-vis the United States. It also was interpreted as a signal to Chinese leaders that Washington might be willing to use similar tactics against China wherever human rights issues might require it—not just in Taiwan but also perhaps in Tibet or Xinjiang.

The debate about whether the United States is China's partner or enemy connects to China's debate about the nature of the international system. Chinese experts believe that a more multipolar order is emerging. They view multipolarity as desirable because of the increased prominence it suggests for China. For the first half of the 1990s, many Chinese believed that America's place in this order would be one of relative decline. In the second half of the 1990s, this view was clouded by dramatic sustained economic growth in the United States, economic difficulty in China, and Washington's assertiveness in the Middle East and Eastern Europe.

U.S. Military Actions and Chinese Military Policy

NATO's war in Kosovo, capped by the embassy bombing, fueled debate in China about its interests in the emerging international order. According to one Chinese analyst, four issues have dominated this debate. Did NATO's war signal a new pattern of American interventionism in the service of a global strategy aimed at imposing global hegemony? Are peace and development still the main streams of world affairs today, or have they been replaced by power politics and hegemonism? Has China's security environment been seriously undermined in recent years? What policy should China adopt toward the United States?[18]

In the scholarly community, there appears to be some caution about drawing alarmist conclusions from the Kosovo war.[19] In August 1999, the Chinese government ended debate by asserting that despite rising concerns about power politics and hegemonism, the main global trends still favored peace and development. But individuals state privately that Chinese leaders are fighting a rear-guard action in defense of the core tenets of Deng Xiaoping's foreign policy: the absence of the prospect of major war permits China to construct partnerships with all of its neighbors so that it may develop and reform, while military improvements are relegated to the bottom of the list of four modernizations. Official documents have begun to reflect the argument that world affairs are defined by competing trends, one toward peace and development and the other toward hegemonism and power politics. There are many signs that the leadership has been unable to close off the debate about which trend prevails.

One American observer suggests that China's way of thinking about the current era is informed by its past, particularly that era when China disintegrated into many warring pieces.[20] Michael Pillsbury argues that the so-called Warring States era is used by Chinese analysts as a model for understanding the dynamics of the more multipolar international order now emerging. This era purportedly teaches that powers in such a situation inevitably compete in a zero-sum game and that the chief dynamic is the rise and fall of individual powers. The Warring States era also teaches that victory goes to those who are wise enough to see through their rivals' conspiracies and patient enough to engage in combat only under favorable circumstances.

U.S. national missile defense fuels the perception that Washington is bent on denying China its rightful place in the sun as a rising great power. In Chinese eyes, NMD confirms fears of encirclement and containment, especially if combined with theater systems in Japan, South Korea, and Taiwan. It confirms the expectation that within that plan is a conspiracy aimed at the strategic misdirection of China, like that perpetrated against the Soviets with the threat of "Star Wars," baiting China into actions that will in turn justify further U.S. efforts to counter China's rise.[21] It confirms for Beijing that the United States is locked into a zero-sum game with the rest of the world for power and influence. In the words of Ambassador Sha: "The real motive of the U.S. government is to make use of the country's unrivaled economic and technological might to grab the strategic high ground for the 21st century in both the scientific and military fields, so as to break the existing global strategic balance, seek absolute security for itself, and realize its ambitions for world domination."[22]

Many Chinese experts also would see the decision to deploy more than limited missile defenses as confirmation that the system is pointed at China. In Ambassador Sha's words, the North Korean missile threat is "an almost absurd pretext."[23] A *China Daily* article argued that "the envisaged NMD cannot stop an all-out Russian nuclear attack. . . . Therefore Beijing can only view the U.S. NMD as being designed to most effectively neutralize China's strategic deterrent. . . . Even interceptors deployed in one single site are enough to knock out all Chinese CSS-4s."[24] Shen Dingli argued:

> It is untenable that the U.S. would spend more than ten billion dollars on a system which has only "rogue" states in mind . . . . Only Russia and China currently have the capability to hit the United States with nuclear warheads on intercontinental ballistic missiles . . . . The envisaged NMD cannot stop an all-out Russian nuclear attack . . . . Given the reported level of China's full-range ICBM force (CSS-4), the NMD plans requiring ABM revision would (if successfully implemented as advertised) compromise China's strategic capability in two respects. Geographically, it will protect the whole United States from being attacked. Numerically, even interceptors deployed on a single site may be enough to knock out all Chinese CSS-4s. Hence China's national security interest is greatly endangered.[25]

If a U.S. interceptor force limited to 100 interceptors is enough to set off alarm bells in Beijing, a more robust NMD certainly would be seen as a decisive threat to China's deterrent capability.[26]

U.S. policymakers tend to dismiss these Chinese concerns. After all, most Americans do not believe that the United States is pursuing a strategy of encirclement, containment, and humiliation of China. Few Americans believe in the capacity of the U.S. government to develop a master plan of any kind, especially one for hegemony, much less to keep it secret. Accordingly, Americans tend to explain complaints about encirclement as little more than the self-serving hyperbole of an ossified regime struggling to find domestic legitimacy in nationalism now that its Marxist-Leninist base is gone. What many Americans fail to appreciate is the depth of Chinese suspicions about the United States and the purposes of the international order that it defends. That suspicion is born of a certain reading of Chinese and twentieth-century history. Chinese experts and leaders have looked for confirmation of their beliefs, expectations, and fears in American behavior since the end of the Cold War, and predictably, they have found that confirmation in a very selective reading of events. In some sense, NMD confirms an understanding born of America's repeated use of force over the last decade and Washington's apparent disregard of Beijing's interests on various matters, including nuclear stability.

The Leadership Factor

The NMD issue comes at a difficult moment for China's leaders and the Communist Party. Basic questions about how to proceed with reform and how to protect China's international interests are under intense debate in China today, raising profound concerns about the legitimacy of the one-party system and the governability of China. Western analysts, and many of their Chinese counterparts, appear to agree on the following interpretations of recent developments:

- Marxism-Leninism has been discredited.
- Economic reform brings with it questions of political reform.
- The Communist Party's grip on power cannot last forever.
- Russia provides a powerful example of how *not* to manage the escape from communism.

What no one can know is the extent to which this uncertainty has weakened the leadership's ability to control events, or where or how a crisis might emerge that calls into question the leaders' continued dominant role in Chinese political life.

Although China has made some difficult choices in pursuing reform, still harder choices lie ahead. The Chinese must decide how to root out corruption in a system built on political favoritism, how to cut deeply into the state enterprise system aimed at providing full employment without inciting unrest, and how to reform China's banking system. Growth is already faltering. Moreover, the Party leadership must deal with a military that believes it has waited long enough for investments in the fourth modernization. Public outrage over the Belgrade embassy bombing also reflected a popular belief that China's leaders have left China too weak on the world stage for too long.

In recent years there also have been setbacks to the regime's foreign policy agenda. China made a major effort to prevent revisions to the guidelines governing U.S.-Japanese military cooperation. This effort failed. The PRC took such a tough line on U.S. theater missile defenses in East Asia that it reinforced regional fears of a rising China threat. China's hard-line response to Indo-Pakistani nuclear developments after the two countries' nuclear tests has increased the likelihood of a buildup of long-range nuclear delivery systems there. China's leaders cut a deal with Russia on no first use, only to see Russia reembrace nuclear weapons and the concept of first use in its national security strategy. China issued strong threats prior to the presidential election in Taiwan, only to see its least-favored candidate elected to office. It bet on improvements in the relationship with the United States that neither side has been able to deliver.

Given these domestic and foreign policy challenges, it would be surprising if China's leaders did not feel besieged. Indeed, President Zhang Zemin is on the defensive politically, as he responds to the accusation that he has made too many concessions to the United States and as he tries to appease the various camps in the Communist Party with an eye toward the 2002 Party Congress. He is attacked in part because of the perception that concessions to Washington have not generated results. It appears, moreover, that the president's style is not to lead decisively but to broker agreements among the multiple powerful constituencies in Beijing. Apparently the government lacks both the internal authority and the self-confidence to make difficult decisions and compel the implementation of governmental initiatives. The challenges of effective governance in Beijing are undoubtedly magnified by the growing role of bureaucratic politics and the growing influence of issue-specific coalitions that cut across traditional political lines.

Thus, in an important political sense, U.S. NMD is yet another test of China's leadership. The prospect of a U.S. NMD system gives new influence to the hard-line elements in the policy process, especially those in the People's Liberation Army and the defense industries, who favor an increase in military spending. It decreases the leadership's ability to close off the debate over Deng Xiaoping's foreign policy. It could allow a growing chorus of voices to participate in the domestic debate about the role of nuclear weapons in China's national security strategy—the voices of those without a stake in the traditional posture of restraint and the doctrine of no first use. A leadership troubled by these various challenges may try to paper over internal differences and look strong on defense by spending more on nuclear forces, not least because spending some money there is undoubtedly less expensive than spending for an across-the-board modernization of conventional forces.

Taiwan

The focal point of Chinese diplomatic and defense concerns is Taiwan. Taiwan is the one place where most Chinese believe that U.S. military power might be exploited to Beijing's detriment, whether through an act of coercion that would be a humiliating loss of face for Beijing or an actual military defeat. The Chinese desire to gain as much leverage as possible fuels the dramatic buildup of short-range missiles across the Taiwan strait. A Taiwan conflict offers one scenario in which the possibility of nuclear confrontation among the major powers is not far-fetched, and in which the PRC can convince itself that Washington's refusal to embrace a policy of no first use may lead to first use by a United States desperate to turn the tide of a losing battle.

It is in relation to Taiwan that Chinese concerns about American hegemonism are most clearly manifested. If Washington is bent on intervening to support its values on a worldwide basis—so goes the argument—then it might be willing to do so in support of a formal declaration of independence by Taiwan. Moreover, Chinese analysts can point to many statements by prominent American politicians making a promise of just this kind. This evokes larger, deeply rooted historical concerns about Chinese sovereignty.

For many experts in China, the prospect of ballistic missile defenses on Taiwan is deeply unsettling. Theater missile defenses are not as troubling to Beijing operationally as they are politically. Operationally, Beijing appears fairly confident of its ability to overwhelm any defenses that Taipei may deploy. The PRC allegedly is well on the way to deploying between 600 and 800 short-range missiles across the strait from Taiwan by 2005. Politically, Beijing is concerned that theater defenses will reinforce Taipei's movement toward formal independence, by signaling both a diminution of Beijing's ability to use missile threats to coerce Taipei and a deepening involvement by the United States in Taiwan's defense. National missile defenses that insulate the United States from coercion by Beijing are understood in China as likely to reduce Beijing's ability to gain what it seeks in time of crisis: a reticence in Washington to come to Taiwan's defense; a willingness not to escalate if the tide of war goes against Taipei; and a strategic retreat from the defense of Taiwan if Beijing resorts to nuclear threats against the United States.

The PRC finds especially troubling the prospect of both theater and national missile defenses being deployed by the United States, defenses that it conceives of as part of a seamless web aimed at denying Beijing any influence over events outside its territory. If NMD consolidates the view that a conflict with Washington is inevitable and that as soon as systems begin to reach the field Washington's advantages in such a conflict will only continue to grow, then the argument may prevail that the time for Beijing to act is now. At the very least, Beijing wants to talk a tough line on ballistic missile defense to try to bluff Taipei and Washington into cutting a deal based on the "One China" principle (according to which Taipei cannot be allowed formally to assert its political independence from the PRC).

For decades China's leaders believed that they could be restrained in their development of their nuclear option and relatively leisurely about dealing with Taiwan. The sense that patience will be its own reward regarding Taiwan, however, appears to be giving way to a new perception that time is not on Beijing's side.

ALTERNATIVE U.S. PATHS AND CHINA'S POSSIBLE REACTIONS

This section reviews the three alternatives for U.S. policy and their likely repercussions in China. The first alternative involves a Russian agreement to modest revisions to the ABM Treaty and deployment of a "thin" U.S. defense focused on small regional powers with limited ballistic missile arsenals. The second involves broad revision of the ABM Treaty and pursuit of a "thick" defense. The third involves withdrawal from the ABM Treaty and pursuit of a "thick" defense that is capable of negating all deterrents except the offensive force deployed by Russia. There is a fourth scenario that was dismissed as unlikely in the introduction, but it is important in the context of Chinese strategic planning: the continuation of the status quo.

Limited Revision, Limited Defense

Had the Clinton administration proceeded only with a plan to deploy twenty interceptors at a single site, it seems unlikely that China would have found many reasons to invest substantially in a larger offensive force. With 200 or more interceptors in the offing, however, there is a greater likelihood that China will deploy a more capable force. It will pursue a combination of measures, including an increase in the number of intercontinental delivery systems and an increased reliance on both multiple independently targetable reentry vehicles (MIRVs) and other technologies to penetrate defenses. It also may adopt a wait-and-see attitude on the performance of system technologies still in development to gauge the likelihood that a few warheads will be able to penetrate U.S. defenses. As newer long-range systems come on line, such as the DF-41 missile, which is slated for deployment late in the decade, China may be able to move to alternative basing modes that enable missiles to reach targets in the United States without crossing through the zone guarded by the site in Alaska.

In the context of a slightly modified ABM Treaty, the United States, perhaps in partnership with Russia, might opt for a regionally based boost-phase intercept system to defeat the missile launches of North Korea or other states. Boost-phase defenses would go a long way toward alleviating Chinese operational concerns about the impact of defense on its deterrent. Indeed, Beijing might welcome the possibility of cooperation with Washington on the deployment of such systems. This might seem especially attractive if such a joint program were part of a larger effort involving cooperation with Russia aimed at boost-phase interception of missiles emanating from the Persian Gulf region. But Chinese leaders have written off such programs given the political climate among China, Russia, and the United States.

China's strategic planning also would be affected by Russian concessions to the United States that would make it possible for Washington to move forward with a defense that is compliant with the ABM Treaty. To Beijing, such concessions would be seen as a sellout. Beijing has lobbied hard in Moscow to "firm up the Russian spine" (as one Chinese expert put it) so that it does not cave in to Washington's preferences. In joint communiqués and U.N. resolutions China's leaders believe they have gained a firm Russian commitment to the preservation of the ABM Treaty. If Moscow gives way under pressure from Washington, Beijing is likely to be disappointed in its long-hoped-for partnership with Moscow to counter U.S. hegemonism. Russian acquiescence also would be read as confirmation of Washington's ability to bully important and powerful countries. Such a political interpretation of events seems likely only to fuel perceptions that China must seek more in its strategic modernization program than simply a restoration of the status quo ante.

Broad ABM Revision Allowing
Pursuit of Advanced Defenses

Washington might persuade Moscow to agree to a more far-reaching revision to the ABM Treaty, permitting it to develop operational capabilities from outer space and all-azimuth protection, perhaps with some fixed timeline for the future expiration of the Treaty. From Beijing's perspective, this would be tantamount to U.S. withdrawal from the ABM Treaty. The commitment to remain ABM compliant for a limited, fixed period of time would likely be read as advance notice of an eventual escape by

Washington from the nuclear balance of power. To Beijing, it would appear that Washington had browbeaten Moscow into an agreement of one-sided benefit—which would be read as yet another sign of Washington's strength and Russia's decline. If the United States were free to go into outer space with core assets of its strategic defense, China would find itself unable to compete in a strategic arms race with the United States (except perhaps with antisatellite weapons). If the United States married defensive systems to naval power projection forces, such an outcome would be perceived as sharply eroding Beijing's ability to influence events near its borders. Accordingly, such a scenario seems likely to generate many of the same Chinese responses as would the end of the ABM Treaty.

Withdrawal from the ABM Treaty

The key issue in this third scenario is whether withdrawal will bring with it deep reductions in offensive missile arsenals. The Chinese might moderate their response if the end of the ABM Treaty is accompanied by reductions in offensive forces. Some proponents of withdrawal see it as the path to a "defense-protected build-down" that leads to far deeper reductions in the nuclear arsenals of the United States and Russia. This position has been favored by Republican administrations (see, for example, Robert Joseph's chapter). Others see withdrawal as an escape from arms control more generally and make no case that stronger defenses should lead to a less robust retaliatory force.

Chinese analysts believe that the U.S. purpose in pursuing defenses is *not* to decrease the size or capability of the U.S. arsenal. Some Chinese experts are conversant with the view that defenses should be used as a tool to secure dominance both offensively and defensively, as a way to protect U.S. preeminence for the period ahead. Some Chinese officials perceive "a well calculated strategy . . . to reinforce U.S. nuclear superiority."[27]

The Chinese expect, moreover, that U.S. withdrawal from the ABM Treaty would bring with it an end to Russian restraint in offensive force deployments. Alarmed as Chinese officials are by the possible collapse of the START process, they are even more alarmed by the Russian promise to walk away from the Intermediate-range Nuclear Forces (INF) Treaty if the United States abandons the ABM Treaty. A Russian push to bolster its theater nuclear forces would have a direct impact on Chinese national security.

In response to the end of the ABM Treaty, China probably would undertake several military initiatives. It would deploy enough delivery systems with advanced warhead and countermeasure technologies to overwhelm U.S. defenses. China also would seek improved capabilities to conduct satellite attacks and information operations aimed at disrupting systems. Accordingly, Chinese officials promise a "new arms race in outer space" if the United States withdraws from the ABM Treaty.[28] Such strategies may well be part of the larger concept of "unrestrained war" that has come into discussion in China in recent years.[29] China seems likely to try to drive a wedge between the United States and its allies, to show the price to be paid for not heeding Beijing's interests.

China also would exploit the grievances created in Moscow by U.S. withdrawal, attempting to deepen strategic cooperation between the two countries. Chinese leaders have spoken frequently in recent years about bringing into being an anti-U.S. global coalition. To date, rhetoric has exceeded reality. But in a world in which both Moscow and Beijing feel aggrieved by American unilateralism, they could cooperate to increase the operational effectiveness of their strategic systems or the unconventional weapons programs and missile delivery systems of other states.

Indeed, China would likely curtail its cooperation with the West in the fields of nonproliferation and arms control. As Ambassador Sha has argued: "The NMD program . . . is designed to gain unilateral strategic superiority by building U.S. security on the insecurity of others. This will undoubtedly undercut the basis for its cooperation with relevant countries. How can you expect progress in [the] arms control field while you yourself are developing NMD at full speed? It's just wishful thinking."[30]

What lies behind this strong statement? As Sha argues further:

Over the decade since the end of the Cold War the international community has achieved remarkable progress in stemming the proliferation of WMD [weapons of mass destruction] and their means of delivery. The basic reason for such progress lies in the relative stability of the global and regional security environments, as well as the willingness of the countries concerned to resolve problems through dialogue instead of confrontation. If the United States is genuinely concerned, as it claims, about the threat to its security caused by the proliferation of WMD and their means of delivery, the right thing to do would be to abandon its hegemonic mentality and behaviour, respect the legitimate security interests of other countries, strengthen international cooperation and dialogue, and shore up—and where possible build on—the international arms control and non-proliferation regime. The development and deployment of NMD and TMD systems may be able to psychologically and temporarily satisfy some people's anxiety for absolute security, but it will do little to reduce the threat of WMD and their means of delivery.[31]

If Chinese leaders act on Sha's assessment, Beijing could end efforts to promote regional restraint in South Asia, the Middle East, and even North Korea. Alternatively, it could take a more obstructionist role, frustrating U.S. efforts in the United Nations Security Council by constructing international political coalitions against U.S. initiatives. It could adopt a more critical attitude toward the Non-Proliferation Treaty (NPT) and play a far more negative role in the 2005 NPT review conference. Worse yet, it could return to its old ways, exporting sensitive technologies associated with the production of nuclear, biological, and chemical weapons and their delivery systems. The United States also must reckon with the possibility that China might opt to export technologies and expertise necessary to counter and penetrate U.S. ballistic missile defenses.

American experts tend to dismiss harsh Chinese pronouncements about ending participation in the NPT as rhetoric aimed at ringing alarm bells in Washington. But China's commitment to nonproliferation and arms control is essentially a remnant of the post–Cold War era, with as yet shallow roots in the Chinese political system. Many Chinese experts adhere to the more traditional view that proliferation serves Chinese interests because it disperses power in the international system, which is both more just in the grand scheme of things, and helpful in curbing U.S. hegemonism.

Lastly, Chinese officials might conclude that a "window of opportunity" is closing and that the time has arrived to seek a military solution to the Taiwan issue.

If withdrawal from the ABM treaty were accompanied by deep reductions in the Russian and American nuclear arsenals, such a move would help reduce Chinese concerns. But this scenario would not alleviate concerns about the survivability and effectiveness of China's nuclear forces against a robust defense. China probably would opt to pursue some technological countermeasure to the problems posed by U.S. defenses, but it would not necessarily resort to more far-reaching political responses intended to complicate U.S. strategic calculations. Continued cooperation on arms control would seem to be in China's interest if offensive force reductions continued, though it also seems likely that China would continue to perceive a significant need to counter American global influence.

No NMD Beyond that Permitted by the ABM Treaty

If Washington opts not to pursue national missile defenses, China's core concerns about the effectiveness of its deterrent presumably would be alleviated. It would still proceed with the modernization of its strategic force and deploy new long-range systems capable of reaching all of the United States. It would likely believe that defenses are inevitable at some later time, when the political constellation again shifts in Washington, or following the next test of a proliferator's missile. China also would still be left to contend with theater missile defenses deployed in neighboring states. In short, the Chinese strategic modernization would likely continue, but in a more measured way.

CHINA'S CHOICES AND U.S. INTERESTS

As the NMD debate grew more intense in 1999 and 2000, several views emerged with regard to the impact of China's reactions on the net assessment that Washington must conduct before making the decision about whether and how to proceed with missile defenses. Some wanted to accord China's reactions considerable significance, given their potential impact on a variety of U.S. interests related to nonproliferation, regional stability, and national security.[32] Others argued that China's reactions matter little because its strategic force modernization will generate only modest improvements in its arsenal, no matter what the United States does.[33] Still others welcomed China's offensive buildup in response to a thin defense, because it helped create in Washington the political will to deploy a more robust NMD system. There also was widespread contempt for China's harsh NMD rhetoric, given China's many contributions to the missile proliferation problem that led to the need for defenses in the first place. China has provided technical assistance to missile programs in a number of countries of concern to Washington, as well as significant assistance to Pakistan's nuclear weapons program. Had it done more to support the global nonproliferation regime, Beijing might not today find itself trying to get Washington to respond to proliferation in ways that also protect Beijing's interests.

This cacophony of views is striking, especially when compared with the single theme emanating from Beijing. This reflects a couple of simple facts. China knows what kind of nuclear relationship it wants with the United States, because it knows what kind of political relationship it wants. It wants to maintain a credible minimum deterrent because it does not want to have thrust upon it a solution to the Taiwan situation that is politically intolerable. But the United States does not know what kind of nuclear relationship it wants with China. Should it respond to China's effort to restore the status quo ante in any way? Can it tolerate a relationship of mutual assured destruction (MAD)? Uncertainty about the nuclear relationship reflects the fact that Americans are deeply divided about what kind of political relationship with China best serves U.S. interests. Is the bilateral relationship one where cooperation or competition should dominate? Are the countries partners or enemies?

Questions about the Sino-American political relationship are unlikely to be settled any time soon in Washington, where China is a political football often exploited for domestic political purposes. If the debate over the Cox committee report is any indication, the U.S. debate about China now more than ever is mired in the worst kinds of emotionalism, rhetorical posturing, and ideology. A new administration and a new Congress must work to restore the bipartisanship necessary to conduct China policy. But Beijing too will have to work hard if it wishes to convince Americans that *its* intentions are not threatening. After all, as much as China raises questions about U.S. behavior on the global scene, there are legitimate and profound questions about the type of international role that decisionmakers in Beijing imagine for themselves in a more multipolar world. As concerned as Beijing is about Washington's intentions to contain China's rise, Washington is concerned about Beijing's intentions to overthrow the norms and institutions of a liberal world order laboriously constructed over the last half century. A strategic dialogue conducted episodically has done little to dispel concerns on either side.

NUCLEAR WEAPONS AND THE SINO-AMERICAN STRATEGIC BALANCE

As the United States contemplates how to respond to China's effort to sustain the status quo, it must answer some strategic questions. What kind of political relationship does it seek with Beijing, both generally and in the continuing confrontation over Taiwan? What role might or should nuclear weapons play in the confrontation over Taiwan, in peace and potentially in war? Only once it answers these questions can the United States determine the kind of strategic nuclear relationship it seeks with the PRC, and how hard it needs to work, if at all, to construct a defense "thick" enough to capture the ICBM and SLBM force that results from the Chinese effort to restore the status quo ante. Whether vulnerability or invulnerability best serves U.S. interests—or whether the effort to secure invulnerability comes at an acceptable political, strategic, and fiscal price—is unclear.

However Washington answers these questions, the relatively benign and static nuclear relationship between the two countries will not endure. To accord the PRC status as a country with which the United States tolerates a MAD relationship means accommodating a substantial buildup of Chinese strategic forces. This buildup is very likely to work against the interests of the United States in deemphasizing strategic nuclear forces at the global level and in ensuring the long-term viability of the nuclear non-proliferation regime.

By contrast, to deny China a credible deterrent means to accept a competitive strategic relationship with the PRC. China cannot acquiesce to a U.S. veto of its strategic modernization program after more than two decades of work, especially at a time of rising concern about U.S. coercion. Moreover, as Chinese experts frequently argue, to treat China as an enemy is to ensure that it becomes one.

It is not uncommon in Washington to simplify the question of what to do about China's responses to NMD to whether the United States can outrace China to the strategic balance it prefers. Indeed, the confidence of Americans in their ability to win any race shapes debate on these questions. Some experts argue that the United States should pursue a strategy vis-à-vis China's strategic modernization that badly taxes its development aspirations while bringing no appreciable gain in China's force-on-force balance vis-à-vis U.S. defenses.[34] Some observers rightly assert that Beijing should not want to commence an arms race with Washington, because Washington is already far ahead and has the technical and fiscal assets to more than compete with China in the production of new strategic arms.

But Americans should not underestimate the depth of the Chinese commitment to escape a world where they are left to be the victims of coercion by Washington without some ability to exert strategic leverage of their own. China's leaders believe history proves that Washington will attempt to coerce Beijing. They also believe that Washington is likely to lend military support to a Taiwanese declaration of independence, and thus dissuade Beijing from challenging that independence. Chinese policymakers want to escape a world in which China's rising power is blocked by U.S. military forces or ignored by Washington.

Washington and Beijing ought to clarify their mutual expectations about their evolving strategic nuclear relationship. Whether it is possible to define a stable "end point" is an open question. It is not at all clear where or how such a line might be drawn, especially because it is not clear where Washington and Moscow might establish their next floor in offensive force reductions. Moreover, it has been difficult to test China's intentions because the arms control dialogue has been regularly sidetracked by other items on the bilateral agenda.

A key question is whether the U.S. political system is capable of making a choice on these strategic questions and sticking to it. If the divisions in Washington on the value of a secure Chinese deterrent run deep, divisions on overall strategy toward China run even deeper. The current debate on China has been poisoned by years of suspicion among rival camps in Washington. It has become difficult to try to understand China's interests without being accused of being a "China sympathizer," just as it is difficult to talk about finding opportunities to advance mutual interests without being accused of contributing to China's rise as a competitor and enemy of the United States. These deep divisions are noticed in Beijing, and they lead Chinese policymakers to the conclusion that any choice a given U.S. administration might make regarding China's deterrent would likely be overturned by a future administration. China's low expectation of continuity in U.S. policy is founded on past experience.

CHINA'S NEIGHBORS

An offensive-defensive arms race between the United States and China would have broad repercussions. In East Asia, the advent of a U.S.-PRC arms race would be unwelcome. East Asians prefer U.S.-PRC interaction that is neither too warm nor too cold. They are loath to see the two dominant powers in the region cooperate over the heads of everyone else. But they do not want to be left to cope with renewed confrontation and the possibility that it will play out in regional frictions, standoffs, or even open hostilities. In Japan, leaders want protection from North Korean missiles—and something that looks like an "answer" to the PRC buildup, that is not based on an increase in offensive nuclear forces. But the Japanese public is unwilling to see the collapse of the arms control regime and the end of restraint by the nuclear weapon states as the price of such defenses. As Brookings analyst Michael Green has argued, the Japanese public sees arms control as a cornerstone of stability. If U.S. ballistic missile defenses undermine the arms control and nonproliferation regime, there likely would be a backlash against the United States, a weakening of the alliance, and an end to the cooperative pursuit of theater missile defenses.[35]

For Russia, a Chinese buildup would present both risks and opportunities. On the one hand, the risk of a new threat to Russia at a time of declining force levels and investments might reduce Russia's willingness to participate in a new START agreement.[36] On the other hand, Russia could have an opportunity to find new partners in the campaign to confound the American unipolar moment. A Chinese buildup also would present the opportunity for increased profits through the sale of advanced Russian technology to China.

A more rapid and far-reaching PRC modernization also would have an impact on strategic relationships in South Asia. India's apparent plans for its nuclear forces are predicated on the notion that it can pursue counterforce capabilities at its leisure, a notion that could be changed if the perception grows that China is accelerating its strategic force modernization. It seems likely that a more intense Sino-Indian nuclear competition would force both parties to create nuclear doctrines based on war-fighting strategies rather than on minimum deterrence.[37]

CONCLUSION

The United States has come late to thinking through China's responses to deployment of American ballistic missile defenses and changes in the ABM Treaty.[38] Its progress in exploring the problem has been inhibited by the intense partisanship surrounding the China issue generally, and by the particular sensitivities generated by the 1999 Cox Report on Chinese espionage. The stove-piping that characterizes policymaking in Washington has also been a problem, as the communities of experts that work on ballistic missile defense, nuclear stability, Asian security, and the U.S.-PRC bilateral relationship rarely interact. Moreover, given the wide range of opinions in Washington about how to deal with China's strategic modernization program, Beijing is left free to select expert opinions that serve its purpose or nourish its paranoia. Beijing's reactions to NMD will not take on a definitive shape until Washington decides whether to use NMD to undermine China's deterrent.

The most benign Chinese reaction to NMD/ABM would follow a U.S. decision to preserve the ABM Treaty in its current form and to continue to reduce offensive nuclear forces. A shift to a boost-phase intercept system rather than a broad national defense could significantly attenuate Chinese concerns and thus reduce the potential pace of China's strategic modernization. A good, but not best, case would be one associated with a revision to the ABM Treaty agreed to by the Russians that imposes some restraints on NMD. In either case, China will continue to modernize forces. But each Chinese deployment of new, longer-range systems will add fuel to the fire of debate in Washington about whether China is America's next great enemy. Each new U.S. deployment of a ballistic missile defense capability will add fuel to the fire of debate in Beijing about whether the United States is bent on global hegemony and containment of China. If Washington wishes to secure the best outcome, it must con-

duct a clear and broad strategic dialogue with Beijing—while also creating a bipartisan basis for continuity in policy.

The worst case is quite stark: China becomes a spoiler. In this case,
China would undermine the stability the United States seeks by sharing
countermeasure technologies and expertise with dangerous governments. It would savage the nonproliferation regime to create an anti-U.S.
coalition. It might generate a highly capable offensive force of its own
that causes new concerns in both Moscow and Washington, concerns
that end the effort to deemphasize nuclear weapons. The relationship between the United States and China would be transformed as questions
are resolved about the "true intentions" of the "new enemy."

To avoid the worst outcome, it would have been best had the United
States not treated China as an afterthought. It is too late for that. It now
may be impossible to achieve the best case outcome, given the strong domestic pressures for unilateral U.S. withdrawal from the Treaty. There is
a tendency in Washington simply to let the chips fall where they may
vis-à-vis China. This is a dangerous way to seek security and stability
between two major nuclear powers. An alternative approach would emphasize a wide-ranging review by Washington and Beijing of the requirements of strategic stability in the decades ahead. Such a dialogue
was not prominent in the Clinton administration's effort to put together
a constructive strategic partnership. It ought to include exploration of
cooperative approaches to the challenges posed by missile proliferation
without generating unwelcome instabilities in major power relations.
Whether China is willing to cooperate and compromise remains an open
question. Testing Chinese intentions remains a priority for U.S. policy.

NOTES

1. Sha Zukang, remarks to the seventh annual nuclear nonproliferation
conference, "Repairing the Regime," Carnegie Endowment for International Peace, Washington, D.C., 13 January 1999.

2. Chinese-Russian press communiqué, "Consultations on Issues Per-
taining to the ABM Treaty," Moscow, 14 April 1999.

3. Sha Zukang, "U.S. Missile Defence Plans: China's View," *Disarmament Diplomacy,* January/February 2000, 5.

4. John Pomfret, "Chinese Official Warns U.S. on Missile Defense," *Washington Post,* 11 November 1999, A1.

5. Joseph Fitchett, "Chinese Nuclear Buildup Predicted," *International Herald Tribune,* 8 November 1999, 1. See also Benjamin Kan Lim, "China Allotting Funds to Counter Nuke Attack," *Washington Times,* 25 October 1999, 18.

6. John D. Holum, senior adviser for arms control and international security, Department of State, "The President's NMD Decision and U.S. Foreign Policy," remarks to the conference "International Reactions to the U.S. National and Theater Missile Defense Deployments," Stanford University, 3 March 2000.

7. Robert Manning, Ronald Montaperto, and Brad Roberts, *China, Nuclear Weapons, and Arms Control* (New York: Council on Foreign Relations, April 2000).

8. Ivo H. Daalder, James M. Goldgeier, and James M. Lindsay, "Deploying NMD: Not Whether, But How," *Survival,* Vol. 42, No. 1, 15.

9. See Manning et al., *China, Nuclear Weapons,* for further elaboration of many of these points and for other references on modernization.

10. National Intelligence Council, "Foreign Missile Developments and the Ballistic Missile Threat to the United States Through 2015," DCI National Intelligence Estimate, Department of Defense, September 1999, 5.

11. House Select Committee on U.S. National Security and Military/ Commercial Concerns with the People's Republic of China, declassified report issued 25 May 1999.

12. See Robert Walpole, "The Ballistic Missile Threat to the United States," statement for the record, Senate subcommittee on International Security, Proliferation, and Federal Services, 9 February 2000.

13. See Michael McDevitt, "Beijing's Bind," *Washington Quarterly,* Vol. 23, No. 3, 177–186.

14. Alastair Iain Johnston, "Prospects for Chinese Nuclear Force Modernization: Limited Deterrence Versus Multilateral Arms Control," *China Quarterly* (June 1996).

15. Erik Eckholm, "China Says U.S. Missile Shield Could Force an Arms Buildup," *New York Times,* 11 May 2000, 1.

16. Shen Dingli, "Ballistic Missile Defence and China's National Security," *Jane's Special Report,* 17 April 2000.

17. Author interviews with Chinese policy analysts, academic specialists, and students.

18. Tao Wenzhao, deputy director of the Institute of American Studies, Chinese Academy of Social Sciences, Beijing, "A Foreign Policy Debate in China After the Tragic Bombing of the Chinese Embassy in Belgrade," discussion paper prepared for the conference "Long-Term Visions of Regional Security," cosponsored by the Asia Pacific Center for Security Studies and Pacific Forum CSIS, Honolulu, Hawaii, 19 April 2000.

19. Ibid.

20. Michael Pillsbury, *China Debates the Future Security Environment* (Washington, D.C.: National Defense University Press, 2000), 314–315.

21. A cynic might argue that China's proliferation of missile technology reflects a secret plan to misdirect American policymakers from the task of containing a rising China.

22. Sha, "U.S. Missile Defence Plans," 3.

23. Ibid.

24. Shao Zongwei, "US Nuke Action Concerns China," *China Daily,* 14 April 2000.

25. Shen, "Ballistic Missile Defence."

26. After Ambassador Sha had received various assurances from the Clinton administration that NMD was not in fact aimed at China, his views softened slightly: "They have assured us it is not directed at China. For that we are grateful, we are happy. But China cannot base its security on assurances only . . . . We cannot sit on our hands, watching our interests compromised, security interests compromised. Impossible." (As quoted in John Leicester, "Official: U.S. Missile Shield Could Force China to Deploy More Warheads," Associated Press, 11 May 2000.)

27. Sha believes this strategy is aimed at marginalizing Russia's nuclear forces; preventing nuclear weapons acquisitions by other states; blocking the programs of small- and medium-weapon states through the Comprehensive Test Ban Treaty (CTBT) and Fissile Material Cutoff Treaty (FMCT); and "immunizing itself [i.e., the United States] from external threats through NMD" (Sha Zukang, "U.S. Missile Defence Plans," 3–4).

28. See the interview with Sha Zukang in *Defense News,* 1 February 1999.

29. Qiao Liang and Wang Xiangsui, *Unrestricted Warfare* (Beijing: PLA Literature and Arts Publishing House, 1999).

30. From introductory remarks by Ambassador Sha to the Second U.S.-China Conference on Arms Control, Disarmament, and Nonproliferation, sponsored by the Center for Nonproliferation Studies, Monterey Institute of International Studies, Monterey, California, May 1999.

31. Sha, "U.S. Missile Defence Plans," 4–6. Similar remarks were made by He Yafei, minister-counselor at the Embassy of the People's Republic of China to the United States, in a presentation to the Carnegie International Non-Proliferation Conference, Washington, D.C., 16 March 2000.

32. Bates Gill and James Mulvenon, "A Look at the China Puzzle," *Washington Post*, 5 March 2000, B-03.

33. Daalder et al., "Deploying NMD."

34. Steve Cambone, presentation to a symposium sponsored by the Center for Nonproliferation Studies, Monterey Institute for International Studies, Washington, D.C., 10 April 2000.

35. Michael Green, remarks to the conference "International Reactions to the U.S. National and Theater Missile Defense Deployments," Stanford University, 3 March 2000.

36. Alexander Pikayev, *The Rise and Fall of START II: The Russian View* (Moscow: Carnegie Center, 1999), 36–37.

37. Roberto Suro, "Study Sees Possible China Nuclear Buildup," *Washington Post*, 10 August 2000, 2.

38. See the statement on NMD by Undersecretary of Defense Walter Slocombe in November 1999, in which he makes no mention of China during a detailed discourse. The text is available on line at http://www.csis.org/html/sf991105Slocombe.html (accessed 14 May 2001).

8

Russia

IVO H. DAALDER AND JAMES M. GOLDGEIER

A little more than three decades ago, when U.S. officials tried to convince their Russian counterparts of the virtues of a strategic relationship based on mutual assured destruction (MAD), the Russians initially reacted as if the Americans were literally mad. The Soviet government took an interest in signing the Anti-Ballistic Missile (ABM) Treaty only after it became convinced that the United States might build a missile defense system. Even after the treaty was signed, the Soviet military's efforts to research and develop ballistic missile defense continued apace. As the twenty-first century opened, there was only one ABM system operating in the world, and it was deployed around Moscow.

The Russian campaign against missile defense today is reminiscent of its public diplomacy in the 1980s. When Ronald Reagan proposed the Strategic Defense Initiative (SDI) in 1983, officials in Moscow grew alarmed. If the Americans with their technological and economic superiority did develop a defensive shield, then Soviet deterrent capabilities might be eviscerated. The Soviets became great devotees of the ABM Treaty and of the virtues of living in a MAD world, once the Reagan administration began to pursue missile defense.

The collapse of the Soviet Union and Russia's subsequent political, economic, and military decline have left Moscow reeling. No longer on a par with the United States militarily, with an economy the size of that of the Netherlands, and a political influence that does not extend much beyond its veto power in the U.N. Security Council, Russia has only two remaining attributes of major power status: territorial size and nuclear weapons. If the United States were to develop an effective missile defense, the Russians would lose confidence in their ability to play a significant role in world affairs, and they might fear that they could no longer deter an American attack. Not having adjusted well to the loss of empire and great power status, Russian officials have reacted with alarm to the increasing U.S. determination to develop a shield that can stop at least a limited nuclear strike consisting of a handful of missiles.

THE SOVIET UNION AND BALLISTIC MISSILE DEFENSE

The Soviet interest in ballistic missile defense (BMD) dates back to the very beginning of the missile age.[1] This interest reflected both an understandable desire to provide as much protection as possible to the Soviet Union and the doctrinal preferences of the Red Army. During the war with Germany, the USSR suffered enormous losses—over 20 million of its citizens were killed in just four short years. The damage inflicted by German V-1 and V-2 rocketry on Britain (not to mention the devastation of Hiroshima and Nagasaki) only added to Moscow's determination to devise ways to limit the destruction missiles could wreak in the nuclear age. Russia's defense efforts accordingly ran the gamut of possibilities, from defense against aircraft, rockets, and missiles, to extensive civil defense measures.

BMD and other defensive measures also were integral to postwar Soviet military doctrine. Although Moscow had little illusion about its ability to emerge unscathed from a nuclear war, Soviet military and political leaders believed that every effort had to be made to limit damage in case of a conflict with the United States and its allies. Counterforce capabilities and the possibility of preemptive war were regarded as offensive means to limit damage; BMD and air and civil defense efforts provided defensive means to the same end (especially in combination with a robust counterforce capability). The idea was not to provide a perfect defense but rather to blunt the devastation of any conflict to the maximum extent possible.

The Soviet BMD program was started in the late 1940s or early 1950s. The first concrete signs of its magnitude emerged in 1960 when a U-2 flight over the Soviet BMD testing area near Saryshagan, in the Kazakh republic, photographed an extensive range of activities. In the early 1960s, a string of Hen House radars appeared on the Soviet periphery, providing a long-range acquisition capability for its interceptor missiles. Next, improved radars and better surface-to-air missile (SAM) capabilities were deployed around Leningrad, providing some defense against sea-launched missile attacks. Beginning in the mid-1960s, the first (and only) Soviet BMD system was built around Moscow.[2]

Once fully operational (in 1970 or 1971), the Moscow ABM system consisted of 64 Galosh interceptors (each larger than the Minuteman missile), armed with nuclear warheads to compensate for their inaccuracy and limited sensors. The system was highly vulnerable to spoofing, nuclear blackout, direct attack, and saturation, and as such provided no more than a psychological defense of the capital city. This may have been one reason why, in the late 1960s, the number of interceptor sites was halved (from eight to four), and the total number of interceptors reduced from the planned 128. Another reason for the slowdown in construction may have been that negotiations with the United States on both offensive and defensive force limitations were beginning to bear fruit.

Soviet leaders had initially appeared hesitant about accepting any limitations on defensive forces (Soviet Premier Aleksei Kosygin noted in February 1967 that defenses were not "a cause of the arms race but designed instead to prevent the death of people").[3] But once the Strategic Arms Limitation Talks got under way in 1969, Moscow made clear its interest in such limitations. Soviet leaders would have been happy to limit BMD to a defense of the national capital area (as Washington originally proposed), but in the end it accepted the idea of allowing BMD at two sites—one surrounding the capital, and the other, an intercontinental ballistic missile (ICBM) field—each with 100 fixed, land-based interceptors. That provision was later amended to limit each country to one site of 100 interceptors, thus allowing Moscow to keep its system, upgraded to 100 missiles, to defend the capital region.

The reason for Moscow's embrace of BMD limitations has been debated ever since. Some have argued that Soviet leaders were motivated primarily by the desire to constrain the U.S. BMD program, which despite the controversy surrounding it in the United States, appeared to be going ahead in the late 1960s and early 1970s. Others claim that Moscow's chief motive was its demonstrated commitment to détente, if not actually an embrace of the logic of mutual vulnerability—a logic that suggested that defensive deployments provided little if any protection and instead stimulated an offensive arms race. Whatever the reason (in reality, it was probably a combination of the two), the United States and the Soviet Union did agree to limit BMD in ways that effectively banned the deployment of strategically significant levels of missile defenses.

Notwithstanding the 1972 ABM Treaty and subsequent additional limitations under the 1974 protocol, Moscow continued development, testing, and deployment of BMD systems. In 1978, it began deploying a new-generation system around Moscow, the ABM-3, even though the United States had abandoned its own limited efforts at Grand Forks three years earlier. The new system consisted of a two-layered defense, combining the exoatmospheric Galosh interceptors and high-speed, endoatmospheric Gazelle interceptors, which were guided by a Pillbox radar at Pushkino.[4] Although the interceptors are armed with nuclear warheads and thus provide Moscow with some chance to intercept a handful of missile warheads directed against the capital region, the ABM-3, like its predecessors, provides no protection against a dedicated attack. U.S. strategic forces could saturate the system easily.

U.S.-RUSSIAN RELATIONS IN THE 1990s

Early in the 1990s, Russia had some reason to hope that it could maintain the status quo in its relations with the United States and participate in the shaping of a new, united Europe. The 1990 Conventional Forces in Europe Treaty ensured a balance in equipment levels on the continent. Strategic Arms Reduction Treaty (START) talks gave hope for maintaining the nuclear balance. In 1991, the North Atlantic Treaty Organization (NATO) began constructing a framework for a relationship with all former Warsaw Pact members. By the end of 1993, the United States had led Russia to believe that rather than taking in new members, NATO would be developing the more inclusive Partnership for Peace program.

As for missile defense, Russian President Boris Yeltsin in February 1992 had called for joint U.S.-Russian efforts, and his summit with U.S. President George Bush in June 1992 seemed to offer tangible evidence that Russians and Americans could make the transition to a world where strategic defenses predominated over offensive missile forces. In an address to the United Nations Security Council on 1 February of that year, Yeltsin stated that Russia saw the United States and the West "not as mere partners but rather as allies." And he called for consideration of "a global system for protection of the world community." Yeltsin explained, "It could be based on a reorientation of the U.S. SDI (Strategic Defense Initiative) to make use of high technologies developed in Russia's defense complex."[5] Presidents Bush and Yeltsin issued a joint statement on this global protection system on 17 June 1992: "The two Presidents agreed that their two nations should work together with allies and other interested states in developing a concept for such a system as part of an overall strategy regarding the proliferation of ballistic missiles and weapons of mass destruction."[6]

Starting in 1994, however, any Russian hopes that the status quo could be maintained seemed to vanish as Russia's domestic and international security position began to deteriorate rapidly. President Bill Clinton told Yeltsin in September 1994 that NATO would be moving forward on enlargement by admitting selected East European states (not Russia). This was most likely the cause of the Russian president's emotional outburst in Budapest at a Council for Security and Cooperation in Europe summit in December of that year.[7] Things only got worse after that. At the same time as Yeltsin's Budapest declaration that a "cold peace" had descended across Europe, the Russian military began its first, disastrous campaign in Chechnya. In 1995, the United States dictated the terms of the Dayton Accords for Bosnia, and Russia could only serve in the implementation force as a junior partner. In 1996, President Clinton announced that he sought the inclusion of new NATO members that would join the alliance in 1999. And in 1999 the United States led NATO into war in Kosovo. As Secretary of Defense William S. Cohen put it in his 2000 *Annual Report to the President and the Congress,* "It's not totally surprising that the Russians see a more threatening environment when they link, for example, NMD with NATO expansion; intervention in Kosovo without United Nations imprimatur; and a general decline in Russian military power."[8]

THE CURRENT STATE OF PLAY

The 1990s were bad enough for the Russian military. Now the United States is talking about forging ahead with missile defense and, if necessary, abrogating the ABM Treaty. With declining conventional capabilities, the Russian military doctrine is relying more heavily on nuclear weapons. Russia's new national security concept states that Russia "considers the possibility of employing military force to ensure its national security, [including the] use of all available forces and assets, including nuclear, in the event of a need to repulse armed aggression, if all other measures of resolving the crisis situation have been exhausted and have proven ineffective."[9]

In a world in which the United States is developing missile defenses and Russia cannot maintain its production of offensive systems, Moscow fears that the American program will nullify its strategic deterrent. This concern contributed to the delay in Russian ratification of the 1993 START II Treaty, even though it was always clear that the treaty was more important to restrain American forces than Russia's, which in any case were rapidly declining below START II ceilings. When the Duma finally ratified the treaty in April 2000, it did so under two conditions. First, it insisted that the treaty would enter into force only after the U.S. Senate had ratified the additional ABM and START protocols agreed to in September 1997. The ABM protocols, in particular, face daunting opposition in the U.S. Senate, making implementation of START II anything but certain. Second, the Duma voted in favor of START II only after acting President Vladimir Putin appeared unexpectedly before Parliament to declare that Russia "will withdraw not only from the START II Treaty, but from the whole system of treaties on limitation and control of strategic and conventional weapons" if the United States abandons the ABM Treaty.[10]

Still, the Russians have shown they are willing to work with the United States to salvage what they can. As it became increasingly evident that NATO would proceed with enlargement, Russia signed the Founding Act with NATO in May 1997. Similarly, Russia worked on an ABM demarcation agreement with the United States later in 1997. The demarcation agreement allowed for theater missile defenses but established that there would be no testing of higher-speed interceptors prior to April 1999.[11]

In Köln, Germany, in the summer of 1999, Clinton and Yeltsin agreed to proceed with an effort to work on an arms control package for both offensive and defensive strategic systems. Discussions in the Clinton administration then proceeded on a regular basis until September 2000, when the president decided to defer a decision on missile defense. U.S. Deputy Secretary of State Strobe Talbott conferred with Russian Deputy Foreign Minister Georgy Mamedov; U.S. arms control negotiator John Holum met with his Russian counterpart Yuri Kapralov; Secretary of State Madeleine Albright discussed the issues with Foreign Minister Igor Ivanov; and President Bill Clinton probed for a deal with Russian President Vladimir Putin.

In October 1999, Talbott sweetened the potential package with an offer that included financial assistance to help Russia finish the partially constructed Mishelevka missile-tracking radar station near Irkutsk; access to early warning data and more intelligence sharing to combat the threat from so-called "rogue" states; and a joint presence at both an American and a Russian radar site.[12]

In January 2000, Holum and Kapralov met in Geneva to discuss the nature of a START III agreement that would be designed to give Russia confidence that the United States was not developing a first-strike capability. The main sticking point in these talks was the ceiling for the number of strategic warheads deployed by both sides. Based on a 1997 study headed by General John Shalikashvili, Chairman of the Joint Chiefs of Staff, the U.S. position was that between 2,000 and 2,500 warheads were required to deter all potential adversaries. By contrast, Kapralov was seeking a commitment to deploy only 1,500 strategic warheads.[13] Albright went to Moscow in late January 2000 to meet with Ivanov, and Clinton and Putin exchanged letters and phone calls to try to work through the remaining differences.

Although the public Russian reaction toward any revision of the Treaty predictably has been highly negative, some prominent Russian officials have stated a willingness to move forward. In December 1999, Colonel General Vladimir Yakovlev, Commander-in-Chief of the Strategic Missile Troops, declared, "There is a chance Russia could reach agreement with the USA on modification of the ABM Treaty."[14] In February 2000, after meeting with President Clinton in Washington, Sergei Ivanov, secretary of the Russian Security Council and a close associate of Putin, said that the possibility existed for "talking about the geographic changes to deploy the system, instead of North Dakota, somewhere else. This is going to be the subject of further discussion." But he sought to distinguish slight modification of the ABM Treaty from deployment of a strategically significant national missile defense. Ivanov, for instance, suggested that the Treaty might be modified to allow the United States to construct its permitted missile defense site in Alaska, rather than near the national capital or an offensive missile base.[15]

Ivanov's statements gave some hope that a deal could be reached at the Moscow summit in June 2000. That was not to be, however. Presidents Putin and Clinton failed to resolve the question of how, or even whether, to amend the ABM Treaty to enable deployment of a limited national missile defense system. At the same time, the door for an eventual agreement on the issue was left partially open by the 16-point joint principles statement made by both presidents, in which Russia agreed with the United States that "the international community faces a dangerous and growing threat of proliferation of weapons of mass destruction and their means of delivery, including missiles and missile technologies."[16] In agreeing to the principles document, Russia went further than it had previously in acknowledging the seriousness of international missile threats.

Putin also suggested before and after the summit that active missile defenses might be an appropriate response to the proliferation of long-range missiles. Putin apparently proposed a cooperative effort with NATO to develop a ground-based, boost-phase intercept system that would defend Europe (and by extension, the United States), although the details of architecture, cost, and timing were murky. Although Clinton administration officials responded by making clear that any joint work with the Russians would not halt U.S. efforts to build its own NMD system, joint exercises with Russia continued on theater missile threats. Such cooperative exercises could prove valuable both in furthering a joint understanding of threats and in developing technologies that could be used in the proposed joint boost-phased system.[17]

During his tour of Europe after the Russian-U.S. summit, Putin also proposed his boost-phase missile defense system to European leaders as a way to deal with theater missile threats "covering all of Europe from the Atlantic to the Urals."[18] Although European heads of state were lukewarm to the U.S. NMD proposal, regarding it as a threat to the ABM Treaty, many of them—most notably German Chancellor Gerhard Schröder—believed that the Russian proposal deserved "thorough consideration."[19] If European countries believe that the system proposed by Russia is the only way to maintain the ABM Treaty, they may look more favorably on developing such a joint system than on a unilateral U.S. decision to deploy a national missile defense system as currently envisioned.

THE THREE WORLDS

After President Clinton deferred a decision on building a missile defense system in September 2000, further negotiations with the Russians were made moot by the impending end of his administration. But Putin's diplomatic moves in mid-2000 appeared to reflect a belief that Russia might gain some constraints on American development of missile defense by agreeing to revisions of the ABM Treaty. A world in which there is a modified treaty has advantages for Russia: keeping agreed-upon limits part of the American debate on this subject; maintaining the broader framework of a strategic relationship based on the precepts of mutual assured destruction; and furthering deep cuts in offensive strategic weapons. Negotiations about the future of the ABM Treaty also could create opportunities for other types of Russian-American strategic cooperation.

Even with these potential advantages, however, Russia would remain concerned about the breakout potential of any American deployment. After all, if the United States has a production line going and can deploy 100 interceptors in Alaska, why would it not be able to deploy hundreds more elsewhere? And if Moscow believes that the George W. Bush administration is intent on developing a full-blown system, Russia might decide that it is not in its interests to play ball; Putin might calculate that the negative global reaction to a U.S. decision to withdraw from the Treaty would improve Russia's security position more than a compromise over the ABM Treaty. This second world—one without treaty constraints on missile defense development—would be the worst-case scenario for Russia. But if the arms control regime limiting strategic defenses collapsed due to an American administration reneging on a deal, or to the failure of the U.S. Senate to ratify a revised treaty, then

Russia would at least come away with a great deal of diplomatic support around the world.

There is a third scenario that is hard to imagine but is certainly not out of the question, depending on Russia's progress toward integration with Western market democracies. In this world, the United States and Russia cooperate to move from the dominance of offensive forces to the dominance of defensive forces. Data sharing and cooperation in developing satellites and other systems might lead to a world in which the two share missile defense technology, as was implied by the Bush-Yeltsin statement of June 1992 and Putin's suggestions in the summer of 2000 regarding a Global Protection System. Thus, although Russians may fear that a world in which there is a modified treaty could lead to a world in which there is no treaty, it is possible that the first scenario could lead ultimately to what for them would be the far better situation—one in which the United States and Russia agreed to cooperate on missile defense.

Nothing the United States is currently planning to deploy would eviscerate the Russian nuclear deterrent. As a *Christian Science Monitor* editorial put it, "Well, of course Russia can overwhelm a limited missile defense. That's the whole point."[20] Russia's two greatest concerns are the breakout potential of any deployed missile defense system, and the lack of restrictions on space-based sensors (which eases the task of knocking down incoming missiles with less sophisticated interceptors). Hence Moscow's dilemma: whether to accept the need to modify the ABM Treaty in the hope that the new limits will continue to constrain U.S. defenses even if future modifications are not ruled out, or to object to any Treaty changes and risk an American decision to abandon the Treaty's constraints altogether. The cooperative approach may buy Moscow a degree of clarity in the short run, even if it cannot guarantee any certainty in the long run; the alternative takes the deployment of U.S. missile defenses as a given and bases Russia's pursuit of its strategic objectives on that reality.[21]

World One: Modified ABM

Following the agreement between Presidents Clinton and Yeltsin in June 1999 to begin discussions on possible modifications of the ABM Treaty, the United States presented Russia with a draft protocol and annex to the Treaty that would allow the United States to deploy a limited defense system in Alaska.[22] The protocol would provide each party to the Treaty the right to deploy a "limited territorial missile defense system," consisting of no more than 100 interceptors and 100 launchers at one site, and one additional ABM radar deployed anywhere on their national territory; and the right to enable existing early warning radars to perform ABM radar functions. These provisions would allow the United States to deploy the first phase of its planned NMD system, including 100 interceptors and associated launchers in Alaska and a new X-band radar in the Aleutian islands, as well as upgrades to the five existing early warning radars in Alaska, California, Maine, Great Britain, and Greenland.

As is consistent with the spirit of the original ABM Treaty, the Clinton administration's draft proposal called for a continued ban on strategically significant defenses, aimed at preserving the stability created by mutual assured destruction in the Russian-American strategic balance. The U.S. talking points used during the presentation of the proposal to Russia in January 2000 went some way toward reassuring Moscow that it would retain the capability to retaliate against the United States with an "annihilating counterattack" in a second strike, even if (as seems likely) Russian offensive forces were reduced to between 1,000 and 1,500 warheads in all. Although worst-case analysis of the kind U.S. and Russian leaders have long applied to the macabre art of nuclear exchanges might indicate that only a few hundred nuclear weapons would survive and penetrate American defenses, it is difficult to see how the prospect of so many weapons exploding on one's national territory would not constitute an effective deterrent. Senior Russian officials appear to agree. Thus, the Kremlin's national security advisor, Sergei Ivanov, suggested that even if Russian forces were reduced to the 1,500 weapons Moscow envisages under START III, that capability would "be ample to penetrate through the national ABM system the Americans hypothetically are going to create over the next 20 to 25 years."[23]

At the same time, it is clear that Russia has little incentive to sign on to a modification of the ABM Treaty simply on the merits of U.S. proposals. For one thing, Russia could not provide a missile defense of its territory (which is much larger than that of the United States) from just one site. For another, Moscow lacks the financial resources to deploy and operate a new defense system that U.S. estimates suggest might cost $60 billion over ten years.

If Moscow is to agree to any modification of the treaty, Washington will have to do more than offer new constraints on future defenses. Specifically, following on the Clinton-Yeltsin talks in Köln in mid-1999, any relaxation on defensive constraints would have to be accompanied by deep reductions in offensive systems. Here, too, however, the two sides remain far apart. Facing dire economic straits, Russia wants to limit offensive weapons to levels that are economically sustainable—about 1,500 weapons. Yet Washington insists that the level agreed to in Helsinki in early 1997—i.e., 2,000–2,500 weapons—must be adhered to, because the upper bound represents the minimum nuclear deterrent U.S. military planners are willing to accept. It is possible that the Bush administration's nuclear posture review could arrive at a lower number; but it is equally plausible that the number of weapons necessary for deterrence may be deemed higher than what the Joint Chiefs said was necessary in 1997.

Whatever the outcome of the review, it is evident that for Washington to get a deal on ABM, it would have to accept Russia's demand for lower levels of offensive systems. This seeming concession might actually serve U.S. interests: Going down to 1,500 weapons or fewer, and reducing alert levels of the forces that remained, would be one clear way to communicate that the United States has no interest in using its limited defenses to gain a strategic advantage over Russia. Moreover, even at this lower level, Washington would still deploy more than enough weapons to deter any conceivable threat. The days in which large numbers of nuclear weapons were necessary for deterrence purposes (if, indeed, they ever were) are long gone.[24]

Cutting a deal with the United States on ABM not only gives Russia some near-term assurances on both the offensive and defensive sides but may also give it leverage in other areas. This deal is something that even the Bush administration might find desirable for diplomatic reasons. And if it does (certainly the Europeans do), the West might be willing to mollify Russia in other areas in exchange for a Russian compromise on modification of the ABM Treaty. For example, Russia's efforts to mute Western criticism of its behavior in Chechnya and of its crackdowns on the Russian press are much more likely to succeed if Russia reaches out in the arms control sphere. And Putin's diplomacy since January 2000 suggests he understands this well. The question therefore is not so much whether a deal can be reached as at what price.

World Two: No ABM Treaty

The nature of this second world would depend to some extent on how it came about. If the United States made a major effort to gain Russian consent to a revised deal and then reluctantly announced that due to Moscow's intransigence no deal was possible, Russia would have less ability to take advantage of the situation. Instead, Russia would be faced with a world in which the United States was unconstrained on the defensive side and had not agreed to START III. In such a world, Russian fears of the U.S. first-strike capability would grow dramatically.

Increasing Russian fears is not in America's interest. Although Russia is weak and will have difficulty maintaining its offensive forces even at START II levels, it could act to decrease U.S. security in a number of ways. Moscow already has warned that a U.S. decision to abrogate the ABM Treaty would lead it to abandon thirty years of arms control restraints, including the START I and II treaties, the Intermediate-Range Nuclear Forces Treaty, and the treaties on Conventional Forces in Europe. Each of these accords placed significant limits on the forces of both countries. Although abandoning them would not immediately result in an unconstrained buildup, it would reduce the predictability and transparency provided by their negotiation and implementation.

Even without expanding force levels significantly, Russia could augment its offensive capabilities in numerous ways.[25] It could retain its aging force of SS-18 monster missiles, each fitted with ten warheads, whose elimination was one of START II's greatest accomplishments. Additional warheads could be fitted onto the new Topol missile force, tripling the offensive firepower of these land-based missiles. Fearing a possible U.S. first strike and lacking an adequate early warning network, Moscow might even decide to increase the alert level of its ballistic missile force, to the point that it would consider launching its forces on warning to ensure their survival in case of attack.

Although an increase in Russian offensive capabilities (or a failure to reduce them) would not in and of itself pose a strategic danger to the

United States, the aging nature of the force, frail command and control capabilities, and lax security over nuclear forces do pose a threat. Moreover, if these forces are placed on ever higher levels of alert so as to enable their launch on tactical warning, the result would be highly destabilizing. Whatever security the United States might gain from deploying a limited defense against a potential "rogue" threat clearly would be negated by a Russian reaction of this kind.

Should the United States forego deployment of a limited defense, lest Moscow react in this adverse manner? Not necessarily. The key is Washington's approach to deployment and its attitude toward Russia's interest in the matter. Washington might insist on the right to deploy missile defenses without any regard to Russia's interests or existing treaty obligations, as some in the U.S. Congress have done. However, a unilateral move to deploy defenses, in open defiance of Russian concerns, would likely lead to a highly destabilizing Russian response, if only because the manner of the deployment would leave Moscow with little doubt that its interests were not being taken into account. In contrast, if the United States offered to modify the ABM Treaty in ways that maintained its strategic essence but allowed for the deployment of a limited defense system, and combined that offer with a willingness to consider very deep cuts in offensive forces, then Moscow's response would likely be more muted—even if it did not agree with the U.S. proposal. Under these circumstances it would still be in the U.S. interest to reduce offensive forces—unilaterally, if necessary—and to lower the alert levels of those that remained, so as to make clear that Washington had no interest in increasing the threat to Russia. In short, if Russia and the United States are to enter into a strategic world without restraints on defensive deployments, the stability of that world depends significantly on how it is entered.

World Three: Cooperative Transition

There is, of course, an alternative to negotiating changes to the ABM Treaty or abandoning the regime altogether, and that is for the United States and Russia to cooperate in deploying defenses to protect both countries against incipient missile threats. Such cooperation could start with joint efforts to build defenses designed to counter the possible missile threat from North Korea, expand to defensive deployments against possible new missile threats from the Persian Gulf region, and end with robust deployments designed to safeguard both countries against ballistic missile attacks. Although mutual offensive deterrence would remain a factor in U.S.-Russian relations in the early phases, a cooperative transition ultimately would aim to supplant offensive deterrence with a regime in which defenses were dominant.

Since the end of the Cold War, the United States and Russia have cooperated extensively in a range of nuclear weapons–related areas. Much of this cooperation has been geared toward safeguarding nuclear materials, production capabilities, and scientific knowledge against possible diversion to other countries. One positive result of these efforts has been a willingness to share information on and generally increase transparency concerning a host of activities and capabilities that, until the early 1990s, were generally regarded in Moscow and Washington as the most sensitive of secrets. Cooperation also has extended to a commitment in principle to exchange early warning data on ballistic missile launches, although mutual suspicions have as yet failed to turn this commitment into a reality.

Efforts were initiated to devise a shared early warning system at the June 2000 U.S.-Russian summit in Moscow. A Joint Data Exchange Center has been set up in Moscow, where continuous, near-real-time data on missile launches are provided by the United States and Russia. The successful Y2K Center for Strategic Stability, operated in fall and winter of 1999–2000, out of Cheyenne Mountain, Colorado, set a successful precedent for the joint sharing of missile launch information.[26]

It may be possible to build on this cooperative record to encourage the joint development of missile defense systems to protect both countries against incipient missile threats. One immediate possibility championed by some who traditionally have opposed missile defenses is the development of boost-phase interceptors. These could be deployed in eastern Russia as a way to defend both the Russian Federation and the United States against strategic-range missiles launched by North Korea.[27] In addition to offering the obvious advantage of attacking the threatening missile at the point of its maximum vulnerability (which therefore eases the technical task of accomplishing an intercept), a boost-phase defense of this kind would not threaten Russian (or Chinese) strategic missiles. If pursued cooperatively, the deployment of such a defense would have the added benefit of further enhancing trust between the United States and Russia. Over time, as evolving threats warrant, it might be possible to build additional defensive sites to deal with potential missile threats from the Persian Gulf region.

Cooperative missile defenses designed to defend the United States and Russia from so-called "rogue state" threats would not in themselves alter the offensive deterrence relationship between the two countries. But it would provide yet another building block in the transition from offense- to defense-dominance. Although it has been an article of faith for many decades that a transition of this kind is undesirable if not actually destabilizing, the underlying assumption of that conclusion has been the persistence of an adversarial political and strategic U.S.-Soviet/Russian relationship. Yet, to the extent that the political and strategic nature of the relationship has changed and continues to do so in the years ahead, the desirability of this kind of transition will be enhanced. Indeed, defenses will provide an extra measure of insurance in a world in which offensive deterrence no longer characterizes the U.S.-Russian strategic relationship—especially if the deployment of missile defenses occurs cooperatively.

To be sure, the two states are still a long way from this point. Mutual suspicion still characterizes much of the Russian-American strategic relationship today. It is doubtful that the two sides can reach agreement on a cooperative deployment of boost-phase defenses. Although Russia now sees the threat of North Korean, Iranian, or Iraqi missiles in much the same light as does the United States, Russia's vague boost-phase proposal has been perceived by U.S. officials as insufficient in scope to deal with ballistic missile threats to the continental United States. Furthermore, it is highly doubtful that any U.S. political leader would be prepared to subject a decision on U.S. national missile defense to Moscow's fiat. Moreover, as the debate about the possible strategic consequences of NMD deployment indicates, the U.S.-Russian strategic relationship may have matured since the end of the Cold War, but it has by no means left offensive deterrence behind.

The road to a cooperative transition is long. It nevertheless is in both countries' interest that they begin the journey. That being the case, an abrogation of the ABM Treaty would appear unwise at this point. It would be better to extend the cooperative effort by pursuing treaty modifications than to act unilaterally. Of course, the critical question for U.S. policymakers then becomes whether Russia is prepared to join in this endeavor.

CONCLUSION

The early moves on strategic arms control suggest that President Putin has not yet made a firm decision on strategy toward the United States with regard to missile defense and the ABM Treaty. In his first year in office he spent a remarkable amount of time on these issues, although he had many difficult domestic political and economic issues on his plate. He garnered Duma ratification of both START II and the Comprehensive Test Ban Treaty, engaged in serious discussions in Moscow with President Clinton on ABM and NMD, and traveled to Europe and Northeast Asia (including North Korea) to show that Russia would not permit its interests to be taken lightly in matters of international security.

The range of efforts and the range of commentary emanating from Moscow during this initial phase of the Putin presidency were indicative of a leadership that was trying tactics that at times fit with world one, and at others, with world two or three. One day, Russian officials would make noises about the changes they could accept to the ABM Treaty; another day, they would insist that the ABM Treaty was nonnegotiable; and the next, President Putin himself would propose joint, cooperative missile defense with the United States.

Two general strategies would be consistent with these tactical maneuvers. One would reflect a desire to establish a good relationship with the United States by cooperating on strategic arms control in return for greater American support for economic assistance and/or debt rescheduling as well as a muted Western response to Russian actions in Chechnya. A Russian deal on ABM would fit comfortably in this strategy, as would Russian cooperation on missile defense with the United States.

It also is possible that these moves were a prelude to a more sustained effort to garner support in Europe, which is increasingly frustrated with American hegemony. Putin may well gamble that no full-scale U.S. BMD is possible technologically or politically, and thus there is no need for

Russia to worry about an America that is unconstrained. But if he can force the United States into abrogating the Treaty, Putin can portray himself to Europeans as the man who tried to keep peace in the world while the United States pursued a reckless course on missile defense. Putin may want to draw closer to Europe, as the United States has long wanted Russia to do, but he may want to do so in a Europe that is distancing itself from America.

Either strategy makes sense. In the first, by keeping U.S.-Russian arms control front and center, Putin would demonstrate Russia's relevance in the twenty-first century as a major world power. In the second, by trying to engage in the familiar Soviet game of splitting Europe from America, he might hope to undermine America's standing (although his effort will likely be too clumsy to succeed).

The main problem for Putin is that having offered suggestions across the board on ABM and NMD, he has conceded too much. He has agreed that the threat is real, and he also has agreed that active defenses are a reasonable component of a strategy to counter present and potential ballistic-missile-capable states. By doing so, he has given the United States and its new president much greater leverage. If the United States takes him up on the offer to develop a joint boost-phase intercept system, then the two states may well be on the way from a world of slight modifications to the ABM Treaty to a defense-dominated world, at least in U.S.-Russian relations.

But the risk for Putin is that instead of getting world three, he may end up making it easier for the United States to move to world two. The United States sought joint cooperation in space programs with the Russians and became profoundly disappointed with Russia's delays in fulfilling its obligations. If the United States pursues boost-phase defense cooperation with Russia, and Russia fails to implement its side of the bargain (or continues to supply advanced technology to problem states), then the United States could legitimately pursue a unilateral course. And since Putin has already agreed on the existence of the threat and on the desirability of defenses, the United States could more easily argue that it has no choice but to abrogate the ABM Treaty in order to counter new missile threats. Putin's activist stance on NMD and ABM—especially if it was adopted before his administration had developed a coherent strategy on missile defense—may well come back to haunt him and his advisers.

NOTES

1. For an overview, see Steven P. Adragna, *On Guard for Victory: Military Doctrine and Ballistic Missile Defense in the USSR* (Cambridge: Institute for Foreign Policy Analysis, 1987); Sayre Stevens, "The Soviet BMD Program," in Ashton B. Carter and David N. Schwartz, eds., *Ballistic Missile Defense* (Washington, D.C.: Brookings Institution Press, 1994), 182–220; and Jeanette Voas, "Soviet Attitudes towards Ballistic Missile Defence and the ABM Treaty," Adelphi Papers, no. 255 (London: International Institute for Strategic Studies, Winter 1990).

2. Stevens, "The Soviet BMD Program," 200–201.

3. Cited in Raymond Garthoff, "BMD and East-West Relations," in Carter and Schwartz, eds., *Ballistic Missile Defense*, 295.

4. Matthew Bunn, *Foundations for the Future: The ABM Treaty and National Security* (Washington, D.C.: Arms Control Association, 1990), 50–51.

5. "Excerpts from Speeches By Leaders of Permanent Members of U.N. Council," *New York Times*, 1 February 2001, A5.

6. "Joint United States–Russian Statement on a Global Protection System, 17 June 1992," *Public Papers of the Presidents of the United States* (1992–93), Book I (Washington, D.C.: Government Printing Office, 1993). See also discussion in Pavel Podvig, "A History of the ABM Treaty in Russia," Project on New Approaches to Russian Security (PONARS), memo no. 109, February 2000.

7. See James M. Goldgeier, *Not Whether But When: The U.S. Decision to Enlarge NATO* (Washington, D.C.: Brookings Institution Press, 1999), 72ff.

8. William S. Cohen, *Annual Report to the President and the Congress* (Washington, D.C.: Department of Defense, 2000).

9. Foreign Policy Concept of the Russian Federation, *Rossiiskaia gazeta*, 11 July 2000 (translated from RIA Novosti for personal use only).

10. Michael Gordon, "Putin Wins Vote in Parliament on Treaty to Cut Nuclear Arms," *New York Times*, 15 April 2000, A1.

11. For the text of the agreed statement of 26 September 1997, see Appendix F.

12. Steven Mufson and Bradley Graham, "U.S. Offers Aid to Russia on Radar Site," *Washington Post*, 17 October 1999, A1; Art Pine, "U.S. Offers Russia Proposal to Renegotiate Missile Pact," *Los Angeles Times*, 17 October 1999.

13. Steven Mufson, "Russia: Cut Arsenals to 1,500 Warheads; U.S. Resists, Prefers 2,000 to 2,500 Units," *Washington Post,* 28 January 2000, A17. Several former prominent officials have argued that the United States could lower these numbers to between 1,000 and 2,000: See Sam Nunn, Brent Scowcroft, and Arnold Kanter, "A Deal with Russia on Arms Control?" *Boston Globe,* 13 September 1999, A13.

14. Quoted in ITAR-TASS, in FBIS-SOV–1999–1217, available on line at http://www.wnc.fedworld.gov.

15. Jane Perlez, "Russian Aide Opens Door a Bit to U.S. Bid for Missile Defense," *New York Times,* 19 February 2000, A3.

16. White House, "Joint Statement By the Presidents of the United States of America and the Russian Federation on Principles of Strategic Stability" (Moscow: Office of the Press Secretary), 4 June 2000.

17. Michael R. Gordon, "Joint Exercise on Missiles Seen for U.S. and Russia," *New York Times,* 29 June 2000, A7.

18. Roger Cohen, "Putin Urges Using Russia for Defense of Europe," *New York Times,* 16 June 2000, A3.

19. Roger Cohen, "Putin Discovers a New Rapport with Germany," *New York Times,* 17 June 2000, A1.

20. *Christian Science Monitor,* 4 November 1999, 10.

21. Alexander Pikayev, "ABM Treaty Revision: A Challenge to Russian Security," *Disarmament Diplomacy,* no. 44 (March 2000), 8–9.

22. The U.S. proposal and accompanying talking points used by U.S. officials were leaked by Russia and printed in the *Bulletin of the Atomic Scientists,* available on line at http://www.thebulletin.org/issues/2000/mj00/treaty_doc.html.

23. "Interview with Sergei Ivanov on the New Military Doctrine of Russia," Vremya ORT, 21:00, 24 April 2000.

24. For a detailed argument along these lines, see Ivo H. Daalder, "Stepping Down the Thermonuclear Ladder: How Low Can We Go?" in Ivo H. Daalder and Terry Terriff, eds., *Rethinking the Unthinkable: New Directions for Nuclear Arms Control* (London: Frank Cass, 1993), 69–102.

25. Pikayev, "ABM Treaty Revision," 7; David Hoffman, "Moscow Warns U.S. on Missile Defense," *Washington Post,* 26 October 1999, A19; Pavel Podvig, "Russian Nuclear Forces in Ten Years With or Without START," PONARS, memo no. 92 (October 1999), available on line at http://www.fas.harvard.edu/~ponars/POLICY%20MEMOS/

Podvig92.html; and "Russia's General Dvorkin Views NMD," *Rossiiskaia gazeta,* 15 February 2000, available on line at ftp://ftp.nautilus.org/ nnnet/news/ 021500rossi.txt.

26. On the Y2K center, see John Donnelly, "Y2K Long Shot: U.S.-Russian Nuclear War," *Boston Globe,* 21 November 1999, A1; Steve Crawshaw, "150 Seconds from Armageddon," *Independent* (London), 26 December 1999, 18–19; Mikhail Shevtsov, "Russia, U.S. to Cooperate in Handling Y2K Bug Problem," FBIS-SOV–1999–0913, 13 September 1999, from ITAR-TASS 1256 GMT. On the Joint Data Exchange Center, see Sergey Merinov, "Following the Events; Okinawa Switches to 21st Century Time," FBIS-EAS–2000–0725, 25 July 2000, from *Rossiiskaia gazeta,* 7; "More on Putin-Clinton Strategic Stability Agreement Initiative," FBIS-SOV–2000–0906, 6 September 2000, from Interfax 1807 GMT; Vladimir Lapskii, "Last Day in Oval Office: Goodbye, Mr. President!" FBIS-SOV–2001–0122, 19 January 2001, from *Rossiiskaia gazeta,* 5.

27. See, for example, Richard Garwin, "Cooperative Ballistic Missile Defense," 17 November 1999, available on line at http://sun00781.dn.net/rlg/991117.htm; Ted Postol, "A Russian-U.S. Boost-Phase Defense to Defend Russia and the U.S. from Postulated Rogue-State ICBMs," analysis presented at the Carnegie Endowment for International Peace, Cambridge, Mass., 12 October 1999; Bruce Blair, "Elements of a Sensible, Responsible NMD Policy," Center for Defense Information, 2 May 2000; and Dean Wilkening, "Amending the ABM Treaty," *Survival,* vol. 42, no. 1, 40–43.

9

South Asia

TIMOTHY D. HOYT

American deployment of national missile defense will affect regional stability around the globe—a consequence often overlooked or ignored by contemporary analysts. The deployment of a national missile defense (NMD) system will shape U.S. security and diplomatic relations with a handful of states that rely either on U.S. extended deterrence guarantees or on their own nuclear forces to deter potentially hostile actions. Although the vast majority of states in the international system do not fall into either of these categories, those states that do play a major role in U.S. foreign and defense policy.

Choices on missile defenses also have indirect implications for states involved in enduring regional rivalries with America's allies or adversaries. Their actions will complicate the security calculations of their neighbors, forcing them to reconsider long-standing policies. Missile defenses, for example, may accelerate modernization programs currently under way—a relatively benign or unthreatening act from an American perspective, but one which could profoundly affect others in the neighborhood of the modernizing state, and which cumulatively may destabilize the international system.

Both advocates and opponents of missile defense characterize NMD's global impact in simplistic terms. This chapter considers the impact of missile defenses on South Asia. It suggests that deployment *could* accelerate the development of a more hostile multipolar nuclear world, the very situation that U.S. nonproliferation policy has sought to prevent. It also demonstrates the difficulties of coordinating increasingly discon-nected U.S. regional and international policies, particularly where non-proliferation concerns are involved.

WHY DOES SOUTH ASIA MATTER?

Current analysis of the deployment of national missile defense systems focuses on the expense and cost-effectiveness of various proposed sys-tems; on potential threats; and on the possible reactions of key players in the international system, particularly Russia, China, and America's NATO allies. These are clearly relevant and important concerns, but they focus on domestic political and security debates and on the impact of missile defense on traditional Cold War allies and adversaries. Yet, NMD deployment will also affect the stability and security of the international system as a whole. Actions by the United States, the most powerful mili-tary actor in the system, shape a global security environment that affects the perceptions of *all* governments in the international system. These ef-fects are most important in regional security competitions involving nu-clear weapons, where various states' responses to U.S. missile defenses may significantly alter regional and global nuclear stability.

For example, U.S. missile defense deployment could have a significant impact on the South Asian nuclear competition, which includes recently nuclearized India and Pakistan. This competition also is affected by the actions of China and by regional rivalries in the Persian Gulf and else-where in the Middle East. The impact of U.S. missile defense deploy-ments on South Asia is a significant policy concern for several reasons. First, in May 1998, both India and Pakistan tested nuclear weapons.[1] From April 1998 through May 2000, each state also tested or paraded missiles with ranges of up to 2,500 kilometers.[2] Although there is no ev-idence that either state currently has the ability or desire to target the United States with missiles, both probably will acquire the ability to do so within the next fifteen years.[3]

Second, the United States is likely to become more involved in South Asia.[4] The March 2000 visit by President Clinton set out a joint vision for a new Indo-U.S. relationship.[5] India's large population and booming informa-tion services economy make it an attractive trading partner. Both India and

Pakistan have increasingly powerful, well-financed, and persuasive political lobbies in the United States which will influence the domestic debate on the region and perhaps also the debate over missile defense deployment.

Third, the subcontinent contains over a billion people, roughly one-fifth of the world's population. This region includes the world's largest democracy and fourth largest economy in terms of purchasing power parity (India) and a state that until recently was viewed as a potential model for Islamic democratization (Pakistan). Areas for potential investment include the internal infrastructure of each of the states in the region; India's growing information technology sector; and newly established energy reserves and infrastructure, including natural gas in Bangladesh and a possible natural gas pipeline through Afghanistan and Pakistan.

Fourth, South Asia is often referred to as the most likely site of a future nuclear war. India's borders with Pakistan and with China remain in dispute. India and Pakistan have fought three major conventional wars in the past 55 years, in addition to a simmering low-intensity conflict at the Siachen Glacier and a major crisis in the summer of 1999 near Kargil. Pakistan provides significant assistance to insurgents and foreign supporters of the insurgency in Kashmir, a province still in dispute with India. From 1983 to 1990, India and Pakistan were involved in at least three crises in which nuclear weapons were a concern. India also confronted China in 1986 and 1987, under circumstances that according to some observers included veiled nuclear threats.[6]

WHY DOES U.S. MISSILE DEFENSE MATTER TO THE REGION?

The primary U.S. security concern in South Asia is the evolving nuclearization of the subcontinent.[7] This nuclearization does not directly affect U.S. strategic interests in the sense that it increases an adversary's capability; rather, it creates difficulties because Americans desire better relations with both India and Pakistan. In the words of the Rumsfeld Commission:

India and Pakistan are not hostile to the United States. The prospect of U.S. military confrontation with either seems at present to be slight. However, beyond the possibility of nuclear war on the subcontinent, their aggressive, competitive development of ballistic missiles and weapons of mass destruction poses three concerns in particular. First, it enables them to supply relevant technologies to other nations. Second, India and Pakistan may seek additional technical assistance through cooperation with their current major suppliers—India from Russia, Pakistan from North Korea and China— because of the threats they perceive from one another and because of India's anxieties about China, combined with their mounting international isolation. Third, their growing missile and WMD [weapons of mass destruction] capabilities have direct effects on U.S. policies, both regional and global, and could significantly affect U.S. capability to play a stabilizing role in Asia.[8]

At present, neither India nor Pakistan has a nuclear deterrence relationship with the United States. Short of extreme measures, neither state has the capability to deliver a nuclear weapon to American soil. Both states maintain diplomatic relations with the United States. Although both states remain under significant U.S. economic, trade, and technology sanctions as a result of their May 1998 nuclear tests, neither views the United States as a significant military threat to its security.[9] So why would a U.S. decision to deploy NMD affect either state?

NMD will have a direct impact on states that rely on the United States for military support and for nuclear deterrence. Many American allies deliberately chose not to develop their own nuclear forces, relying instead on U.S. extended deterrence. This decision strengthened the nonproliferation regime and earned them some economic benefits (in the form of reduced defense spending). Actions that appear to endanger, or in some way to alter, American willingness or capability to honor U.S. extended deterrent threats, are of great concern to these allies.

NMD also affects states that rely on their nuclear forces to deter potential U.S. threats to their security, however ill-founded the United States may believe those threat perceptions to be. Much of the NMD debate has revolved around two such countries, Russia and China. The impact of NMD on these countries is sometimes dismissed as insignificant. If both bilateral relationships remain "manageable" from a security and diplomatic standpoint despite U.S. NMD, and if NMD counters potential threats from small states that are extremely hostile to the United States or its allies, this theoretically represents a net gain for U.S. security.

This vision is too simplistic, however, because it ignores the indirect impact that missile defense decisions have on regions adjoining China. It also ignores the spillover effect of force modernization from one region to another, and the impact of *accelerated* modernization on security decision making in adjacent regions. South Asia is especially relevant because of its intricate interrelationship with China. India justified its May 1998 nuclear tests with specific reference to the Chinese threat.[10] It has repeatedly criticized the United States for failing to respond to China's transfer of nuclear and missile technologies and facilities to Pakistan in violation of a wide range of nonproliferation treaties and regimes. India also seeks recognition as a great power, and many Indians believe that nuclear weapons will help their country achieve that recognition. Some even argue, given the U.S. role as the primary military power in the international system, that India must deploy an intercontinental ballistic missile (ICBM) as rapidly as possible, copying China's small ICBM force, to deter U.S. power and match China's international status.

Pakistan's situation is more complicated. Pakistani security is defined primarily in terms of rivalry with India—a larger, more powerful, and far more influential state than Pakistan. Pakistan has attempted to find a niche for itself as a leader of the Islamic community, in either symbolic or nuclear terms.[11] Although Pakistan's development of unconventional weapons has been partly indigenous, it has mostly relied on either covert acquisition or outside assistance.[12] Its most important external partners have been Iran and North Korea—the very states that U.S. NMD appears aimed against—and China.

Both India and Pakistan have refused to sign important nonproliferation agreements, including the Nuclear Non-Proliferation Treaty (NPT), the Comprehensive Test Ban Treaty (CTBT), and the Missile Technology Control Regime. Both countries are now under international sanctions directed at their nuclear and scientific sectors as a result of the May 1998 nuclear tests.

NMD deployment, therefore, can have both direct and indirect implications for India and Pakistan. The direct impact tends to be underestimated by U.S. analysts, and the indirect effects are often ignored.

U.S. OBJECTIVES IN SOUTH ASIA

U.S. policymakers do not anticipate a significant nuclear threat from either India or Pakistan. India has never been labeled a "rogue state," and its diplomacy and military policies can be described as stable, responsible, and relatively unaggressive. Although Indo-U.S. relations during the Cold War were never warm, neither state viewed the other as an adversary.[13] Pakistan was a U.S. ally in the Cold War—it was a member of both the Central Treaty and Southeast Asian Treaty Organizations—but the relationship soured when Pakistan began using U.S.-supplied weapons to fight India in 1965. A close relationship resumed in 1979 after the Soviet invasion of Afghanistan, but it was threatened almost immediately by reports of Pakistan's nuclear capability and Congressional action to strengthen U.S. and global nonproliferation efforts. Pakistan has been denied access to U.S. arms and certain types of technology since the early 1990s, and its ties with extremist Islamic groups such as the Taliban are a matter of some concern.

U.S. policy seeks to cap, reduce, and eliminate nuclear and missile stockpiles. In South Asia, American policies are intended to prevent the mating of warheads with delivery systems, and their deployment; to assure treaty compliance with CTBT and the Fissile Material Cutoff Treaty (FMCT); to avoid an arms race between India and Pakistan; and to prevent proliferation from South Asia to other regions. American policymakers have adopted a specific agenda aimed at reducing both the demand for nuclear arsenals and the supply of nuclear materials in the region:

- Halt further nuclear testing by India and Pakistan;
- Gain acceptance of the Comprehensive Test Ban Treaty;
- Stop the weaponization of nuclear devices;
- Stop the testing and deployment of long-range missiles;
- Cut off fissile material production for nuclear weapons;
- Gain Indian and Pakistani cooperation in FMCT negotiations;
- Maintain and formalize export controls and bans on proliferation of sensitive technologies;
- Reduce bilateral tensions, especially in Kashmir, by creating a series of confidence building measures.[14]

American policymakers hope to contain and eventually eliminate the proliferation virus in the region. U.S. policy is driven by fear of regional nuclear escalation and by concerns that further overt acts of nuclearization in South Asia will endanger U.S. efforts toward global nonproliferation. Both India and Pakistan currently are progressing slowly in the development and deployment of nuclear weapons.[15]

HOW WILL NMD DEPLOYMENT AFFECT INDIAN NUCLEAR POLICY?

India's current nuclear policy, codified unofficially in a draft nuclear doctrine released in the heat of the summer 1999 election campaign, names no specific adversaries.[16] It articulates a uniquely Indian conception of nuclear deterrence based on a sophisticated triad like those fielded by other nuclear powers but relying on a no-first-use strategy that includes the ability to absorb multiple strikes and still assure nuclear retaliation.

The nuclear forces and infrastructure necessary to carry out this doctrine are quite expensive and largely unavailable on the international market. Current programs for domestic production of these types of capabilities, like most Indian military-industrial endeavors, have experienced significant delays and inadequate administration.[17] Some analysts have questioned whether India can have a truly credible deterrent force without additional nuclear testing.[18]

Three issues will be crucial in determining India's response to NMD: the impact of the Chinese threat on Indian security; India's perception of the way U.S. defenses influence international security and arms-race and crisis stability; and its domestic security debate.

China

The key question for India will be how the Chinese respond to NMD deployment. Three aspects of the Chinese response are likely to be of particular concern. China could respond with qualitative improvements to its nuclear forces and delivery systems. It also could respond by increasing the number and range of existing forces. Finally, it could resume more overt types of proliferation, providing complete weapons and production facilities to interested customers.

China already has begun to modernize its forces, replacing older, liquid-fuel missiles with more accurate, solid-fuel designs. Indians view this Chinese force modernization with some concern.[19] Much of China's current buildup, however, appears to be directed at the Pacific Rim, particularly its plans to deploy hundreds of accurate, short-range missiles in the Taiwan region.[20] The difficulty with the Chinese qualitative buildup is that the most negative ramifications for India will result from U.S. theater missile defense (TMD) deployments, not NMD. A natural response for China will be to increase the range of the missiles threatening Taiwan so as to bypass the intercept envelope of TMD interceptors. Deployment of a force containing hundreds of long-range, solid-fuel, more accurate medium-range ballistic missiles (MRBMs) and intermediate-range ballistic missiles (IRBMs) of the DF-21 and DF-25 types would pose a greater threat to India than the current short-range M-series missiles (DF-11 and DF-15).

Qualitative shifts in current Chinese forces, then, can be converted into an increased quantitative threat to India. Indian decisionmakers appear to accept current Chinese force levels, recognizing that China has multiple foes and that the modernization of a few dozen ICBMs would not fundamentally change the Chinese threat to India.[21] Additionally, the limited range of the DF-11 and DF-15 missiles provides India with the opportunity to obtain strategic and tactical warning of an impending attack. If they are to be deployed against major Indian urban targets, these forces will have to be moved to the Tibetan plateau. Indian intelligence analysts would have the opportunity to place their nuclear forces on alert if they obtained indications that China was moving its missiles into a position to attack. A Chinese shift from short-range missiles to medium- and intermediate-range missles, however, significantly increases the threat to Indian targets, and decreases the possibility of tactical warning of a missile launch during a crisis. This undermines Indian efforts to achieve minimal deterrence with small nuclear forces that are maintained at very low alert rates in peacetime, and its efforts to provide rudimentary missile defenses based on Russian S-300V and S-300PMU surface-to-air missiles.

The third Chinese response that could directly affect India would be the resumption of Chinese proliferation of ballistic and cruise missiles, or other forms of unconventional technology. India has been the greatest victim of past Chinese proliferation because of the close relationship between the People's Republic of China and Pakistan.[22] China has contributed substantially to Pakistani nuclear and missile capability, providing Islamabad with M-11 missiles and production facilities.[23] Further transfers to Pakistan via China—even the transfer of North Korean Scud and No Dong technology and missiles—would complicate India's security calculations.

Impact on the International System

India traditionally has viewed the international system as a potential source of support against hegemonic states in the developed world. India's primary objection to international efforts to control proliferation of nuclear weapons is that these weapons should not be found only in the hands of a few superpowers. Given the choice between nuclear deployment and global disarmament, India until recently chose the latter, and it continues to espouse global disarmament as its eventual goal.

Deployment of missile defenses by the United States would increase India's perception of the already overwhelming American military edge over potential rivals. Combined with the projected decline in Russian strategic forces, it would leave the United States in a position to use military force to dominate the international system. This would be a matter of serious concern to India, which aspires to a greater role in international relations. Indian analysts are particularly suspicious of the new U.S. willingness to intervene in ethnic conflicts, given the ethnic nature of the Kashmir dispute.

NMD will be seen as a symptom of a greater U.S. effort to change strategic direction in the twenty-first century. Changes in nonproliferation policy and arms control, and U.S. efforts to intervene alone or multilaterally in regional disputes or localized, civil disorders, will be scrutinized in connection with NMD to determine whether deployment represents a threat to Indian security interests. NMD deployment synchronized with U.S. unilateral or bilateral nuclear force reductions will be viewed as much less destabilizing than the deployment of NMD with no reduction in offensive forces. Similarly, NMD deployment accompanied by what India views as more equitable stances by the major powers in nonproliferation talks will be interpreted as less threatening than a combination of NMD and renewed U.S. intransigence on CTBT, FMCT, and NPT. In short, the "defensive" nature of NMD will be judged on the basis of U.S. actions in other areas. If NMD appears to be a means of assuring U.S. military dominance rather than an attempt to substitute defense for deterrence, India may reconsider its current policies.[24]

Domestic Security Debate

India has steadfastly pursued a "nuclear option" throughout its fifty-two years as an independent state, but it has been extraordinarily cautious regarding the codification of doctrine or the actual deployment of forces. The nuclear option, which included technological development of weapons capabilities and stockpiling of fissile materials, now appears to have given way to the policy of "minimum deterrence"—the acquisition of credible weapon designs and deployment of appropriate delivery vehicles.

The nuclear debate is no longer between "hawks" (favoring testing and deployment) and "doves" (favoring the development of a nuclear option, but nondeployment).[25] It is now between moderates and hawks, with both sides supporting the current policy of minimal deterrence, but each having different concepts of the forces, command structure, and doctrine necessary for achieving deterrence and the pace at which Indian deterrent forces should be deployed.[26] Moderates call for ultimate deployment of up to 200 nuclear weapons, but not necessarily high-yield thermonuclear warheads. Hawks call for a large nuclear force, and some call for development and deployment of tactical nuclear weapons or enhanced radiation devices.[27]

Perhaps most important, hawks are calling for a new round of nuclear tests to ensure the credibility of India's nuclear deterrent, focusing particularly on the implied failure of the 11 May 1998 thermonuclear test.[28] Further tests would undermine U.S. nonproliferation policy in the region, including efforts at building support for the CTBT and initiatives to cool tensions over Kashmir. Some hawks also call for deployment of an ICBM, which may already be under development.[29] India also is pursuing programs that include ship-launched short-range ballistic missiles, submarine-launched ballistic missiles, and cruise missiles deliverable by a nuclear-powered submarine (one is on the drawing board).[30] Potential Indian threats to U.S. territory might eventually materialize, and the process could be accelerated by U.S. actions. The ramifications of NMD deployment will be seen in the balance between hawks and moderates in Indian security debates, in the acceleration of Indian nuclear development and deployment, and in the influence of hawks in Indian foreign policy.

Potential Indian Responses to U.S. NMD Deployment

If the United States were to deploy the threshold NMD option outlined in this book's Introduction, it would have little or no direct impact on Indian policy; but unilateral deployment in the absence of Russian agreement or appropriate modification of the ABM Treaty would raise Indian suspicions regarding U.S. intentions. It is possible, however, to imagine a chain of events started by limited U.S. missile deployment that could affect Indian interests. For example, if threshold deployments are linked to U.S.-supplied theater missile defenses on Taiwan, China might respond by greatly enhancing its nuclear and missile arsenals. This would create quite a stir in New Delhi, bolstering hawks who argue for a significant increase in the Indian nuclear arsenal.

If handled with diplomatic finesse, U.S. deployment of limited missile defenses could occur without significant disruption of U.S.-Indian relations or significant degradation of U.S. policy in South Asia. If deployments were linked to a reduction in Russian and American strategic offensive forces, the net effect in the region might even be positive. The U.S. decision to deploy limited defenses might strengthen U.S.-Indian strategic relations, leading India to join with the United States in an effort to counterbalance a growing Chinese threat. Indian sensitivity to alignment and perceived hegemonic powers, however, makes this a marginal possibility.[31]

U.S. deployment of a more substantial missile defense architecture would raise a series of more complicated questions. The deployment of TMD and NMD capabilities on U.S. ships would represent a direct threat to Indian deterrence policy. Stationed in the Indian Ocean or Persian Gulf for use in contingencies involving Iran or Iraq, these defenses might also be able to blunt or destroy an Indian retaliatory strike against Pakistan or China. These advanced defenses also could provide significant cover for U.S. intervention in the region. These developments would greatly strengthen the position of advocates of a strong nuclear force in India.[32]

Although the direct impact of a C3-plus system deployment on Indian security would be far greater than would a threshold C1 deployment, other states' responses to enhanced U.S. deployments will greatly affect Indian interests. If the Chinese respond vigorously to U.S. missile deployment, India's leaders will expand their arsenal and adjust their doctrine to counter Chinese nuclear modernization. If deployment occurs outside the confines of an arms control regime, significant concerns will be raised about U.S. intentions. India could interpret U.S. deployment of enhanced missile defenses as a significant step towards U.S. hegemony in the international system, leading it to consider an alliance with other states (e.g., Russia). Some form of cooperation with China also may be viewed as preferable to U.S. dominance and unilateralism.[33] This tilt away from the United States would lead to a transformation of Indian security policy and force structure.

Unless extraordinary steps are taken in the realm of U.S.-Indian relations, collapse of the ABM Treaty combined with unrestricted U.S. NMD deployments would probably result in a fundamental reassessment of Indian security policy. Indian leaders would be increasingly preoccupied with balancing against U.S. power and perceived ambitions. In the worst case, this could lead New Delhi to reevaluate India's strategic position vis-à-vis Pakistan, which as the major U.S. ally in the region, would be perceived as more threatening. A perception that the United States intended to guarantee its security through unilateral measures would probably produce an Indian policy aimed at securing regional dominance. In terms of military strategy, Indian armed forces would attempt to strengthen their capabilities and doctrine to deny the U.S. military access to operating areas within striking distance of the subcontinent. In the domestic debate about India's nuclear future, moderates who advocate restrained nuclearization and accommodation with the United States would be discredited. If the nonproliferation regime collapses, India also might consider supplying dual-use technologies to states seeking to enhance their space and missile programs to counter U.S. missile defenses.

HOW WILL NMD
DEPLOYMENT AFFECT PAKISTAN?

Pakistan faces much more serious security problems than does India. Pakistan is dwarfed by the capabilities of its larger and wealthier neighbor. It also faces significant threats to internal order, including rampant corruption, poverty, and a growing Islamic fundamentalist movement with significant international ties. Pakistan's security policy is supply-driven, dependent on outside sources of technology and weapons for most of its conventional and unconventional force structure. But if U.S. actions lead India to undertake a major acceleration of its nuclear program, Pakistani leaders will feel that their security is being undermined and will redouble their efforts to match India's nuclear capability.

Pakistan's options are limited when it comes to responding to any type of U.S. missile deployment or matching Indian or Chinese policies set in motion by a changing strategic situation. Pakistani forces lack the reach, and Pakistan lacks the political incentive, to establish a deterrence relationship with the United States. Pakistan, therefore, will seize upon other opportunities created by U.S. NMD deployments to enhance its security.

The impact of NMD deployment on other states also is of interest to Pakistan. China and North Korea both are suppliers of missiles and possibly also of nuclear technology to Pakistan.[34] If these states respond to NMD deployments by increasing the flow of military technology to third parties, Pakistani capabilities will improve as an indirect result of decisions made in Washington about missile defenses.

Iran and Israel also could affect the way Pakistan's leaders develop their strategic capabilities. Iran is a neighbor and sometime partner of Pakistan, and has ties to the North Korean missile industry. Pakistan and Iran currently disagree strongly over Afghanistan, however; Pakistan supports the Taliban government, and Iran supports opposition forces. Pakistan and Afghanistan have become the new center of Islamic extremism, and Iran may be moving towards a more secularized democracy. There is, therefore, the possibility for significant tension between these states. Iran's response to NMD deployment will help determine Pakistani policies, and vice versa.

Israel is a current beneficiary of U.S.-developed theater missile defense technologies. Enhanced Israeli missile defenses could lead Pakistan to strengthen its links to the Arab world and emphasize its status as a Muslim state. Israel will be monitoring closely the growth of Pakistan's nuclear arsenal and its delivery capabilities, in addition to its links with Islamic terrorists. Given growing Indo-Israeli defense ties, it would not be surprising to see some form of cooperation between these two states to develop missile technology—a situation that would be unsettling in Islamabad.

Pakistan's nuclear policy is more coherent than India's, partly because of the vastly different nature of civil-military relations in the two countries. India's nuclear policy has remained largely in the hands of politicians and scientists, who have only partial information about defense issues. In contrast, Pakistan's military traditionally plays a crucial role in defense planning under both civilian and military regimes, and Pakistani military officers have been closely involved in their nation's nuclear program from its inception.[35] Pakistani military and civilian leaders believe that their nuclear deterrent played a crucial role in preventing escalation during multiple conflicts with India in the 1980s and 1990s.[36] Pakistan is constructing a carefully planned and clearly articulated command and control system, has rejected the notion of matching Indian force posture, and has refused decisively to rule out the first use of nuclear weapons.[37]

To outsiders, Pakistan's nuclear doctrine seems deliberately vague. Because it is inferior to India in conventional capabilities, Pakistan must maintain the ability to use nuclear weapons in a tactical role to avert possible disaster on the battlefield.[38] Pakistan also has attempted to exploit the "stability-instability" paradox in the South Asian nuclear competition by waging a low-intensity, geographically-limited conflict in Kashmir to force outside political intervention to resolve the dispute in its favor.[39] Pakistani delivery systems include a variety of short-range, mobile missiles based on both North Korean and Chinese designs, as well as a number of U.S., Chinese, and French strike aircraft.[40] Given Pakistan's weak navy, poor economy, and limited resources, deployment of a sea-based nuclear force appears unlikely without considerable foreign assistance.

Ultimately, Pakistan's response to NMD deployment will affect the United States by creating regional instability or by facilitating proliferation of nuclear materials or delivery systems.[41] A second possibility is that U.S. NMD deployment will accelerate centrifugal forces that already are weakening the cohesion of the Pakistani state. In these circumstances, control of Pakistan's nuclear forces could become a significant concern for U.S., Indian, and even Israeli policymakers, particularly if nuclear weapons fell into the hands of militant Islamic elements.[42]

Potential Responses of Pakistan to NMD Deployment

Pakistan's response to a threshold C1 level deployment would almost certainly be opportunistic. Insofar as limited missile defense deployments create third-party resentment or additional cracks in the nonproliferation regime, Pakistan will seek to take advantage of them, obtaining whatever weapons and production facilities it can afford. Pakistan also would seek to maintain the appearance that it is complying with existing regimes to the maximum extent possible, and would make an effort to acquire TMD systems—perhaps as part of a tacit bargain for adherence to certain nonproliferation norms such as those of the CTBT. A U.S. decision to deploy a modest number of interceptors in Alaska would have a minimal impact on the Pakistani security calculus, because Pakistan is far more focused on regional competition with India than on the international ramifications of the strategic balance among Russia, China, and the United States. Until the threat becomes extreme, Pakistan will seek to bandwagon with a great power (the United States if possible, or China if necessary) in order to obtain outside military and technical assistance for its competition with India.

A U.S. decision to deploy more advanced missile defenses would have a greater impact on Pakistani security interests. Already concerned about the possibility of being labeled a supporter of terrorism, Pakistan would view the deployment of robust sea-based ballistic missile defenses (or sea-based, boost-phase defenses) with alarm, as a possible U.S. threat aimed at guaranteeing Islamabad's good behavior. Pakistan currently relies heavily on the Ghauri, a North Korean Scud derivative, and is anticipated to be a prime candidate for purchases of the Taepo Dong missile when North Korea puts it on the market.[43] These are the same types of weapons that U.S. systems will be optimized to destroy, potentially jeopardizing the effectiveness of Pakistani deterrent forces that would be used in a regional conflict. Pakistan has some options to overcome the arrival of missile defenses in the region. It can use short-range systems such as the M-11, or it can station its missiles far enough inland to minimize the impact of sea-based defenses while still maintaining the capability to threaten India.[44] These kinds of changes could be costly for Pakistan. But a hostile international response to a U.S. decision to deploy enhanced defenses also could damage the nonproliferation regime, thereby opening new opportunities for Pakistan to fulfill a new set of missile requirements.

If the United States abandons the ABM Treaty and proceeds to construct highly capable missile defenses, it would create difficult problems for Pakistan. Pakistan might be tempted to balance against the United States. To do so, Pakistan would have to be willing to accept a minor role in a China-led alliance, which might include cooperation with India. Pakistan also might attempt to lead an Islamic alliance formed for the purpose of devising a variety of asymmetric responses to American military superiority. Another option would be to bandwagon with the United States to obtain support against India. Any significant response by Pakistan, however, would be dictated by the availability of foreign supplies of aid, technology, or weapons, which is in turn a function of the alliance choices made in Islamabad.

One response seems certain: Pakistan will respond to any Indian action that threatens the credibility of the Pakistani deterrent or that gives India regional hegemony.[45] Early in the Pakistani nuclear program, Foreign Minister Zulfikar Bhutto told reporters that if India became a nuclear power, Pakistanis would eat grass if necessary to match that capability. This determination to match India does not appear to have faded now that Pakistan has the bomb.

FURTHER RAMIFICATIONS

If U.S. NMD deployments evoke a significant response from either India or Pakistan, the resultant changes will produce a cascading effect from South Asia—the most overtly nuclearized region in the developing world—to neighboring regions. Iran will view any acceleration of Pakistani nuclear programs with concern, particularly if tensions increase over the Taliban and Afghanistan. Iran's actions, of course, will have repercussions for Iraq and probably also for Israel. Israel also will view Pakistani programs with concern, particularly if there is evidence that internal fissures in Pakistani society threaten the power of the central government. Pakistani acquisition or deployment of longer-range missiles will threaten Israeli territory, possibly strengthening Pakistani claims to Islamic leadership. China, and eventually Russia, would probably feel compelled to respond to increased force structures in the South Asian region. Long-range Indian missiles also will threaten Southeast Asian states and perhaps Japan. These states responded with alarm to increases in Indian naval forces during the 1980s, and it would be reasonable for them to be concerned about developments in the nuclear arena that might allow India to project force into East and Southeast Asia.

CONCLUSION

The impact of American NMD deployment on South Asia could range from utterly insignificant to disastrous. A U.S. decision to deploy highly capable defenses, especially if undertaken in a context of diplomatic rancor following the collapse of ABM Treaty negotiations, would likely undermine U.S. nonproliferation objectives in the region. India would have a good reason to consider resumption of nuclear testing, particularly to validate more advanced thermonuclear weapon designs. NMD deployment may lead Indian leaders to doubt the persuasiveness of the last set of tests, and may encourage a third round of tests or a refusal to sign the Comprehensive Test Ban Treaty. Similarly, if NMD leads to an acceleration of Chinese strategic force modernization, India may feel compelled to increase its own arsenal, threatening the viability of the Fissile Material Cutoff Treaty. Any change in Indian strategic forces or doctrine will create pressure in Islamabad to mount a Pakistani response, which will undermine the potential of confidence-building measures to quell the simmering Indo-Pakistani nuclear and territorial rivalry.

Some tentative policy conclusions can be drawn from this discussion. First, the single most important factor in determining South Asian responses to U.S. NMD deployments will be Chinese actions. An aggressive Chinese response to U.S. missile deployments would force New Delhi to pour more resources into its nuclear program, especially if the Chinese saw it in their interests to provide Pakistan with more dual-use technology to undermine U.S. nonproliferation policies. It would be a mistake not to consider the impact of the Chinese response to U.S. NMD deployments on South Asian regional rivalries.

Second, nuclear modernization programs are underway in all the nuclear powers in the region. NMD deployment may accelerate these programs, eventually leading to larger arsenals. The proliferation of more substantial arsenals could reduce the positive security impact of missile defenses for the United States by raising the number of threats from states that are not traditionally viewed as rogues. Increases in the size and capability of South Asian arsenals also will raise concerns about the adequacy of existing or emerging nuclear deterrent forces in adjacent regions.

Third, the importance of renegotiating the ABM Treaty in conjunction with any NMD deployment should not be underestimated. If the United States acts unilaterally to deploy NMD despite the objections of its friends and adversaries, its missile deployments could have catastrophic effects on the nonproliferation regime and adverse effects on Indian and Pakistani policies. The United States must appear to be acting in good faith in introducing even a limited missile defense of American territory. By tying NMD deployments to further reductions in the strategic arsenal, U.S. policymakers might be able to reassure Indian officials about U.S. security objectives. The "rogue threat" justification for NMD is not credible to states that could never seriously consider fielding the numbers of nuclear weapons the United States currently deploys. Deployments in the absence of sincere and sustained diplomacy may induce smaller nuclear and near-nuclear powers to increase their forces, creating the multipolar nuclear world that the United States has sought to avoid for thirty years. This outcome would make limited NMD a poor security investment indeed.

NOTES

1. For a discussion of India's test of its first nuclear device (in 1974), see George Perkovich, *India's Nuclear Bomb* (Berkeley: University of California Press, 1999), 161–189.

2. "The Arms Race," *Frontline*, available on line at http://www.the-hindu.com/fline/fl1609/16090230.htm; "Pak missile has a range of 2,500 km," *Hindu*, 6 April 2000.

3. See Gregory S. Jones, "From Testing to Deploying Nuclear Forces: The Hard Choices Facing India and Pakistan," RAND Issue Paper IP–192, available on line at http://www.rand.org/IP/IP192; "U.S. Defends Anti-Missile System Need," *Huntsville Times,* 2 May 2000.

4. "U.S., India have turned a new page in their relationship, says Inderfurth," *Indian Express,* 17 May 2000. See http://www.indian-express.com/ie/daily/20000517/ian17046.htm.

5. "Clinton-Vajpayee Joint Vision Statement," United States Information Agency, available on line at http://www.usia.gov/regional/nea/mena/india1.htm.

6. "On the nuclear brink, no room for error," MSNBC, available on line at http://www.msnbc.com/news/378873.

7. Thomas R. Pickering, Under Secretary of State for Political Affairs, "U.S. Policy in South Asia: The Road Ahead," speech delivered at the Paul H. Nitze School of Advanced International Studies, Johns Hopkins University, Washington, D.C., 27 April 2000, 7.

8. *Report of the Commission to Assess the Ballistic Missile Threat to the United States: Executive Summary,* Pursuant to Public Law 201, 104th Congress (Washington, D.C.: Government Printing Office, 15 July 1998), 16–17.

9. For a perspective different from the one presented in this chapter, see Gaurav Kampani, "How a U.S. National Missile Defense Will Affect South Asia," Center for Nonproliferation Studies, Monterey Institute of International Studies, available on line at http://www.CNS.MIIS.EDU/pubs/reports/usmslsa.htm.

10. "India's Letter to Clinton on Nuclear Testing," *New York Times,* 13 May 1998, A14. See also Jaswant Singh, "Against Nuclear Apartheid," *Foreign Affairs* 77:5, 41–52; "Paper Laid on the Table of the House on Evolution of India's Nuclear Policy," available on line at http://www.meadev.gov.in/govt/evolution.htm.

11. See Thomas Perry Thornton, "Pakistan: Fifty Years of Insecurity," in Selig Harrison, Paul Kreisberg, and Dennis Kux, eds., *India and Pakistan: The First Fifty Years* (Washington, D.C.: Woodrow Wilson Center and Cambridge University Press, 1999), 170–188.

12. See Rodney W. Jones and Mark G. McDonough with Toby F. Dalton and Gregory D. Koblenz, *Tracking Nuclear Proliferation: A Guide in*

Maps and Charts, 1998 (Washington, D.C.: Carnegie Endowment for International Peace, 1998), 131–146.

13. Dennis Kux, *Estranged Democracies* (Washington, D.C.: National Defense University Press, 1993).

14. "After the Tests: U.S. Policy Toward India and Pakistan," Report of an Independent Task Force, Richard N. Haass and Morton J. Halperin, co-chairs (Council on Foreign Relations, 1998); "Fact Sheet: India and Pakistan Sanctions" (Washington, D.C.: U.S. Department of State, Bureau of Economic and Agricultural Affairs, 18 June 1998); Paul Leventhal, "An End to Nuclear Proliferation, or to Nuclear *Non*-Proliferation?," presented to the Conference on the Impact of the South Asian Nuclear Crisis on the Non-Proliferation Regime, Carnegie Endowment for International Peace, 16 July 1998, available on line at http://www.nci.org/sp71698.htm.

15. The Indo-Pakistani competition has occasionally been referred to as an "arms crawl," rather than an arms race (P. R. Chari, "India's Slow-Motion Nuclear Deployment," *Issue Brief,* Vol. III, No. 26 [Carnegie Endowment for International Peace, Non-Proliferation Project]).

16. The current government has stepped back from some of the more aggressive pronouncements of the Draft Nuclear Doctrine. The text of the document can be found at http://www.indianembassy.org/policy/CTBT/nuclear_doctrine_aug_17_1999.html.

17. See Timothy D. Hoyt, "Rising Regional Powers," Ph.D. dissertation (Johns Hopkins University, 1997), 62–198; and Raju G.C. Thomas, *Indian Security Policy* (Princeton: Princeton University Press, 1986).

18. See P. K. Iyengar (former Indian Atomic Energy Commission chief), "In Testing Times," *Times of India,* 17 February 2000, 12.

19. "China adding modern missiles: Expert," *Deccan Herald,* 13 June 2000, 7. See also "No cause for India to lower its N-guard," *National Herald,* 19 May 2000, available on line at http://www.meadev.gov.in/opn/2000may/19nh.htm.

20. See Brad Roberts, Robert Manning, and Ronald Montaperto, "China: The Forgotten Nuclear Power," *Foreign Affairs* 79:4 (July/August 2000), which reports that the number of Chinese SRBMs rose from 20 in the mid-1990s to about 160–200 in 1999, with estimates as high as 500–650 for 2005.

21. "Delhi says no nuclear race with China," *Dawn* (Pakistan), 7 February 2000. This article quotes Indian National Security Advisor Brajesh

Mishra as having asserted, "[W]e are not, definitely not, attempting to catch up with China."

22. Singh, "Against Nuclear Apartheid."

23. *Report of the Commission,* 10, 16.

24. See Achin Vanaik, "On the verge of a new nuclear age," *Hindu,* 17 June 2000, 13. The article raises questions about how NMD will affect international stability, and about the forces propelling the U.S. towards NMD deployment.

25. See "The great Indian nuclear debate," *Hindu,* 12 November 1999, 12.

26. The moderate position is articulated by two leading nuclear proponents, General K. Sundarji and K. Subramanyam. Sundarji, a proponent of existential deterrence, called for the ability to detonate fifteen warheads, each being between 14 and 20 kilotons (these could be fission devices), and argued that 150 warheads, with a delivery force of 45 Prithvi and 90 Agni missiles and dual-use aircraft, would be sufficient to deter China and Pakistan. Subramanyam, for decades India's leading public advocate of nuclearization, has called for a force of sixty warheads in the 125-kiloton range (boosted fission or thermonuclear). See K. Sundarji, "Imperatives of Indian Nuclear Deterrence," and K. Subramanyam, "Nuclear Force Design and Minimum Deterrence Strategy for India," both cited in Verghese Koithara, *Society, State and Security: The Indian Experience* (New Delhi: SAGE, 1999), 346–347.

27. P. K. Iyengar has argued for enhanced radiation tests ("India should test neutron bomb, says AEC ex-chief," *Times of India,* 1 May 2000, 5). On tactical nuclear weapons, see Brahma Chellaney, "Tactical nukes," *Hindustan Times,* 26 January 1999, p. 13; Gurmeet Kanwal, "Does India Need Tactical Weapons?" *Strategic Analysis,* available on line at http://www.idsa-india.org/an-may–03.html.

28. Iyengar, "In Testing Times;" V. R. Raghavan, "Dangerous Nuclear Uncertainties," *Hindu,* 13 March 2000, 12; and Srinivas Laxman, "Hard decisions for minimum N-deterrence needed," *Times of India,* 13 March 2000, 16.

29. The Indian Space Research Organization is currently pursuing a Global Space Launch Vehicle and a Polar Space Launch Vehicle, both of which could be converted to ICBM-type ranges if deployed as missiles. Contradictory reports late last year suggested that ICBM development

was under way. See "India plans to build 5,000 km ICBM," *Deccan Herald,* 14 December 1999, 1; "India admits plan to test missile," Australian Broadcasting Corporation, available on line at http://www.abc.net.au:80/news/newslink/weekly/newsnat–6nov1999–108.htm (which attributed the story of a 5,000-kilometer-range missile to a junior defense minister named Bachchi Singh Rawat); and "Report on 'Surya' denied," *Hindu,* 8 November 1999, 12. This last article denies the Australian report.

30. For more information on Indian missile programs, see the Federation of American Scientists (http://www.fas.org), and the Center for Disarmament and International Security Studies (http://www.cdiss.org). On the recent test of the ship-launched Dhanush SRBM, see "Dhanush missile test-fired," *Hindu,* 11 April 2000, 13; Rahul Bedi, "Missile test is 'partial success,' says India," *Jane's Defence Weekly,* 19 April 2000. Ship-launched missiles were considered to be an important threat to the territory of the United States in the Rumsfeld Commission Report. See *Report of the Commission,* 1.

31. See Brahma Chellaney, "An American Umbrella for India," *International Herald Tribune,* 10 April 2000, 10.

32. Ship-based deployment of boost-phase interceptors would cause the same level of concern in New Delhi.

33. See the comments of the Chinese ambassador to New Delhi in "U.S. trying to upset global strategic equilibrium," *Times of India,* 19 January 2000, 12.

34. See "China behind N Korean shipment: DRI," *Times of India,* 18 July 1999, 8. The story refers to the discovery of Scud parts on a North Korean vessel in India during the crisis. See also "N Korean yet to challenge Indian charge that its ship was carrying missile manuf" [sic], *Indian Express,* 25 May 2000, available on line at http://www.indian-express.com/ie/daily/20000525/ina25043.htm. The crew apparently told their captors that the final destination for the cargo was North Africa. The cargo included designs, drawings, and reports about the manufacture of Scud-C and Scud-B missiles, test equipment, components, and equipment for inspection and calibration of components.

35. "Pak to consolidate N-Capability," *Times of India,* 28 May 2000, 1. According to this report, Pakistan established a National Command Authority in February 2000, including the three service chiefs, several cabinet-level ministers, and a group of key scientists. See also "Nuclear com-

mand authority established," *Islamabad,* 3 February 2000, available on line at http://www/fas.org/news/pakistan/2000/boo203-pak-app1.htm.

36. "Nuke deterrence prevented conflicts with India: Sattar," *Times of India,* 27 February 2000.

37. For a discussion, see Rodney W. Jones, "Nuclear Command and Control Issues in Pakistan," presentation to Islamabad Council on World Affairs—Institute of Strategic Studies Seminar on Command and Control of Nuclear Weapons in South Asia, 21–22 February 2000. See also "N-bombs to be used as last resort: Musharraf," *Times of India,* 20 January 2000, 14.

38. See Rodney W. Jones, "Pakistan's Nuclear Posture: Quest for Assured Nuclear Deterrence—A Conjecture," *Spotlight on Regional Affairs* XIX:1 (Islamabad: Institute of Regional Studies, January 2000), especially 17–21.

39. See *From Surprise to Reckoning: The Kargil Review Committee Report* (New Delhi: SAGE, April 2000), 183. On the "stability-instability paradox," see Robert Jervis, *The Meaning of the Nuclear Revolution* (Ithaca: Cornell University Press, 1989), 19–22.

40. "Pakistan more capable of putting warheads on missiles: Expert," *Indian Express,* 18 January 2000, available on line at http://www.indian-express.com/ie/daily/20000118/news.htm.

41. One recent report from the United Kingdom claimed that Pakistan already was exporting nuclear materials. Given the small fissile stockpile available to Pakistan, this seems unlikely. See "Pakistan denies exporting N-material," *News International* (Pakistan), 30 May 2000.

42. Fear of "an Islamic bomb" long has been associated with Pakistan's nuclear program. See Stephen D. Bryen, "The New Islamic Bomb," *Washington Times,* 10 April 2000.

43. See statement by Robert Walpole, "U.S. Defends Anti-Missile System Need," *Huntsville Times,* 2 May 2000.

44. See "Second round completed: Short range Shaheen missile tested," *DAWN (Pakistan),* 16 April 1999, 1; "Pak missile has a range of 2,500 km," *Hindu,* 6 April 2000, 13; "Pakistan's ballistic response," *Frontline,* available on line at http://www.the-hindu.com/fline/fl1609/16090290.htm. Pakistan has tested or paraded two versions of the Ghauri (derived from the North Korean No Dong) and two versions of the solid-fueled Shaheen (derived from the Chinese DF-11 and -15).

45. "Pak won't allow India 'to become superpower,'" *Hindustan Times,* 29 February 2000, 14.

1 0

The Allies

CHARLES BALL

The likely reactions of America's allies to the Bush administration's plans to deploy a global or a national missile defense (NMD) system will have a significant impact on how the administration proceeds with defense deployments. Although many U.S. policymakers in recent times have indicated that the deployment of some type of missile defense is inevitable, the support of key U.S. allies for the effort is critical—not only because missile defenses will be dependent on early warning radars located outside the United States but also because the continued strength of U.S. alliances is essential to the overall success of defense efforts. The Bush administration will be keen to ensure that the anticipated improvements in U.S. security provided by limited protection against ballistic missile attacks are not diminished by a serious rupture with U.S. allies over missile defenses. As Secretary of Defense Donald Rumsfeld has stated, "The United States has no interest in deploying defenses that would separate us from our allies."[1]

This chapter surveys the issues that America's allies find troubling about U.S. deployment of ballistic missile defenses. It begins with an outline of the objections raised by America's European allies about what appears to be an impending decision to deploy ballistic missile defenses. It then describes the different diplomatic stances adopted by Britain, France, and Germany to deal with renewed U.S. interest in missile defense. The chapter then explores how America's allies outside Europe may react to the deployment of missile defenses.

259

NMD AND GROWING UNEASE IN EUROPE

The proposed U.S. national missile defense system has provoked greater transatlantic controversy than any U.S. program since President Ronald Reagan's Strategic Defense Initiative (SDI), outlined in March 1983. Although there is no official European position or consensus about the implications of U.S. deployment of missile defenses, the broad outlines of Europe's reaction have emerged. Allied officials believe that U.S. NMD threatens to upset global stability. Specifically, European allies contend that NMD deployments would ignite an arms race by undermining the ABM Treaty, and would severely damage U.S. relations with Russia and China. Many European governments argue that American ballistic missile defenses would bolster U.S. conventional superiority by rendering U.S. territory immune to counterattack from nations against which the United States may want to conduct military operations. If these countries cannot retaliate against the United States, they will be tempted to strike against an unprotected Europe. In other words, European allies are worried that the United States and its partners in the North Atlantic Treaty Organization (NATO) would no longer share similar risks in dealing with emerging threats and that U.S. and European security interests might become "decoupled." Some allies voice additional concerns about the future effectiveness of the French and British nuclear deterrent forces if highly capable missile defenses proliferate, and about the consequences of a growing technological gap between the U.S. defense establishment and its European allies.

Decoupling

European officials worry that the deployment of a U.S. national missile defense system could lead to the decoupling of U.S. and European security. During the Cold War, the term *decoupling* described European doubts about the credibility of U.S. extended nuclear deterrent guarantees to NATO allies.[2] Used in the context of NMD debates in Europe, it refers to the idea that a missile shield deployed over the United States, in the absence of corresponding protection for Europe, would lead to zones of unequal security. U.S. missile defenses would undermine the shared risk that is essential to transatlantic security. Many European officials fear that unless the United States and its allies are subject to similar threats and risks, Americans will retreat into "Fortress America," reducing their involvement in situations that might be viewed in Washington as posing a threat only to Europe.

Europeans also are concerned that U.S. NMD deployment might increase the possibility of missile attacks against Europe. They suggest that if the United States became involved in a conflict with a country that possessed nuclear, chemical, or biological weapons and long-range missiles, Europe, unprotected by missile defenses, would be the logical target for retaliation. They also suspect that the critical missile defense radars based outside of the United States could invite attacks from states wishing to diminish the effectiveness of NMD as a prelude to attacks against American territory.

Germans have been especially vocal with their concerns about the possibility that NMD could lead to decoupling within NATO. According to German Foreign Minster Joschka Fischer, "There is no doubt that this [NMD deployment] would lead to split security standards within the NATO alliance." Fischer also suggested that Germany's renunciation of nuclear weapons was "always based on the trust that the United States would protect our interests, that the United States as the leading nuclear power would guarantee some sort of order."[3]

Fischer's statement should not be misconstrued as a threat to renounce Germany's nonnuclear status in response to U.S. NMD deployment; but it does reveal the origins of German, and by extension NATO, objections to NMD. The fact that Fischer would broach the highly sensitive issue of the conditions that Germans believe underlie their commitment to nonnuclear status shows how troubled West Europeans are by the prospect of NMD deployment. Fischer's statement about split security standards is equally revealing: It seems to suggest that the major problem produced by NMD will be a tendency for American and European views to diverge over specific threats to international security and the best ways to counter those threats so as to preserve international order. Fischer apparently is suggesting that U.S. officials have lost sight of the fact that a unilateral pursuit of security could undermine the treaties and relations that form the bedrock of international order and stability.

262   Charles Ball

Preserving the Arms Control Regime

Most European leaders believe that U.S. NMD deployments would do grave damage to the global arms control regime and to U.S. relations with Russia, outweighing the security gains derived from protection against missile attacks launched by small, hostile states. For European governments, it is axiomatic that security depends on upholding existing arms control agreements and maintaining good relations with Russia. Allied European leaders are concerned that the expansion of NATO, the continued deterioration of Russia's early warning system, and Moscow's growing inability to maintain its strategic nuclear forces at the lower levels agreed to in the Strategic Arms Reduction Treaty (START II) have set the stage for deteriorating relations with the Kremlin. Under these circumstances, U.S. NMD deployments would only heighten the sense of insecurity among Russian officials.[4]

NATO allies also regard the ABM Treaty as a cornerstone of strategic stability. They often note that the Treaty made possible subsequent reductions in strategic offensive forces, and that it is a major safeguard against a rekindling of the nuclear arms race. They consider the U.S. Senate's rejection of the Comprehensive Test Ban Treaty in 1999 a disturbing manifestation of America's disregard for international agreements, which when coupled with potential abrogation of the ABM Treaty, would undermine the implicit foundations of the nonproliferation regime, and even the Nonproliferation Treaty itself. NATO members also believe that modifying the ABM Treaty would set back NATO-Russian relations.

These European sentiments have been bolstered by dire Russian warnings about the implications of U.S. abrogation of, or withdrawal from, the ABM Treaty. Russian leaders have stated that in response to a U.S. decision to abandon the ABM Treaty, they not only would refuse to abide by the START II agreement but would also retaliate by withdrawing from all arms control agreements, including the 1989 Intermediate-range Nuclear Forces (INF) Treaty.

Another salient feature of the controversy within NATO surrounding the U.S. NMD deployment decision is the extent to which Russian and American officials have attempted to court European public opinion so as to gain support for their different positions on missile defenses. The

U.S. administration under President Bill Clinton attempted to convince Europeans that NMD deployment could be achieved without jeopardizing arms control agreements or relations with Russia. U.S. government officials explained in various European forums that Washington intends to make negotiated changes to the ABM treaty by convincing Moscow that limited defenses will not affect the credibility of Russia's strategic nuclear deterrent. The Clinton administration's efforts to win over European public opinion, however, proved less than successful. The advent of the new Bush administration significantly changed the dynamics of the transatlantic debate. Bush's unequivocal statement that missile defenses would be deployed has shifted the focus of debate onto the more practical questions of how and when the deployment will occur. Thus, although European states' substantive objections remain unchanged, they are now accommodating themselves to the inevitability of NMD.

Russian officials appreciate European opposition to NMD, and portray themselves as paragons of reasoned restraint in the face of irresponsible and dangerous U.S. proposals. To reinforce this perception, in the spring of 2000 Russian President Vladimir Putin made a proposal of his own, apparently designed in large measure to divide the United States from Europe. The Russian proposal called for a joint West European–Russian theater missile defense to defend Europe. Although the particulars of Putin's plan were vague and it was not taken particularly seriously, the Russian proposal demonstrated that Moscow believes Europe is a key constituency in the effort to block U.S. NMD deployment. As long as President Putin remains opposed to amending the ABM Treaty to allow for NMD, the prospect of U.S. missile defenses will continue to trouble NATO relations.

Differing Threat Perceptions

American and allied European viewpoints diverge when it comes to assessing the immediate threat posed by the proliferation of weapons of mass destruction and ballistic missiles. European governments believe, for example, that the United States is exaggerating the threat posed by the Iranian or North Korean missile programs. Even if European allies shared American perceptions of the severity of today's ballistic missile threat, they do not believe that current technologies can be effective against this threats, especially against the countermeasures that proliferators are likely to adopt in an attempt to penetrate U.S. defenses.[5]

These different perceptions of threats and technological capabilities are reflected in a related transatlantic disagreement concerning how best to deal with proliferant countries. French Prime Minister Lionel Jospin characterized NMD as "a project the logic of which would tip the balance between efforts towards nonproliferation and efforts centered on counterproliferation."[6] The French foreign minister's statement suggests that the United States is attempting to devise military or technical solutions to the fundamentally political problem of weapons proliferation. Indeed, some Europeans are concerned that this turn toward a military solution to the proliferation problem could be counterproductive. If NMD gave the United States protection from limited attacks, Washington might be more inclined to launch preventive or preemptive attacks against the arsenals of small adversaries, secure in the knowledge that no effective ballistic missile attack would be forthcoming. By contrast, European allies believe that this type of cure is worse than the disease of proliferation. They prefer a policy of engagement, contending that this is the best way to assuage grievances and reduce the tensions that give rise to proliferation and conflict.

The United States as "Rogue Superpower"

The United States' pursuit of NMD has given fresh impetus to the European charge, usually articulated *sotto voce*, that the United States is becoming a rogue superpower. Increasingly, NATO allies are charging that the United States refuses to play by the same rules as other nations. They see the American intention to deploy NMD as further evidence of disturbing proclivities that were in evidence even before the NMD dispute arose: unilateralism, isolationism, and excessive foreign interventionism.[7] NMD also evokes feelings of impotence vis-à-vis the United States, insofar as many Europeans believe that they have little power to deflect U.S. policymakers from a course that is self-evidently deleterious to European (and American) interests. These feelings are further exacerbated by the complaint that despite the enormous impact NMD would have on European security, European governments were not part of the decisionmaking process regarding whether to proceed with NMD. To be sure, the United States consulted with its allies; but some Europeans believe that ultimately the decision will be made irrespective of their concerns.

The British and French Nuclear Deterrents

There is concern in Britain and France that U.S. NMD deployments could reduce the effectiveness of the British and French nuclear deterrents. British and French officials believe that American NMD deployments would be followed by a Russian decision to expand the ABM system currently surrounding Moscow. Although these Russian ABM deployments might not significantly affect the ability of the U.S. strategic nuclear force to strike targets in the Russian capital, the smaller French and British nuclear forces probably would be unable to penetrate enhanced Moscow missile defenses. This would reduce the likelihood that America's NATO partners would be prepared to forge a more independent European defense identity and policy. France and Britain also would be forced to invest significant resources in the effort to overcome improved Russian defenses, or else abandon the effort to hold key targets within the Russian capital at risk.

The demise of an independent French and British deterrent against Moscow would heighten European concerns about American military and diplomatic unilateralism. A strongly held premise during the Cold War was that the British and French nuclear forces "coupled" the strategic fate of Europe to that of the United States, because American policymakers would have to assume that a British or French attack on Russia would bring Soviet retaliation against the United States.[8] Today, fears that a Russian-NATO confrontation might lead to nuclear war are slim. However, the fear that Russia might retain the only credible deterrent in Europe, with Washington appearing increasingly willing to go it alone, make officials in Paris and London highly uncomfortable.

THE BIG THREE:
BRITAIN, FRANCE, AND GERMANY

America's NATO allies generally hold similar views about the potential implications of NMD deployment; but the attitudes they take toward the U.S. position, and their diplomatic responses to various American initiatives and positions, vary. There are several important differences, for example, among the most important NATO allies: Britain, France, and Germany.

The British are the most sympathetic to the U.S. point of view. Although they do not entirely share U.S. concern over the proliferation of small nuclear, chemical, or biological arsenals and ballistic missiles, the government of Prime Minister Tony Blair has accepted the U.S. premise that there is a growing missile threat. At times, however, internal divisions on the question of NMD have beset Blair's government. The foreign ministry has adopted a generally negative stance toward NMD, whereas the defense ministry is far less hostile. The opposition Tory Party has attempted to exploit this division, making it clear that the Conservatives favor the project.[9] The Clinton administration's proposal for missile defenses strengthened the special relationship that exists between the United States and Britain. In keeping with its traditional role as a bridge between Europe and the United States, the British government has attempted to mediate the transatlantic controversy engendered by NMD. Accordingly, Britain has not been as vociferous in its criticism of proposed U.S. NMD deployments as have some other allies, although it has indicated that should NMD deployment occur, Britain also should be protected.

The French, by contrast, are the most openly hostile and dismissive of NMD. Interpreting NMD as yet another manifestation of American unilateralism, the French government has pulled no punches in deriding the Clinton administration's proposals. Prime Minister Jospin announced that "the global strategic equilibrium would be threatened" if the international community "does not succeed in reining in an arms race which is clearly reviving," and if the temptation of the United States "to free itself from international discipline in the field of strategic weapons were to take a more concrete form." The French government is concerned not only that NMD might ruin relations with Russia but also that it could upset the balance of power in Asia. Foreign Minister Hubert Vedrine went so far as to write a letter to U.S. Secretary of State Madeleine Albright warning of the destabilizing consequences of including Taiwan and Japan in any prospective ballistic missile defense.[10]

German officials, although they oppose NMD, have refrained from expressing their opposition with the same vehemence as their allies in Paris. More than any other European country, however, Germany is concerned with the effect that missile defenses might have on arms control and East-West relations. Thus, the German government has been the strongest advocate of finding a *modus vivendi* with Moscow that would prevent the collapse of the ABM Treaty.

IS RESOLUTION POSSIBLE?

Sorting out the relative importance that European governments attach to the various potential implications of NMD deployment, as well as assessing the validity of these concerns, can help chart a path to building a U.S. missile defense system that Europeans might find acceptable, or at least tolerable.

Although European officials consistently cite the fear of decoupling when explaining their opposition to NMD, that is neither the most important nor most cogent European objection to the U.S. plans for missile defense. As in prior transatlantic debates about ballistic missile defense, Europeans argue that if the United States were protected from ballistic missiles, it would be less likely to defend Europe. Today, Europeans seem to fear that NMD gives Americans a choice about whether to come to their aid, and that Europe might be left alone to bear the consequences of an overly aggressive U.S. counterproliferation policy.

Past arguments about decoupling reflected a different strategic setting and a different logic. The credibility of the U.S. nuclear guarantee to Europe was first seriously called into question in the 1950s, when the United States lost its invulnerability to Soviet nuclear attack. Subsequently, NATO's great challenge was to make U.S. nuclear threats credible against the Soviet Union, as American territory became increasingly vulnerable to cataclysmic Soviet retaliation for any NATO use of nuclear weapons. This led to a series of doctrinal and operational changes in

NATO policy, such as flexible response, intermediate range nuclear force deployments, and in 1983, the Strategic Defense Initiative, all of which evoked European concerns about decoupling.

During the Cold War, virtually every major alliance initiative that suggested an alteration in NATO policy, whether it involved changes in doctrine, force structure, or missile defense, was seen in Europe as prima facie evidence that decoupling had occurred. The reason that U.S. proposals engendered concerns about decoupling had little to do with the proposals per se. Europeans were anxious because these proposals indicated that U.S. officials had become worried about the credibility of the American extended deterrent over Europe. Weapons deployments that arguably enhanced the credibility of America's extended deterrent (thus enhancing coupling) often raised European fears that Americans would abandon them during a crisis. The fact that U.S. policymakers thought policy initiatives were necessary was enough to remind Europeans about the difficulty of making extended nuclear deterrence to Europe credible in a Soviet-American strategic relationship characterized by mutual assured destruction. This dilemma—a Cold War manifestation of the alliance paradox, in which members of a coalition fear entrapment or abandonment—was never resolved.[11] It simply disappeared from NATO policy agendas following the demise of the Soviet Union.

The current debate about modifying the ABM Treaty and U.S. national missile defense is no different, in the sense that any U.S. initiative that affects NATO security is bound to stir up acrimony. Today, when European allies argue that American missile defenses would decouple the United States from Europe by creating two different security zones, they are wrong on two accounts. First, America and Europe already occupy different zones of security, even in the absence of U.S. missile defenses. Middle Eastern countries have missiles with ranges sufficient to strike Europe but not the United States. Just as it did during the Cold War, geography, as much as technology, affects the nature of the threat each NATO member faces. Second, protecting the United States would not decouple U.S. security interests from those of NATO; rather, it would make Americans more secure and therefore more likely to engage in conflicts that threaten Europe's interests. In this sense, U.S. NMD could prevent a convergence of the security threats faced by the United States and Europe as a result of the proliferation of intercontinental ballistic missiles.

If the two security zones did converge, the *absence* of U.S. missile defense would likely lead to decoupling in transatlantic security relations.

In contrast, U.S. and NATO officials are rightly concerned about the effect NMD deployments might have on the existing arms control regime. Russia is in a position to withdraw from existing arms treaties if the United States deploys NMD, a possibility that has Europeans extremely alarmed. If limited defenses corresponding to the proposed threshold C1 deployments could be undertaken with Russian consent, European allies would be mollified. Although they might still harbor reservations about the necessity of U.S. missile defenses, revision of the ABM Treaty would reassure all concerned, proving that international relations are not going to deteriorate into mutual suspicion and arms races.

Despite Europe's distinct lack of enthusiasm for U.S. national missile defense deployment, there is some joint work occurring on lower-tier ballistic missile technologies. The United States, Germany, and Italy are cooperating in the Medium Extended Air Defense System. This is a rather low-key effort that builds on the capabilities of elements from existing theater missile defense (TMD) weapons systems, such as the Patriot Advanced Capability (PAC)-3.[12]

JAPAN

Ballistic missile defense has been less controversial in Japan than in Western Europe. The Japanese government generally shares Washington's perspective about the threat posed by the proliferation of ballistic missiles and weapons of mass destruction. Japanese officials know that they already are well within range of North Korean ballistic missiles. North Korea's August 1998 test of the Taepo Dong-1 ballistic missile, which overflew Japan, made missile defense a vital Japanese security concern. But Japanese officials prefer to proceed quietly in developing defenses, hoping to avoid unnecessary domestic and international controversy.

Because the North Korean threat is perceived to be real and immediate, Japanese officials are not preoccupied with the implications of U.S. NMD for arms control or the ABM Treaty. Japanese officials remain supportive of arms control and improved relations with Russia, but they also tend to view Japanese missile defense as an issue of vital national security. Japanese leaders are sensitive to the possibility that the People's Republic of China might respond negatively to increased Japanese collaboration with the United States in creating missile defenses. Yet these concerns are overshadowed by the threat posed by North Korean ballistic missiles and the fear that these could someday be armed with nuclear warheads.

U.S.-Japanese Cooperation on Theater Missile Defenses

The United States and Japan have been cooperating on TMD research for many years. This cooperation recently has intensified in response to North Korean missile tests.[13] During the 1980s, as a part of SDI, the Reagan administration forged partnerships with key allies to develop technologies and conduct studies on ballistic missile defense. On 27 July 1987, for example, Japan and the United States signed a formal Memorandum of Understanding (MOU) regulating their cooperation on ballistic missile defense research. Japan's decision to sign the MOU was made out of loyalty to Washington and the desire to gain technological benefits rather than from a shared perception of the strategic necessity of deploying ballistic missile defenses.

One of the first significant results of the U.S.-Japanese collaboration was the West Pacific Missile Defense Architecture (WESTPAC) study. Its charter was to investigate the requirements of building a "highly viable theater missile defense capability for the U.S. overseas forward-deployed forces and U.S. Allies and friendly nations." Out of the 1988–1989 WESTPAC meetings was born the theater missile defense option. The interest in pursuing TMD, however, waned as the Cold War came to an end.

Japanese interest in TMD was rekindled by North Korea's 29 May 1993 missile test and by subsequent public speculation that North Korea possessed enough plutonium for one or two nuclear weapons. Interest in TMD was further heightened in 1995 and 1996 when China conducted missile drills around Taiwan. In 1994 the United States proposed a number of options to respond to the burgeoning missile threat facing the Japanese. The most promising option entailed a combination of space-based early warning systems, upgraded Aegis air defense systems and Patriot PAC-3 missiles, and the Theater High Altitude Air Defense (THAAD). This option was extremely expensive, and some observers doubted that it was compatible with Japan's constitution. Although Japanese leaders had begun to see the acquisition of missile defenses as a possible option for Japan, a consensus had not yet emerged to move forward with some sort of defense system.

This state of affairs changed dramatically on 31 August 1998 when North Korea conducted a missile test that overflew Japan, starkly exposing the country's vulnerability to missile attack and highlighting North Korea's rapid progress in extending the range of its ballistic missiles. In the charged atmosphere immediately following the North Korean tests, Japan's vice minister of defense stated that Japan needed atomic weapons. He was forced to resign as a result of his ill-considered remarks. Nonetheless, this outburst from a high-ranking official gives an indication of the widespread fear that the North Korean test generated in Japan. One year later, Japan and the United States signed an agreement to accelerate research on the technologies and architecture necessary to field a theater missile defense.[14]

Japanese TMD systems designed to counter North Korean missile threats are a separate program from the NMD systems proposed by the Clinton administration. The Japanese are investigating technologies designed to intercept missiles with a range of between 80 and 3,000 kilometers and relatively low reentry speeds. The 16 August 1999 U.S.-Japanese agreement called for a five-year effort to investigate TMD options, including "analysis and design of an advanced sensor, advanced kinetic warhead, second stage propulsion and lightweight nose cone."[15] The Japanese are interested primarily in two systems: the PAC-3 and the U.S. Navy's Theater Wide system. The latter would be deployed on Aegis-equipped cruisers that already are operated by the Japanese navy. This is regarded as the most promising existing technology for combating the threat of North Korean missiles. What remains unclear is whether Japan will field a TMD system that has the capability to operate independently from U.S. missile defense systems. Japan's neighbors are concerned that Japan will eventually develop such an independent system. More likely, Japan will possess capabilities that in theory could provide an independent defense but that in practice would require American or jointly controlled assets (such as early-warning satellites) in order to work effectively.

Although the Japanese debate on missile defense focuses almost exclusively on TMD, Japan's support for TMD implies support for NMD. It would hardly be credible for Japanese officials to state a need for protection from North Korean missiles yet deny this option to America, their partner in the joint development of TMD technologies. Because the Japanese are already hard at work on what amounts to their own national missile defense, U.S. NMD proposals generate little controversy in Japan, especially in comparison to that generated in Western Europe.

Japan's China Problem

Chinese officials take a far more sanguine view of the threat posed by recent North Korean activities. Japanese advocacy of TMD has strained relations with China's leaders, who believe that the alarm expressed by U.S. and Japanese policymakers conceals ulterior motives. Chinese officials believe that Japanese and American missile defense efforts are directed primarily against China, and they have become major supporters of the ABM Treaty by joining Russia in strongly opposing plans for U.S. NMD. Chinese leaders also are concerned that Japanese-American TMD cooperation might be expanded to include Taiwan. The U.S. Navy's upper-tier program that forms the foundation of Japanese-American defense cooperation is sea-based, and its warships also could be deployed elsewhere, to protect other countries from ballistic missile attack. Chinese leaders fear that new TMD systems would have the capability to intercept a wide variety of Chinese missiles aimed at targets throughout East Asia. The possibility that missile defense programs will adversely affect relations with China is a source of concern in Japan. These concerns have not dissuaded Japan from joining the United States in TMD research. But if the threat posed by North Korean ballistic missiles to Japan were mitigated, Japanese support for TMD would diminish in the face of Chinese opposition.

SOUTH KOREA

No country is more affected by the threat from North Korea than South Korea. Seoul does not, however, evince keen interest in joining U.S. and Japanese TMD efforts. It would rather support the development of offensive ballistic missiles to deter North Korea. The different nature of the threat to South Korea dictates its position. South Korea is targeted by short-range ballistic missiles (SRBMs)—a situation that predates the highly publicized medium- and intermediate-range ballistic missile threat that spawned renewed U.S.-Japanese cooperation on TMD. The United States has long deployed Patriot missiles on the Korean Peninsula to counter this SRBM threat, and it upgraded its Patriot capability by deploying the PAC-3 system in 2001. Given the economic constraints facing the government in Seoul, it makes more sense for South Koreans to rely on TMD systems operated by the United States than to purchase or develop their own systems.

For South Korean officials, missile defenses take second place to Seoul's effort to build SRBMs with the range needed to reach all potential military targets in North Korea. A 1979 agreement between the United States and South Korea prohibited Seoul from deploying ballistic missiles with a range of more than 180 kilometers. This restriction placed a large number of North Korean military targets beyond the range of Seoul's rocket forces. South Korean officials argued that this lack of capability undermines South Korea's deterrent, and they intensified calls for a modification of these range limits as North Korea expanded its missile program.[16]

South Korea's effort to have this restriction lifted was not sidetracked by the June 2000 summit between North Korean President Kim Jong Il and South Korean President Kim Dae-jung. On 15 July 2000, Washington and Seoul agreed that South Korea could deploy missiles with a range of 300 km. Seoul also will be allowed to conduct research and development of missiles with a range of up to 500 km. Once this agreement is codified, South Korea will join the Missile Technology Control Regime, which prohibits its members from deploying missiles with ranges exceeding 300 km. This compromise still leaves a significant portion of North Korea out of range, but it demonstrates Seoul's determination not to allow North Korean missile deployments to go unanswered.

With Russia and China playing increasingly active roles in effecting a rapprochement between North and South Korea, it is possible that South Korea will become embroiled in the NMD debate. A key component of the Russian and Chinese campaigns against proposed U.S. missile deployments is an effort to reduce the perception that North Korea is engaged in dangerous activities. Increased cooperation between Seoul and Pyongyang would greatly reduce the so-called rogue missile threat that preoccupies many American policymakers. These Russian and Chinese efforts high-light a salient feature of the campaign to block NMD deployment: the ex-ertion of additional pressures on Washington by influencing the opinions and perceptions of U.S. allies. Russia and China apparently view this as an effective way to sidetrack the deployment of missile defenses.

TAIWAN

Taiwan faces a significant threat from China's SRBMs, and it manifests a strong interest in upgrading its TMD capabilities to confront this threat. Chinese missile tests in 1995 and 1996, and subsequent Chinese SRBM deployments, have pushed Taipei to acquire both indigenous and Amer-ican-supplied TMD capabilities. Currently, Taiwan deploys Tien Kung-1 and Tien Kung-2 (Sky Bow) surface-to-air antiaircraft missiles, which are radar guided and capable of tracking objects at distances of about 300 km. Taiwanese officials claim that these missiles have a TMD capability equivalent to the U.S. Patriot missile defense system. In addition, Taiwan deploys the PAC-2/Modified Air Defense System and is anxious to up-grade this system to PAC-3. Taiwan also is keen to acquire a sea-based TMD capability by purchasing Aegis-equipped destroyers.

Despite the clear military justification for these requests, Taiwan's as-pirations to improve its missile defense systems are likely to touch off a political firestorm in Asia. Officials in Beijing regard Taiwan as a rene-gade province and react negatively to any suggestion that the United States might upgrade Taipei's TMD capability. Chinese officials are par-ticularly alarmed about the prospect of Taiwan and the United States de-ploying interoperable TMD systems. Chinese leaders view this as evi-dence that American leaders are backing away from a "one-China" policy. In the view of policymakers in Beijing, both Taiwanese TMD and recent U.S. NMD proposals are manifestations of U.S. hostility and an on-going U.S. effort to deprive China of military options essential to the ac-complishment of important political goals.

Despite concerns in Beijing about diminished Chinese military capabil-ities, the political significance of U.S. efforts to help Taiwan augment its TMD program is probably more important than the military benefits provided by better missile defenses. Advanced TMD systems could vastly complicate Chinese military calculations and ensure that enough critical Taiwanese military assets survived to mount an effective response to Chinese invasion attempts. TMD, however, would not prevent Taiwan from suffering significant damage in the event that China launched hundreds of missiles at the island. Taiwanese officials believe that the ultimate guarantor of their security is the perception in Beijing that Washington will intervene to prevent China from solving the Taiwan problem by force. The extent to which Washington is willing to furnish Taiwan with TMD is seen as a concrete manifestation of this commitment. In an ironic twist, the Taiwanese see theater missile defenses as a way to couple their security fate to that of their American patron, and to bolster deterrence—the exact opposite of the consequences many NATO allies believe will flow from national missile defense deployments.

ISRAEL

Israel faces significant ballistic missile threats from hostile neighbors, a fact that was brought home during the 1991 Gulf War when Iraq launched a series of Scud missile attacks against Tel Aviv. Israeli officials are very interested in deploying theater missile defenses. During April 2000, Israel deployed the first battery of its ballistic missile defense system, the Arrow, a U.S.-Israeli project that began under the auspices of SDI.

Israeli officials were reluctant to embrace American offers to participate in SDI research during the 1980s. This reluctance later gave way to enthusiastic collaboration as Israeli policymakers became concerned about the accuracy of their adversaries' medium- and short-range missiles and possible nuclear, chemical, or biological payloads. Despite the waning of SDI and the end of the Cold War, Arrow development persisted, receiving a significant boost in the aftermath of the Scud missile attacks during the Gulf War. In addition to the deployment of interceptors, co-development work included a tracking radar to complement the Arrow, as well as the requisite command and control systems needed to manage missile engagements. Israeli officials also are working with their U.S. counterparts to make it possible for Arrow to utilize the early warning and battle management systems that will be available to American forces for theater missile defense.

Israel and the United States also are collaborating on the Tactical High-Energy Laser advanced concepts technology demonstrator. This system is designed to use lasers to destroy small battlefield missiles as well as anti-ship missiles. Although it is not yet operational, the system achieved success in a June 2000 test when it destroyed a 122-mm Russian-built Katyusha rocket. Once deployed, this system is designed to protect Northern Israel from rocket attacks launched by Hezbollah guerrillas in southern Lebanon.[17]

The American deployment of NMD is not a controversial issue in Israel. Given the close U.S.-Israeli cooperation in missile defense research and Israel's recent Arrow deployment, America's desire to protect its forces and homeland from some of the same countries that threaten Israel is understood in Tel Aviv. Israel's relations with Russia and China have improved since the end of the Cold War, and Israelis do not believe that their security would be significantly affected by strains in U.S. relations with Russia and China caused by U.S. NMD deployment.[18]

CONCLUSION

The dynamics of the ballistic missile debate between the United States and its allies underwent a significant shift after George W. Bush came to office. America's European allies understood that President Clinton and his administration shared many of their misgivings about deploying ballistic missile defenses, and recognized that American domestic politics was driving the Clinton administration toward NMD. As a result, European officials continued to register their strong objections to deployment, hoping that the combination of their misgivings, Russia's strenuous objections, technological hurdles, and a shift in the U.S. political scene would delay the deployment of NMD indefinitely. Those hopes evaporated in early 2001.

The Bush administration has diplomatically yet emphatically stated that it will deploy ballistic missile defenses, preferably with the cooperation of key allies and the acquiescence of Russia, but if necessary without them. Many Europeans initially chafed at the Bush administration's peremptory manner on BMD, but a significant shift in the allied position undeniably occurred once the United States signaled its desire to deploy national missile defenses. The European allies now view deployment as inevitable. Accordingly, they are concentrating on influencing the process by which deployment occurs rather than trying to block it.

The end result of this shift in the debate should be salutary. The debate prior to the new Bush presidency mostly revolved around old strategic disagreements between the United States and its European allies, acting as a metaphor for more deep-seated problems. Only thus can one explain Europeans' mutually contradictory complaints that U.S. ballistic missile defense deployments would lead to American isolationism and to excessive American interventionism. The ballistic missile debate is occurring at a time when Europe seeks to define an identity more independent of the United States, and it is in this context that the debate must be judged. U.S. ballistic missile deployments remind Europeans of the overwhelming military and technological prowess of the United States, a prowess from which they want both protection and distance. These competing desires explain Europe's deeply ambivalent stance toward American offers to extend the reach of ballistic missile deployment to encompass European territory. Although such protection might be welcome, it comes at a price. It would reinforce European dependence on the United States and retard efforts toward a more independent defense identity. Perhaps more worrisome is the extent to which European involvement in ballistic missile deployments would alienate Moscow, an outcome that European governments are eager to avoid.

Yet, the perception concerning the inevitability of NMD deployment that now reigns in Europe is sure to exercise a powerful effect on Russia as well. Once Moscow concludes that deployment is inevitable, it is reasonable to assume that Russian officials will want to have a hand in influencing the scope and type of systems deployed—influence that it would forfeit, should it remain completely opposed. Russia's inability to fund a renewed strategic nuclear competition, combined with the U.S. desire for a negotiated end to the current ABM regime, bodes well for a compromise that includes Russian acquiescence to limited deployments. Should this occur, U.S. problems with its European allies will be greatly diminished.

In Asia, the effect of President George W. Bush's strong support for BMD deployment is less apparent. Yet, the clear move to strengthen U.S. relations with Japan, and a reduced U.S. reluctance to confront China, are factors that should expedite TMD efforts already under way in the East Asian theater. At the same time, such developments are unlikely to receive the blessing of the Chinese government. Beijing sees TMD as a stalking horse for U.S. deployment of defenses against Chinese ICBMs. And although limited American defenses against long-range missiles would not affect Russia's deterrent capability vis-à-vis the United States, the same cannot be said of China's. Even a modest American deployment would compromise the credibility of China's small long-range missile force. The consternation that this will provoke in China will certainly affect Beijing's relationship not only with the United States but also with America's allies in Asia, who will be seen as abetting these developments.

NOTES

1. "U.S. Will Build Missile Shield, EU Allies Told," *Los Angeles Times*, 4 February 2001, A1.

2. The issue of decoupling was raised by West German chancellor Helmut Schmidt in his 1977 Alastair Buchan Memorial Lecture, delivered to the International Institute of Strategic Studies. See Helmut Schmidt, "The 1977 Alastair Buchan Memorial Lecture," *Survival*, January/February 1978, 2–10.

3. William Drozdiak, "Possible Missile Shield Alarms Europe," *Washington Post*, 6 November 1999, A1.

4. "French Premier Jospin Warns of Renewed Arms Race," in FBIS-WEU–1999–1022.

5. "National Missile Defense and the Alliance After Kosovo," NATO Parliamentary Assembly Committee Reports, paragraph 8, available on line at http://www.naa.be/publications/comrep/2000/at–243-e.html#2.

6. "French Premier Jospin Warns."

7. Drozdiak, "Possible Missile Shield Alarms Europe."

8. Paul Taylor, "U.S. Allies Split on 'Son of Star Wars,'" Reuters, 25 November 1999.

9. Bob Roberts, "UK Tories Urge Missile Defense Cooperation," PA News in FBIS-WEU–1999–1004.

10. "France: Richard Skeptical of US ABM Program Assurances," AFP News in FBIS-WEU–1999–1022, 2 December 1999.

11. On the alliance paradox, see Glenn Snyder, *Alliance Politics* (Ithaca: Cornell University Press, 1997), 180–181.

12. "Nuclear Forces and Missile Defenses," 2001 DoD Report to Congress, chapter 6, available on line at http://www.dtic.mil/execsec/adr2001/Chapter06.pdf.

13. "Theater Missile Defense in Northeast Asia: An Annotated Chronology, 1990–Present," *DPRK Report,* June 2000, Center for Nonproliferation Studies, Monterey Institute of International Studies, Monterey, Calif., available on line at http://cns.miis.edu/research/neasia/index.htm

14. "Theater Missile Defense in Northeast Asia," August 1999.

15. Ibid.

16. "US, South Korea to Discuss Missiles," AP News, 14 July 2000, available on line at http://www.nytimes.com/pages/aponline/news/index.html (cited 15 May 2001).

17. "US-Israeli Arrow Deployability Project," Joint Theater Ballistic Missile Defense Programs Efforts, Ballistic Missile Defense Organization, Washington, D.C. Available on line at http://www.acq.osd.mil/bmdo/bmdolink/html/arrow.html (cited 15 May 2001).

18. Ibid.

Conclusion

JEFFREY A. LARSEN

The debate over deploying a national missile defense (NMD) system and the corresponding discussion about revising the thirty-year-old treaty limiting deployment of anti-ballistic missile (ABM) systems is vitally important to the future security of the United States. Our goal in this book was to explore the spectrum of likely consequences produced by decisions to deploy missile defenses and to change the Anti-Ballistic Missile Treaty, especially possible unintended or unanticipated consequences.

A changing international threat environment and growing domestic political support for deploying missile defenses suggest the Cold War status quo is unlikely to persist much longer. Our opening assumption was that some sort of missile defense and modification to the ABM Treaty were likely in the near term. Our considerations of three alternative deployment scenarios convey no normative judgments about the desirability of various missile defense architectures or Treaty modifications. Instead, they merely suggest that in keeping with current trends, future Treaty formats will place few if any restrictions on missile defenses.

The decision to deploy a modest national missile defense has, in fact, already been made—it was signed into law in 1999. President Clinton announced four criteria for determining whether and when to implement that decision: the nature of the threat; the technological capabilities of the system; its cost; and the impact on the international system, including relations with allies and potential adversaries. This book focuses on that last criterion.

THREE NMD ALTERNATIVES: LIKELY SYSTEMIC CONSEQUENCES

The systems approach introduced at the beginning of this book would suggest that although the ABM Treaty is a bilateral agreement, it has had a global effect on international politics because the parties to the Treaty were the superpowers of the day. Evidence that the Treaty produced systemic effects can be found every time one of our authors makes reference to the way in which nonparties to the ABM Treaty might view changes to the agreement or how they might be forced to respond to U.S. NMD deployments. The United States and the Soviet Union agreed to limit defenses, thereby avoiding a costly arms race and increasing crisis stability. This decision had the effect of reducing significant missile defenses across the global strategic landscape, because many states were able to "free ride" on the absence of missile defenses. But the ABM agreement came at the cost of American and Russian cities' remaining vulnerable to ballistic missile attack. Today, U.S. policymakers are reassessing the value of this deal, especially as missile technology and nuclear, chemical, and biological weapons are acquired by states that are highly hostile to the United States. The free ride appears to be coming to an end.

Limited Defenses: Threshold C1

Our limited defense scenario was based on the Clinton administration's plan for an initial deployment of between 20 and 100 ground-based interceptors at a single site that would allow a limited defense of the United States, designated as threshold C1 capability. This scenario placed relatively strict limits on the radars or other sensors and command and control networks needed to make these defenses operational. These limited defenses, however, embody what in fact would be a major change in the existing arms control regime: a negotiated change in the ABM Treaty to permit limited national missile defenses. Yet, our limited defense scenario would not affect the bargain at the heart of the ABM Treaty, because it would not reduce the vulnerability of the American people to a Russian nuclear attack. The systemic consequences produced by this type of treaty modification should, therefore, be modest.

Our contributors confirm this expectation. Countries with small missile arsenals that were seeking to use these arsenals to gain leverage over the United States would see the value of their strategic investments diminish. The United States might become more active in world affairs, intervening more in regional disputes or engaging in preventive attacks to block missile proliferation in the developing world. Indeed, Charles Ball points out that this is the sort of activity that worries America's European allies. They fear that the absence of strategic defenses will make them the logical target of retaliation for U.S. military action. But by strengthening U.S. escalation dominance, missile defenses could increase the ability of U.S. military forces to deter the outbreak of war. Herein lies one of the paradoxes of the NMD debate: Threshold C1 might undermine crisis stability because it could embolden U.S. policymakers to become more interventionist, at the same time as it makes confrontation less likely in the first place by strengthening deterrence.

The possibility of negotiating a revision to the ABM Treaty to permit limited national missile defense is quite likely. Negotiations could remain a bilateral affair, which would greatly ease the task of reaching a settlement. Russian leaders have a strong incentive to constrain U.S. defensive missile deployments by keeping the Treaty viable. They also might find it expedient to use ABM negotiations to obtain concessions from the United States on further reductions in offensive strategic forces, or concessions of other kinds. Robert Joseph suggested that ABM negotiations could be used to move the Russian-American strategic relationship away from the Cold War model based on mutual vulnerability. Negotiations could be used to chart a new course in Russian-American relations to increase the role of defense in some sort of mutual security arrangement.

The real source of international concern about a threshold C1 deployment is that many see it as a harbinger of things to come. Chinese leaders, for example, believe that the United States will continue to enlarge its defense capabilities, diminishing the benefits China is likely to gain from its strategic force modernization programs and making Washington more willing to intervene in future disputes over Taiwan. NATO allies worry that the United States might be tempted to withdraw into a Fortress America, even though 100 interceptors at a single site would offer a weak defense of the battlements. The sale of advanced countermeasures to small missile states in response to threshold C1 deployments would do little to ease these kinds of concerns, and it could make matters worse by increasing pressures on U.S. policymakers to upgrade missile defenses.

Moderate Defenses: C3-Plus

In this scenario, we expanded the Clinton administration's C3 proposal to deploy 250 ground-based interceptors by adding sea-based and air-based systems currently under development. This "C3-plus" system would have limited restrictions on radars and associated command and control networks, permitting the maximum operational effectiveness of planned systems (including the Navy Theater Wide missile defense system) to bolster national missile defenses. This scenario would require extensive changes to Articles I, III, V, and VI of the ABM Treaty. Although a C3-plus system would not overturn the ABM bargain between Russia and the United States, it would "raise the bar" for any country wishing to hold U.S. cities at risk. C3-plus would produce significant systemic consequences because it would greatly reduce American, and in some cases allied, vulnerability to missile attack.

A C3-plus system would have its greatest systemic impact in challenging China's quest to modernize its strategic nuclear forces, eliminating China's free ride on Russian-American cooperation in limiting missile defenses. A vigorous Chinese response to these deployments, according to Brad Roberts and Tim Hoyt, could set off a chain reaction in Asia affecting Indian, Pakistani, Japanese, and Taiwanese defensive doctrines and deployments. Chinese efforts to complicate the defense problems faced by American policymakers by providing advanced missile or weapon technologies to America's adversaries also could destroy the nonproliferation regime. A shift in China's arms transfer policy or an acceleration in its strategic programs could produce the cascading international effects identified by systems theory.

C3-plus would strain the international arms control regime because it would be difficult to construct a treaty that would curb the breakout potential inherent in such a robust defense deployment. In other words, if Russian and American offensive forces continue to decline in numbers, a C3-plus system might be expanded rapidly to deny Russians the ability to hold large numbers of U.S. targets at risk. Moreover, Chinese officials would have an interest in the details of a renegotiated treaty, because they would want to discern exactly how a new treaty might interact with their plans for modernizing their strategic forces. An ABM Treaty that accommodates a C3-plus system might have to become multilateral. But as Julian Schofield explained in his chapter, it can be difficult to construct a multilateral arms control treaty of sufficient issue depth to restrict missile defenses in a meaningful way. Russian officials might cooperate in renegotiating the ABM Treaty under these circumstances, but the negotiations could be a source of acrimony unless a political agreement were reached about how best to integrate defenses into the Russian-American strategic relationship.

Because it affects Chinese interests and because China is a key player in international relations, a C3-plus deployment is likely to produce the systemic effects often identified by critics of national missile defenses. Brad Roberts even suggested that U.S. deployment of significant missile defenses could create a perception among Chinese leaders that a "window of opportunity" was about to close, increasing pressures in Beijing to settle the Taiwan issue by force. This sort of event probably would spur a global increase in strategic offensive and defensive armaments and regional crisis instability.

Unlimited Defenses, Unconstrained by Treaty

The end of the ABM Treaty would immediately produce new systemic effects and amplify existing trends because it would signify that American policymakers, or Russian leaders for that matter, had decided that unilateral measures offered a path preferable to cooperation as a means of guaranteeing their national security. An abrupt end to the ABM Treaty might of course be caused by some diplomatic failure produced by domestic political pressures or miscalculation. But a U.S. decision to withdraw from or abrogate the Treaty also could be a response to an abrupt change in the strategic environment. In this case, an end to the

ABM Treaty would constitute a consequence rather than a primary cause of systemic change.

Arms-race and crisis instability would prevail in a world of strategic defenses left unconstrained by any treaty, or in the absence of a new consensus among the great powers about the role of defenses in national security. Russia might decide that the effort to run an arms race with the United States was not worth the cost, and might seek a new basis for Russian-American strategic relations. Equally likely, however, would be a Russian decision to join with China in a diplomatic campaign to resist American unilateralism. Sentiments among America's NATO allies probably would swing between the traditional dual fears of abandonment and entrapment. America's Asian allies might work quickly to integrate their defenses into an emerging American defense architecture to protect themselves against an increasingly suspicious China. Small states such as Pakistan, Iraq, North Korea, Israel, and Iran might quickly improve their offensive and defensive missile capabilities by capitalizing on a resulting breakdown in the Missile Technology Control Regime or the Nonproliferation Treaty. In sum, the United States could find its real security actually diminished despite the deployment of robust defenses.

RECURRING THEMES IN THE DEBATE ABOUT NMD AND TREATY REVISION

Because the NMD deployment debate touches upon many of the security issues that preoccupy American policymakers, our contributors' analyses identified at least six unexpected and noteworthy observations about the strategic situation facing national governments at the dawn of the twenty-first century.

First, NMD and ABM Treaty revision is a litmus test for Russian-American relations. The way Russia leaders respond to American negotiating overtures will convey much about Moscow's desires to improve its security relationship with the United States. Indeed, as Kerry Kartchner, Dennis Ward, Robert Joseph, and James Goldgeier and Ivo Daalder suggested in their surveys of past and present Russian attitudes toward the ABM Treaty, the Russian response to U.S. plans to deploy missile defenses will give a good indication of how accustomed Russians have

TABLE C.1   Likely reactions to U.S. Missile Defense Options

	Limited Defenses	Moderate Defenses	Unlimited Defenses
U.S. Option	*(Based on C1 plan: 20–100 interceptors, single site, upgraded radars and sensors, deployed by 2010)*	*(Based on "C3-plus" plan: 250 interceptors, two sites, improved sensors, layered defense including Navy Theater Wide, airborne laser; deployed no earlier than 2011)*	*(Unconstrained by treaty: sensors run free; ground-, sea-, and space-based systems, including space-based laser; deployment 2020 at the earliest)*
Inter- national System Reaction	Minor impact. Would strengthen U.S. extended deterrence, but diminish crisis stability. Third parties may seek asymmetric alternatives to direct military confrontation (for example, using delivery means other than ballistic missiles).	Major Impact. U.S. more willing to engage in regional crises and conflicts; China's strategic forces marginalized and concerns over Taiwan enhanced. Russia's secure 2nd strike questionable at lower force levels.	Major impact. Decline in security cooperation, increased autarky. Possible Russian alliances with other states. U.S. allies may seek greater independence. Withdrawal from Treaty could also reflect a systemic change that required unilateral response.
Arms Control Effects	Minor impact if U.S. and Russia agree to amend ABM Treaty; major changes to Treaty necessary. Underlying strategic vulnerability of both states would remain.	Moderate impact if U.S. and Russia agree to amend treaty, although some doubts as to U.S. commitment to regime and concerns over U.S. break-out capability. Treaty would require substantial rewrite. Potential for great acrimony in negotiations for Treaty amendment.	U.S. withdrawal from ABM Treaty would potentially destroy the international arms control regime. Arms races, crisis instability, and proliferation would prevail. End of the MTCR and NPR. (Optimistic alternative: the world agrees to transition from an offense- to a defense- dominant paradigm.)
Russia	Likely to agree to negotiated changes to ABM Treaty to constrain U.S. defensive systems and gain other concessions.	ABM bargain still in effect, but U.S. break-out capabilities concern Russia, especially given its reduced strategic forces under START III and economic weakness.	Russia accepts second- rate power status or joins other European states to form collective defense arrangement.

(continues)

TABLE C.1   (continued)

	Limited Defenses	Moderate Defenses	Unlimited Defenses
China	Fears this as a beginning of U.S. defensive arms race, threatening China's rise as great power. China might sell countermeasures to U.S. adversaries.	NMD challenges China's strategic offensive force modernization program. May respond with vigorous growth. May even see window of opportunity closing, and choose to act precipitously.	Fear. Expect an offensive buildup, technology transfer to U.S. opponents, proliferation, intentional undermining of arms control regime to disperse threats and undercut U.S. hegemony.
East Asian allies	Japan supports NMD, cooperating with U.S. on TMD. South Korea and Taiwan are ambivalent about NMD as long as they get TMD protection against North Korea and China. Both see defenses as bolstering deterrence.	Japan wants TMD to protect against North Korea, but doesn't want to antagonize China. South Korean rapprochement with the North would undermine U.S. worries about Pyongyang.	All three allies would want to be covered under the U.S. NMD umbrella for protection against larger or more aggressive neighbors (China and North Korea). Taiwan may declare independence if it gets TMD protection and U.S. support.
South Asia	No response as long as China does not change policies. India will react to China, Pakistan to Indian reactions. Pakistan will attempt to bandwagon with a great power, preferably the U.S.	Chain reaction in response to Chinese offensive arms programs. India will increase its strategic forces, which will cause Pakistan to do the same. Both will particularly worry about sea-based boost-phase defenses.	India will undergo fundamental reassessment of its security policy, and will attempt to achieve regional dominance by building up forces in response to Chinese actions, including IRBMs and naval weapons that can reach the United States. Pakistan will seek alternative political alliances to counter U.S. influence.

(continues)

TABLE C.1 (continued)

	Limited Defenses	Moderate Defenses	Unlimited Defenses
European allies	Britain supports U.S. NMD program, agrees there is a growing missile threat from rogue states. France opposes NMD because it smacks of unilateralism. Germany thinks NMD undercuts global arms control regime; seeks a modus vivendi with Russia. Concerns about U.S. "decoupling" raised.	Britain supports U.S. program, requests to be included in defensive coverage. French fear entrapment under U.S. leadership, and U.S. abandonment of NATO and Europe inside its "Fortress America." Germans opposed and uncertain of next steps.	France: greater independence from U.S., possible alignment with Britain to create European nuclear deterrent. Germany might reconsider its non-nuclear pledge in a world of self-defense. UK and France must devote resources to ensure their nuclear deterrents can penetrate improved Moscow BMD.
Israel	Supportive. Israel is also deploying Arrow and PAC III TMD systems and benefits from the U.S. programs.	Supportive. Israel doesn't believe its security would be hurt by strained U.S. relations with Russia or China.	Supportive. Some concern over possible Pakistani reactions to U.S. NMD.

grown to strategic vulnerability. Although it has been an article of faith for many decades that a transition to a world of defense dominance is undesirable if not actually destabilizing, the underlying assumption has been the persistence of an adversarial political and strategic relationship between Russia and the United States. To the extent that the political and strategic nature of the relationship has changed and will continue to do so in the years ahead, the desirability of this kind of transition will be enhanced. It remains to be seen whether the U.S. drive to build limited missile defenses will rekindle old Russian desires to limit damage in a nuclear exchange, or whether Russian leaders will agree to provide U.S. policymakers with some treaty relief to deal with small-scale threats and growing domestic pressures to deploy defenses.

Whether the Soviets used arms control, and the ABM Treaty negotiations in particular, to mask their buildup of forces and foreclose an arms race with the United States in the 1960s and 1970s is an open question.

The fact is that they pursued arms control and a major strategic offensive buildup simultaneously. Similar competing motivations are reflected in present Russian foreign and defense objectives. Thus, Russian reactions to U.S. NMD deployments and efforts to modify the ABM Treaty will be affected by their own internal debates about the benefits mutual vulnerability has to offer as the continuing basis of a Russian-American strategic relationship.

Second, unintended consequences not only will follow in the wake of efforts to modify the ABM Treaty but also will be produced by continuing to abide by a Treaty that no longer reflects strategic or technical realities. For example, as Dennis Ward explained, theater ballistic missiles have grown far more capable in the thirty years since the Treaty was signed, but the restrictions placed by the ABM Treaty on national missile defenses are beginning to impede the effort to develop theater missile defenses. Although many hoped that the ABM Treaty would be a "living document" that could be adapted to changing technical and strategic circumstances, that hope has not been realized. The proliferation of theater offensive capability, defensive responses to meet that capability, and the technological advances that made such responses possible, all combine to raise treaty conflicts. It would appear that the ABM Treaty is producing an effect never intended by its negotiators: it is stopping the United States from deploying tactical ballistic missile defenses. Today the United States is prevented from responding to threats that did not exist when the Treaty was signed (e.g., North Korean ICBMs), but it is difficult to imagine that the ABM bargain with the Soviets really was intended to leave Americans vulnerable to a North Korean missile threat. The key questions are whether the objectives that the Treaty was intended to meet are still valid as we enter the twenty-first century, and whether the Treaty can be modified to meet legitimate security concerns now that the Cold War is over.

Third, although most observers agree that national missile defenses will enhance U.S. power projection capabilities, they disagree about the political and strategic consequences that will flow from this new capability. Would the deployment of missile defenses lead the United States to stronger isolationist tendencies, as the European allies fear, or to a greater propensity for intervention in international relations, as China and many other states believe? Richard Harknett's analysis suggests that limited

NMD capabilities would increase the ability of the United States to project power into regional trouble spots with less fear of retaliation. This would degrade crisis stability, but it could help deter the outbreak of conflicts in the first place. The impact of defense deployments will vary, depending on the amount of offensive missile capability possessed by potential U.S. opponents. Ultimately, he says, the diplomatic path to deployment, reflected in efforts to renegotiate the ABM Treaty, may have a greater impact on crisis and arms-race stability than the specific capabilities of American missile defenses. Some believe that missile defenses will reduce crisis stability or make unprotected allies likely targets for reprisals following U.S. military intervention. Others believe missile defenses will strengthen deterrence, making military conflict less likely. Ironically, as Charles Ball points out, U.S. policymakers believe NMD would strengthen extended deterrence, whereas America's NATO allies express concerns over the possibility of U.S. decoupling from European security.

Fourth, although national missile defense is a U.S. issue, it often is framed in different regional and national contexts. For example, several of our case study authors considered scenarios different from those suggested in the introduction because they believed that their modified scenarios better reflected the way U.S. NMD was viewed by the national leaders they considered. Their deviation from the path we set out in the introduction has more than just methodological implications. The scenarios we outlined at the beginning of the volume were vetted before several groups of mid-level Washington policymakers, who seemed satisfied that these scenarios reflected the most plausible ways of thinking about various NMD and Treaty options. The lesson for Washington policymakers is clear: Failure to consider the way U.S. policy will be interpreted "outside the Beltway" could lead to some nasty surprises when it comes to the reactions of other states to NMD deployments or changes in arms control policy.

Fifth, although European, and especially Russian, responses to the NMD issue preoccupy U.S. policymakers, modification of the ABM Treaty and deployments of theater and national missile defenses eventually will be viewed as an Asian issue. In part, this is because U.S. NMD deployments were planned primarily in response to the actions of North Korea. Reactions in China to the possibility that Chinese strategic force modernization might no longer be able to capitalize on Russian-American security cooperation raise the possibility that U.S. missile defense

deployments could lead to negative repercussions in the Asia-Pacific region, as China's neighbors react to its security decisions. As Timothy
Hoyt points out, both proponents and opponents of NMD neglect the serious ramifications of their decisions in faraway parts of the globe. South
Asia is the region most likely to experience a cascading effect following a
U.S. decision to deploy NMD, but both Japan and Taiwan also would
have to adjust their defense policies to reflect any American decision. For
better or worse, U.S. NMD deployments and changes to the arms control
regime governing strategic defenses are likely to clarify Chinese national
security objectives in the years ahead. China's decisions may not be to
Washington's liking. China, after all, sees a dark side to U.S. plans to deploy NMD—one that includes American desires for global hegemony,
and an overt U.S. campaign to stem China's emergence as a great power.
If the United States wants to salvage its relationship with China, it needs
to be more proactive in considering and cultivating China's interests and
friendship, rather than simply "letting the chips fall where they may."
Brad Roberts also points out that the United States needs to decide
whether it considers China a "Little Russia" or a "Big Rogue." If the former, then it behooves the United States to help China develop a secure
retaliatory capability for reasons of stability, in accordance with the clas-
sic deterrence model. If the latter, however, then NMD is directed at the
potential Chinese threat.

Finally, this book points out the dangers of making short-sighted policy decisions that fail to take into account either current international reactions or longer-term systemic consequences. The United States must
recognize the critical importance of diplomacy in assuaging the fears of
allies and adversaries facing even a minimal U.S. missile defense deployment decision. As Julian Schofield points out, U.S. arms control policy is
intended to preserve arms-race and crisis stability, thereby reducing the
risks of war and preserving America's freedom of action. Today, the
three primary strategies for achieving these goals include minimal deterrence with Russia, limited disarmament initiatives, and constrained proliferation of nuclear weapons and associated delivery systems. The ABM
Treaty has served these goals.

If the United States deploys missile defenses while continuing to advocate arms control, it will be seen as hypocritical and could become the target of political assaults by states that seek to change the current regime

and the balance of power. "What is missing," Schofield says, "is a vision of how U.S. policymakers hope to use arms control and national missile defense to shape the future international security environment." The NMD debate focuses on today's threats; but treaty revision has to take into account the probable strategic setting twenty years from now, when mature defense systems finally are deployed. If it fails to do this, the United States will find itself wedded to an increasingly irrelevant arms control treaty.

FINAL THOUGHTS

Throughout this book, we have considered U.S. efforts to deploy missile defenses and to modify the ABM Treaty primarily as a cause, not a consequence, of changes in international affairs. But recent U.S. interest in developing missile defenses is itself a consequence of more fundamental changes in the international scene. Cold War bipolarity seems to be in decline, and American policymakers focus increasingly on regional threats. Chinese strategic calculations and policies, although not central to U.S. strategic planning today, appear likely to increase in importance on future policy agendas.

In a sense, Americans have been lucky. Strategic policies and systems inherited from the Cold War have served U.S. strategic interests well for more than a decade following the demise of the Soviet Union. A cornerstone of these policies, the ABM Treaty, is now being stretched to the breaking point as advances in technology outpace our diplomacy. Change is in the air.

So what are America's options? The threat from rogue states does appear to pose a real danger to the United States that could justify a limited missile defense system. Michael O'Hanlon draws the conclusion that the American people want a limited NMD system, and that the U.S. Senate in its current makeup is likely to vote to create such a defense, with or without Russian acquiescence to a revised ABM Treaty. But no decisions are likely to be cast in stone. Given the findings in this book, it would appear that neither the current C1 nor the C3-plus option is necessarily the best choice for the United States right now. Either choice would antagonize both allies and adversaries and have ripple effects throughout the international system. This is not to deny the validity of the threat facing the United States, nor the eventual need (from a U.S. perspective) for some type of ballistic missile defense system.

One possible solution would be to postpone deployment of the C1 program and instead pursue the development of a boost-phase intercept program. Based at sea, mobile, and developed jointly with Russia, such a system would appear less threatening to China and probably would have a reduced domino effect throughout East and South Asia. Under the George W. Bush administration such a system is more likely.

The United States finds itself on the horns of a dilemma. On the one hand, it can seek to increase its security through largely unilateral action, but at the risk of a harsh international response. Arms-race and crisis instability, unleashed by highly capable defenses deployed in the absence of a revised ABM Treaty, probably would undermine America's strategic position over the long term. Given the likely international ramifications, are missile defenses and ABM Treaty modifications worth the modest protection NMD will provide? On the other hand, can the United States avoid defense deployments, given the proliferation of ballistic missile threats and domestic demands for protection? No matter how American policymakers attempt to resolve this missile defense dilemma, real choices will have to be made concerning U.S. strategic interests— choices that must not be made without full consideration of the potential long-term international consequences.

Appendix A

Treaty Summary and Text of the 1972 ABM Treaty

In the Treaty on the Limitation of Anti-Ballistic Missile Systems the United States and the Soviet Union agree that each may have only two ABM deployment areas (subsequently reduced to one area in the 1974 ABM Protocol), so restricted and so located that they cannot provide a nationwide ABM defense or become the basis for developing one. Each country thus leaves unchallenged the penetration capability of the other's retaliatory missile forces.

The Treaty permits each side to have one limited ABM system to protect its capital and another to protect an ICBM launch area. The two sites defended must be at least 1,300 kilometers apart, to prevent the creation of any effective regional defense zone or the beginnings of a nationwide system.

Precise quantitative and qualitative limits are imposed on the ABM systems that may be deployed. At each site there may be no more than 100 interceptor missiles and 100 launchers. Agreement on the number and characteristics of radars to be permitted had required extensive and complex technical negotiations, and the provisions governing these important components of ABM systems are spelled out in very specific detail in the Treaty and further clarified in the "Agreed Statements" accompanying it.

Both Parties agreed to limit qualitative improvement of their ABM technology—e.g., not to develop, test, or deploy ABM launchers capable of launching more than one interceptor missile at a time or modify existing launchers to give them this capability, and systems for rapid reload of launchers are similarly barred. These provisions, the Agreed Statements clarify, also ban interceptor missiles with more than one independently guided warhead.

Treaty summary from United States Arms Control and Disarmament Agency, "Treaty Between the United States of America and the Union of Soviet Socialist Republics on the Limitation of Anti-Ballistic Missiles Systems," *Arms Control and Disarmament Agreements: Texts and Histories of the Negotiations, 1996 Edition* (Washington, D.C.: U.S. Government Printing Office, 1996), 113.

There had been some concern over the possibility that surface-to-air missiles (SAMs) intended for defense against aircraft might be improved, along with their supporting radars, to the point where they could effectively be used against ICBMs and SLBMs, and the Treaty prohibits this. While further deployment of radars intended to give early warning of strategic ballistic missile attack is not prohibited, such radars must be located along the territorial boundaries of each country and oriented outward, so that they do not contribute to an effective ABM defense of points in the interior.

Further, to decrease the pressures of technological change and its unsettling impact on the strategic balance, both sides agree to prohibit development, testing, or deployment of sea-based, air-based, or space-based ABM systems and their components, along with mobile land-based ABM systems. Should future technology bring forth new ABM systems "based on other physical principles" than those employed in current systems, it was agreed that limiting such systems would be discussed, in accordance with the Treaty's provisions for consultation and amendment.

The Treaty also provides for a U.S.-Soviet Standing Consultative Commission to promote its objectives and implementation. The Commission was established during the first negotiating session of SALT II, by a Memorandum of Understanding dated December 21, 1972. Since then, both the United States and the Soviet Union have raised a number of questions in the Commission relating to each side's compliance with the SALT I agreements. In each case raised by the United States, either the Soviet activity in question has ceased, or additional information has allayed U.S. concern.

Article XIV of the Treaty calls for review of the Treaty five years after its entry into force, and at five-year intervals thereafter. . . .

Since the October 1993 Treaty review, numerous sessions of the Standing Consultative Commission have been held to work out Treaty succession—to "multilateralize" the Treaty—as a result of the breakup of the Soviet Union, and to negotiate a demarcation between ABM and non-ABM systems.

Treaty Between the United States of America and the Union of Soviet Socialist Republics on the Limitation of Anti-Ballistic Missile Systems

Signed at Moscow May 26, 1972
Ratification advised by U.S. Senate August 3, 1972
Ratified by U.S. President September 30, 1972
Proclaimed by U.S. President October 3, 1972
Instruments of ratification exchanged October 3, 1972
Entered into force October 3, 1972

The United States of America and the Union of Soviet Socialist Republics, hereinafter referred to as the Parties,

Proceeding from the premise that nuclear war would have devastating consequences for all mankind,

Considering that effective measures to limit anti-ballistic missile systems would be a substantial factor in curbing the race in strategic offensive arms and would lead to a decrease in the risk of outbreak of war involving nuclear weapons,

Proceeding from the premise that the limitation of anti-ballistic missile systems, as well as certain agreed measures with respect to the limitation of strategic offensive arms, would contribute to the creation of more favorable conditions for further negotiations on limiting strategic arms,

Mindful of their obligations under Article VI of the Treaty on the Non-Proliferation of Nuclear Weapons,

Declaring their intention to achieve at the earliest possible date the cessation of the nuclear arms race and to take effective measures toward reductions in strategic arms, nuclear disarmament, and general and complete disarmament,

Desiring to contribute to the relaxation of international tension and the strengthening of trust between States,

Have agreed as follows:

ARTICLE I

1. Each Party undertakes to limit anti-ballistic missile (ABM) systems and to adopt other measures in accordance with the provisions of this Treaty.

2. Each Party undertakes not to deploy ABM systems for a defense of the territory of its country and not to provide a base for such a defense, and not to deploy ABM systems for defense of an individual region except as provided for in Article III of this Treaty.

ARTICLE II

1. For the purpose of this Treaty an ABM system is a system to counter strategic ballistic missiles or their elements in flight trajectory, currently consisting of:

(a) ABM interceptor missiles, which are interceptor missiles constructed and deployed for an ABM role, or of a type tested in an ABM mode;
(b) ABM launchers, which are launchers constructed and deployed for launching ABM interceptor missiles; and
(c) ABM radars, which are radars constructed and deployed for an ABM role, or of a type tested in an ABM mode.

2. The ABM system components listed in paragraph 1 of this Article include those which are:

(a) operational;
(b) under construction;
(c) undergoing testing;
(d) undergoing overhaul, repair or conversion; or
(e) mothballed.

ARTICLE III

Each Party undertakes not to deploy ABM systems or their components except that:

(a) within one ABM system deployment area having a radius of one hundred and fifty kilometers and centered on the Party's national capital, a Party may deploy: (1) no more than one hundred ABM launchers and no more than one hundred ABM interceptor missiles at launch sites, and (2) ABM radars within no more than six ABM radar complexes, the area of each complex being circular and having a diameter of no more than three kilometers; and
(b) within one ABM system deployment area having a radius of one hundred and fifty kilometers and containing ICBM silo launchers, a Party may deploy: (1) no more than one hundred ABM launchers and no more than one hundred ABM interceptor missiles at launch sites, (2) two large phased-array ABM radars comparable in potential to

corresponding ABM radars operational or under construction on the date of signature of the Treaty in an ABM system deployment area containing ICBM silo launchers, and (3) no more than eighteen ABM radars each having a potential less than the potential of the smaller of the above-mentioned two large phased-array ABM radars.

ARTICLE IV

The limitations provided for in Article III shall not apply to ABM systems or their components used for development or testing, and located within current or additionally agreed test ranges. Each Party may have no more than a total of fifteen ABM launchers at test ranges.

ARTICLE V

1. Each Party undertakes not to develop, test, or deploy ABM systems or components which are sea-based, air-based, space-based, or mobile land-based.

2. Each Party undertakes not to develop, test or deploy ABM launchers for launching more than one ABM interceptor missile at a time from each launcher, not to modify deployed launchers to provide them with such a capacity, not to develop, test, or deploy automatic or semi-automatic or other similar systems for rapid reload of ABM launchers.

ARTICLE VI

To enhance assurance of the effectiveness of the limitations on ABM systems and their components provided by the Treaty, each Party undertakes:

(a) not to give missiles, launchers, or radars, other than ABM interceptor missiles, ABM launchers, or ABM radars, capabilities to counter strategic ballistic missiles or their elements in flight trajectory, and not to test them in an ABM mode; and

(b) not to deploy in the future radars for early warning of strategic ballistic missile attack except at locations along the periphery of its national territory and oriented outward.

ARTICLE VII

Subject to the provisions of this Treaty, modernization and replacement of ABM systems or their components may be carried out.

ARTICLE VIII

ABM systems or their components in excess of the numbers or outside the areas specified in this Treaty, as well as ABM systems or their components prohibited by this Treaty, shall be destroyed or dismantled under agreed procedures within the shortest possible agreed period of time.

ARTICLE IX

To assure the viability and effectiveness of this Treaty, each Party undertakes not to transfer to other States, and not to deploy outside its national territory, ABM systems or their components limited by this Treaty.

ARTICLE X

Each Party undertakes not to assume any international obligations which would conflict with this Treaty.

ARTICLE XI

The Parties undertake to continue active negotiations for limitations on strategic offensive arms.

ARTICLE XII

1. For the purpose of providing assurance or compliance with the provisions of this Treaty, each Party shall use national technical means of verification at its disposal in a manner consistent with generally recognized principles of international law.

2. Each Party undertakes not to interfere with the national technical means of verification of the other Party operating in accordance with paragraph 1 of this Article.

3. Each Party undertakes not to use deliberate concealment measures which impede verification by national technical means of compliance with the provisions of this Treaty. This obligation shall not require changes in current construction, assembly, conversion, or overhaul practices.

ARTICLE XIII

1. To promote the objectives and implementation of the provisions of this Treaty, the Parties shall establish promptly a Standing Consultative Commission, within the framework of which they will:

(a) consider questions concerning compliance with the obligations assumed and related situations which may be considered ambiguous;

(b) provide on a voluntary basis such information as either Party considers necessary to assure confidence in compliance with the obligations assumed;

(c) consider questions involving unintended interference with national technical means of verification;

(d) consider possible changes in the strategic situation which have a bearing on the provisions of this Treaty;

(e) agree upon procedures and dates for destruction or dismantling of ABM systems or their components in cases provided for by the provisions of this Treaty;

(f) consider, as appropriate, possible proposals for further increasing the viability of this Treaty; including proposals for amendments in accordance with the provisions of this Treaty;

(g) consider, as appropriate, proposals for further measures aimed at limiting strategic arms.

2. The Parties through consultation shall establish, and may amend as appropriate, Regulations for the Standing Consultative Commission governing procedures, composition and other relevant matters.

ARTICLE XIV

1. Each Party may propose amendments to this Treaty. Agreed amendments shall enter into force in accordance with the procedures governing the entry into force of this Treaty.

2. Five years after entry into force of this Treaty, and at five-year intervals thereafter, the Parties shall together conduct a review of this Treaty.

ARTICLE XV

1. This Treaty shall be of unlimited duration.

2. Each Party shall, in exercising its national sovereignty, have the right to withdraw from this Treaty if it decides that extraordinary events related to the subject matter of this Treaty have jeopardized its supreme interests. It shall give notice of its decision to the other Party six months prior to withdrawal from the Treaty. Such notice shall include a statement of the extraordinary events the notifying Party regards as having jeopardized its supreme interests.

ARTICLE XVI

1. This Treaty shall be subject to ratification in accordance with the constitutional procedures of each Party. The Treaty shall enter into force on the day of the exchange of instruments of ratification.

2. This Treaty shall be registered pursuant to Article 102 of the Charter of the United Nations.

Done at Moscow on May 26, 1972, in two copies, each in the English and Russian languages, both texts being equally authentic.

FOR THE UNITED STATES OF AMERICA:
RICHARD NIXON
President of the United States of America

FOR THE UNION OF SOVIET SOCIALIST REPUBLICS:
L. I. BREZHNEV
General Secretary of the Central Committee of the CPSU

1972 Memorandum
of Understanding
Regarding the ABM Treaty

MEMORANDUM OF UNDERSTANDING BETWEEN THE GOVERNMENT OF THE UNITED STATES OF AMERICA AND THE GOVERNMENT OF THE UNION OF SOVIET SOCIALIST REPUBLICS REGARDING THE ESTABLISHMENT OF A STANDING CONSULTATIVE COMMISSION

I.

The Government of the United States of America and the Government of the Union of Soviet Socialist Republics hereby establish a Standing Consultative Commission.

II.

The Standing Consultative Commission shall promote the objectives and implementation of the provisions of the Treaty between the USA and the USSR on the Limitation of Anti-Ballistic Missile Systems of May 26, 1972, the Interim Agreement between the USA and the USSR on Certain Measures with Respect to the

Limitation of Strategic Offensive Arms of May 26, 1972, and the Agreement on Measures to Reduce the Risk of Outbreak of Nuclear War between the USA and the USSR of September 30, 1971, and shall exercise its competence in accordance with the provisions of Article XIII of said Treaty, Article VI of said Interim Agreement, and Article 7 of said Agreement on Measures.

III.

Each Government shall be represented on the Standing Consultative Commission by a Commissioner and a Deputy Commissioner, assisted by such staff as it deems necessary.

IV.

The Standing Consultative Commission shall hold periodic sessions on dates mutually agreed by the Commissioners but no less than two times per year. Sessions shall also be convened as soon as possible, following reasonable notice, at the request of either Commissioner.

V.

The Standing Consultative Commission shall establish and approve Regulations governing procedures and other relevant matters and may amend them as it deems appropriate.

VI.

The Standing Consultative Commission will meet in Geneva. It may also meet at such other places as may be agreed.

Done in Geneva, on December 21, 1972, in two copies, each in the English and Russian languages, both texts being equally authentic.

Appendix C

Agreed Statements, Common Understandings, and Unilateral Statements Regarding the ABM Treaty, May 1972

AGREED STATEMENTS, COMMON UNDERSTANDINGS, AND UNILATERAL STATEMENTS REGARDING THE TREATY BETWEEN THE UNITED STATES OF AMERICA AND THE UNION OF SOVIET SOCIALIST REPUBLICS ON THE LIMITATION OF ANTI-BALLISTIC MISSILES

1. AGREED STATEMENTS

The document set forth below was agreed upon and initialed by the Heads of the Delegations on May 26, 1972 (letter designations added):

Agreed Statements Regarding the Treaty Between the United States of America and the Union of Soviet Socialist Republics on the Limitation of Anti-Ballistic Missile Systems

[A]

The Parties understand that, in addition to the ABM radars which may be deployed in accordance with subparagraph (a) of Article III of the Treaty, those non-phased-array ABM radars operational on the date of signature of the Treaty within the ABM system deployment area for defense of the national capital may be retained.

[B]

The Parties understand that the potential (the product of mean emitted power in watts and antenna area in square meters) of the smaller of the two large phased-array ABM radars referred to in subparagraph (b) of Article III of the Treaty is considered for purposes of the Treaty to be three million.

[C]

The Parties understand that the center of the ABM system deployment area centered on the national capital and the center of the ABM system deployment area containing ICBM silo launchers for each Party shall be separated by no less than thirteen hundred kilometers.

[D]

In order to insure fulfillment of the obligation not to deploy ABM systems and their components except as provided in Article III of the Treaty, the Parties agree that in the event ABM systems based on other physical principles and including components capable of substituting for ABM interceptor missiles, ABM launchers, or ABM radars are created in the future, specific limitations on such systems and their components would be subject to discussion in accordance with Article XIII and agreement in accordance with Article XIV of the Treaty.

[E]

The Parties understand that Article V of the Treaty includes obligations not to develop, test or deploy ABM interceptor missiles for the delivery by each ABM interceptor missile of more than one independently guided warhead.

[F]

The Parties agree not to deploy phased-array radars having a potential (the product of mean emitted power in watts and antenna area in square meters) exceeding three million, except as provided for in Articles III, IV, and VI of the Treaty, or except for the purposes of tracking objects in outer space or for use as national technical means of verification.

[G]

The Parties understand that Article IX of the Treaty includes the obligation of the United States and the USSR not to provide to other States technical descriptions or blueprints specially worked out for the construction of ABM systems and their components limited by the Treaty.

2. COMMON UNDERSTANDINGS

Common understanding of the Parties on the following matters was reached during the negotiations:

A. Location of ICBM Defenses

The U.S. Delegation made the following statement on May 26, 1972:

Article III of the ABM Treaty provides for each side one ABM system deployment area centered on its national capital and one ABM system deployment area containing ICBM silo launchers. The two sides have registered agreement on the following statement: "The Parties understand that the center of the ABM system deployment area centered on the national capital and the center of the ABM system deployment area containing ICBM silo launchers for each Party shall be separated by no less than thirteen hundred kilometers." In this connection, the U.S. side notes that its ABM system deployment area for defense of ICBM silo launchers, located west of the Mississippi River, will be centered in the Grand Forks ICBM silo launcher deployment area. (See Agreed Statement [C].)

B. ABM Test Ranges

The U.S. Delegation made the following statement on April 26, 1972:

Article IV of the ABM Treaty provides that "the limitations provided for in Article III shall not apply to ABM systems or their components used for development or testing, and located within current or additionally agreed test ranges." We believe it would be useful to assure that there is no misunderstanding as to current ABM test ranges. It is our understanding that ABM test ranges encompass the area within which ABM components are located for test purposes. The current U.S. ABM test ranges are at White Sands, New Mexico, and at Kwajalein Atoll, and the current Soviet ABM test range is near Saryshagan in Kazakhstan. We consider that non-phased-array radars of types used for range safety or instrumentation purposes may be located outside of ABM test ranges. We interpret the reference in Article IV to "additionally agreed test ranges" to mean that ABM components will not be located at any other test ranges without prior agreement between our Governments that there will be such additional ABM test ranges.

On May 5, 1972, the Soviet Delegation stated that there was a common understanding on what ABM test ranges were, that the use of the types of non-ABM radars for range safety or instrumentation was not limited under the Treaty, that the reference in Article IV to "additionally agreed" test ranges was sufficiently clear, and that national means permitted identifying current test ranges.

C. Mobile ABM Systems

On January 29, 1972, the U.S. Delegation made the following statement:

Article V(1) of the Joint Draft Text of the ABM Treaty includes an undertaking not to develop, test, or deploy mobile land-based ABM systems and their components. On May 5, 1971, the U.S. side indicated that, in its view, a prohibition on development of mobile ABM systems and components would rule out the deployment of ABM launchers and radars which were not permanent fixed types. At that time, we asked for the Soviet view of this interpretation. Does the Soviet side agree with the U.S. side's interpretation put forward on May 5, 1971?

On April 13, 1972, the Soviet Delegation said there is a general common understanding on this matter.

D. Standing Consultative Commission

Ambassador Smith made the following statement on May 22, 1972:

The United States proposes that the sides agree that, with regard to initial implementation of the ABM Treaty's Article XIII on the Standing Consultative Commission (SCC) and of the consultation Articles to the Interim Agreement on offensive arms and the Accidents Agreement,[1] agreement establishing the SCC will be worked out early in the follow-on SALT negotiations; until that is completed, the following arrangements will prevail: when SALT is in session, any consultation desired by either side under these Articles can be carried out by the two SALT Delegations; when SALT is not in session, ad hoc arrangements for any desired consultations under these Articles may be made through diplomatic channels.

Minister Semenov replied that, on an ad referendum basis, he could agree that the U.S. statement corresponded to the Soviet understanding.

E. Standstill

On May 6, 1972, Minister Semenov made the following statement:

In an effort to accommodate the wishes of the U.S. side, the Soviet Delegation is prepared to proceed on the basis that the two sides will in fact observe the obligations of both the Interim Agreement and the ABM Treaty beginning from the date of signature of these two documents.

In reply, the U.S. Delegation made the following statement on May 20, 1972:

---

[1]See Article 7 of "Agreement to Reduce the Risk of Outbreak of Nuclear War Between the United States of America and the Union of Soviet Socialist Republics," signed September 30, 1971.

The United States agrees in principle with the Soviet statement made on May 6 concerning observance of obligations beginning from date of signature but we would like to make clear our understanding that this means that, pending ratification and acceptance, neither side would take any action prohibited by the agreements after they had entered into force. This understanding would continue to apply in the absence of notification by either signatory of its intention not to proceed with ratification or approval.

The Soviet Delegation indicated agreement with the U.S. statement.

3. UNILATERAL STATEMENTS

The following noteworthy unilateral statements were made during the negotiations by the United States Delegation:

A. Withdrawal from the ABM Treaty

On May 9, 1972, Ambassador Smith made the following statement:

The U.S. Delegation has stressed the importance the U.S. Government attaches to achieving agreement on more complete limitations on strategic offensive arms, following agreement on an ABM Treaty and on an Interim Agreement on certain measures with respect to the limitation of strategic offensive arms. The U.S. Delegation believes that an objective of the follow-on negotiations should be to constrain and reduce on a long-term basis threats to the survivability of our respective strategic retaliatory forces. The USSR Delegation has also indicated that the objectives of SALT would remain unfulfilled without the achievement of an agreement providing for more complete limitations on strategic offensive arms. Both sides recognize that the initial agreements would be steps toward the achievement of complete limitations on strategic arms. If an agreement providing for more complete strategic offensive arms limitations were not achieved within five years, U.S. supreme interests could be jeopardized. Should that occur, it would constitute a basis for withdrawal from the ABM Treaty. The United States does not wish to see such a situation occur, nor do we believe that the USSR does. It is because we wish to prevent such a situation that we emphasize the importance the U.S. Government attaches to achievement of more complete limitations on strategic offensive arms. The U.S. Executive will inform the Congress, in connection with Congressional consideration of the ABM Treaty and the Interim Agreement, of this statement of the U.S. position.

B. Tested in an ABM Mode

On April 7, 1972, the U.S. Delegation made the following statement:

Article II of the Joint Text Draft uses the term "tested in an ABM mode," in defining ABM components, and Article VI includes certain obligations concerning such testing. We believe that the sides should have a common understanding of this phrase. First, we would note that the testing provisions of the ABM Treaty are intended to apply to testing which occurs after the date of signature of the Treaty, and not to any testing which may have occurred in the past. Next, we would amplify the remarks we have made on this subject during the previous Helsinki phase by setting forth the objectives which govern the U.S. view on the subject, namely, while prohibiting testing of non-ABM components for ABM purposes: not to prevent testing of ABM components, and not to prevent testing of non-ABM components for non-ABM purposes. To clarify our interpretation of "tested in an ABM mode," we note that we would consider a launcher, missile or radar to be "tested in an ABM mode" if, for example, any of the following events occur: (1) a launcher is used to launch an ABM interceptor missile, (2) an interceptor missile is flight tested against a target vehicle which has a flight trajectory with characteristics of a strategic ballistic missile flight trajectory, or is flight tested in conjunction with the test of an ABM interceptor missile or an ABM radar at the same test range, or is flight tested to an altitude inconsistent with interception of targets against which air defenses are deployed, (3) a radar makes measurements on a cooperative target vehicle of the kind referred to in item (2) above during the reentry portion of its trajectory or makes measurements in conjunction with the test of an ABM interceptor missile or an ABM radar at the same test range. Radars used for purposes such as range safety or instrumentation would be exempt from application of these criteria.

C. No-Transfer Article of ABM Treaty

On April 18, 1972, the U.S. Delegation made the following statement:
In regard to this Article [IX], I have a brief and I believe self-explanatory statement to make. The U.S. side wishes to make clear that the provisions of this Article do not set a precedent for whatever provision may be considered for a Treaty on Limiting Strategic Offensive Arms. The question of transfer of strategic offensive arms is a far more complex issue, which may require a different solution.

D. No Increase in Defense of Early Warning Radars

On July 28, 1970, the U.S. Delegation made the following statement:
Since Hen House radars [Soviet ballistic missile early warning radars] can detect and track ballistic missile warheads at great distances, they have a significant ABM potential. Accordingly, the United States would regard any increase in the defenses of such radars by surface-to-air missiles as inconsistent with an agreement.

Appendix D

Summary and Text of the 1974 Protocol to the ABM Treaty

At the 1974 Summit meeting, the United States and the Soviet Union signed a protocol that further restrained deployment of strategic defensive armaments. The 1972 ABM Treaty had permitted each side two ABM deployment areas, one to defend its national capital and another to defend an ICBM field. The 1974 ABM Protocol limits each side to one site only.

The Soviet Union had chosen to maintain its ABM defense of Moscow, and the United States chose to maintain defense of its ICBM emplacements near Grand Forks, North Dakota. To allow some flexibility, the protocol allows each side to reverse its original choice of an ABM site. That is, the United States may dismantle or destroy its ABM system at Grand Forks and deploy an ABM defense of Washington. The Soviet Union, similarly, can decide to shift to an ABM defense of a missile field rather than of Moscow. Each side can make such a change only once. Advance notice must be given, and this may be done only during a year in which a review of the ABM Treaty is scheduled. The Treaty prescribes reviews every five years; the first year for such a review began October 3, 1977.

Upon entry into force, the protocol became an integral part of the 1972 ABM Treaty, of which the verification and other provisions continue to apply. Thus the deployments permitted are governed by the Treaty limitations on numbers and characteristics of interceptor missiles, launchers, and supporting radars. The system the United States chose to deploy (Grand Forks) has actually been on an inactive status since 1976.

Treaty summary from United States Arms Control and Disarmament Agency, "Protocol to the Treaty Between the United States of America and the Union of Soviet Socialist Republics on the Limitation of Anti-Ballistic Missiles Systems," *Arms Control and Disarmament Agreements: Texts and Histories of the Negotiations, 1996 Edition* (Washington, D.C.: U.S. Government Printing Office, 1996), 131.

PROTOCOL TO THE TREATY BETWEEN THE UNITED STATES OF AMERICA AND THE UNION OF SOVIET SOCIALIST REPUBLICS ON THE LIMITATION OF ANTI-BALLISTIC MISSILE SYSTEMS

Signed at Moscow July 3, 1974
Ratification advised by U.S. Senate November 10, 1975
Ratified by U.S. President March 19, 1976
Instruments of ratification exchanged May 24, 1976
Proclaimed by U.S. President July 6, 1976
Entered into force May 24, 1976

The United States of America and the Union of Soviet Socialist Republics, hereinafter referred to as the Parties,

Proceeding from the Basic Principles of Relations between the United States of America and the Union of Soviet Socialist Republics signed on May 29, 1972,

Desiring to further the objectives of the Treaty between the United States of America and the Union of Soviet Socialist Republics on the Limitation of Anti-Ballistic Missile Systems signed on May 26, 1972, hereinafter referred to as the Treaty,

Reaffirming their conviction that the adoption of further measures for the limitation of strategic arms would contribute to strengthening international peace and security,

Proceeding from the premise that further limitation of anti-ballistic missile systems will create more favorable conditions for the completion of work on a permanent agreement on more complete measures for the limitation of strategic offensive arms,

Have agreed as follows:

ARTICLE I

1. Each Party shall be limited at any one time to a single area of the two provided in Article III of the Treaty for deployment of anti-ballistic missile (ABM) systems or their components and accordingly shall not exercise its right to deploy an ABM system or its components in the second of the two ABM system

deployment areas permitted by Article III of the Treaty, except as an exchange of one permitted area for the other in accordance with Article II of this Protocol.

2. Accordingly, except as permitted by Article II of this Protocol: the United States of America shall not deploy an ABM system or its components in the area centered on its capital, as permitted by Article III(a) of the Treaty, and the Soviet Union shall not deploy an ABM system or its components in the deployment area of intercontinental ballistic missile (ICBM) silo launchers as permitted by Article III(b) of the Treaty.

ARTICLE II

1. Each Party shall have the right to dismantle or destroy its ABM system and the components thereof in the area where they are presently deployed and to deploy an ABM system or its components in the alternative area permitted by Article III of the Treaty, provided that prior to initiation of construction, notification is given in accord with the procedure agreed to in the Standing Consultative Commission, during the year beginning October 3, 1977, and ending October 2, 1978, or during any year which commences at five-year intervals thereafter, those being the years of periodic review of the Treaty, as provided in Article XIV of the Treaty. This right may be exercised only once.

2. Accordingly, in the event of such notice, the United States would have the right to dismantle or destroy the ABM system and its components in the deployment area of ICBM silo launchers and to deploy an ABM system or its components in an area centered on its capital, as permitted by Article III(a) of the Treaty, and the Soviet Union would have the right to dismantle or destroy the ABM system and its components in the area centered on its capital and to deploy an ABM system or its components in an area containing ICBM silo launchers, as permitted by Article III(b) of the Treaty.

3. Dismantling or destruction and deployment of ABM systems or their components and the notification thereof shall be carried out in accordance with Article VIII of the ABM Treaty and procedures agreed to in the Standing Consultative Commission.

ARTICLE III

The rights and obligations established by the Treaty remain in force and shall be complied with by the Parties except to the extent modified by this Protocol. In particular, the deployment of an ABM system or its components within the area selected shall remain limited by the levels and other requirements established by the Treaty.

ARTICLE IV

This Protocol shall be subject to ratification in accordance with the constitutional procedures of each Party. It shall enter into force on the day of the exchange of instruments of ratification and shall thereafter be considered an integral part of the Treaty.

Done at Moscow on July 3, 1974, in duplicate, in the English and Russian languages, both texts being equally authentic.

FOR THE UNITED STATES OF AMERICA:
RICHARD NIXON
President of the United States of America

FOR THE UNION OF SOVIET SOCIALIST REPUBLICS:
L. I. BREZHNEV
General Secretary of the Central Committee of the CPSU

Appendix E

Text of the 1997 Helsinki Joint Statement Concerning the ABM Treaty

JOINT STATEMENT CONCERNING THE ANTI-BALLISTIC MISSILE TREATY

Helsinki, Finland
21 March 1997

President Clinton and President Yeltsin, expressing their commitment to strengthening strategic stability and international security, emphasizing the importance of further reductions in strategic offensive arms, and recognizing the fundamental significance of the Anti-Ballistic Missile (ABM) Treaty for these objectives as well as the necessity for effective theater missile defense (TMD) systems, consider it their common task to preserve the ABM Treaty, prevent circumvention of it, and enhance its viability.

The Presidents reaffirm the principles of their May 10, 1995 Joint Statement, which will serve as a basis for reaching agreement on demarcation between ABM systems and theater missile defense systems, including:

- The United States and Russia are each committed to the ABM Treaty, a cornerstone of strategic stability.
- Both sides must have the option to establish and to deploy effective theater missile defense systems. Such activity must not lead to violation or circumvention of the ABM Treaty.

- Theater missile defense systems may be deployed by each side which (1) will not pose a realistic threat to the strategic nuclear force of the other side and (2) will not be tested to give such systems that capability.
- Theater missile defense systems will not be deployed by the sides for use against each other.
- The scale of deployment—in number and geographic scope—of theater missile defense systems by either side will be consistent with theater ballistic missile programs confronting that side.

In this connection, the United States and Russia have recently devoted special attention to developing measures aimed at assuring confidence of the Parties that their ballistic missile defense activities will not lead to circumvention of the ABM Treaty, to which the Parties have repeatedly reaffirmed their adherence.

The efforts undertaken by the Parties in this regard are reflected in the Joint Statement of the Presidents of the United States and Russia issued on September 28, 1994, as well as in that of May 10, 1995. Important decisions were made at the U.S.-Russia summit meeting on April 23, 1996.

In order to fulfill one of the primary obligations under the ABM Treaty—the obligation not to give non-ABM systems capabilities to counter strategic ballistic missiles and not to test them in an ABM mode—the Presidents have instructed their respective delegations to complete the preparation of an agreement to ensure fulfillment of this requirement.

In Standing Consultative Commission (SCC) negotiations on the problem of demarcation between TMD systems and ABM systems, the United States and Russia, together with Belarus, Kazakstan and Ukraine, successfully finished negotiations on demarcation with respect to lower-velocity TMD systems. The Presidents note that agreements were also reached in 1996 with respect to confidence-building measures and ABM Treaty succession. The Presidents have instructed their experts to complete an agreement as soon as possible for prompt signature on higher-velocity TMD systems.

Neither side has plans before April 1999 to flight test, against a ballistic target missile, TMD interceptor missiles subject to the agreement on demarcation with respect to higher-velocity TMD systems. Neither side has plans for TMD systems with interceptor missiles faster than 5.5 km/sec for land-based and air-based systems or 4.5 km/sec for sea-based systems. Neither side has plans to test TMD systems against target missiles with MIRVs or against reentry vehicles deployed or planned to be deployed on strategic ballistic missiles.

The elements for the agreement on higher-velocity TMD systems are:

- The velocity of the ballistic target missiles will not exceed 5 km/sec.
- The flight range of the ballistic target missiles will not exceed 3,500 km.
- The sides will not develop, test, or deploy space-based TMD interceptor missiles or components based on other physical principles that are capable of substituting for such interceptor missiles.

- The sides will exchange detailed information annually on TMD plans and programs.

The Presidents noted that TMD technology is in its early stages and continues to evolve. They agreed that developing effective TMD while maintaining a viable ABM Treaty will require continued consultations. To this end, they reaffirm that their representatives to the Standing Consultative Commission will discuss, as foreseen under the ABM Treaty, any questions or concerns either side may have regarding TMD activities, including matters related to the agreement to be completed on higher-velocity systems, which will be based on this joint statement by the two Presidents, with a view to precluding violation or circumvention of the ABM Treaty. These consultations will be facilitated by the agreed detailed annual information exchange on TMD plans and programs.

The Presidents also agreed that there is considerable scope for cooperation in theater missile defense. They are prepared to explore integrated cooperative defense efforts, inter alia, in the provision of early warning support for TMD activities, technology cooperation in areas related to TMD, and expansion of the ongoing program of cooperation in TMD exercises.

In resolving the tasks facing them, the Parties will act in a spirit of cooperation, mutual openness, and commitment to the ABM Treaty.

Appendix F

1997 Agreed Statements Relating to the ABM Treaty

STANDING CONSULTATIVE COMMISSION

First Agreed Statement Relating to the Treaty Between the United States of America and the Union of Soviet Socialist Republics on the Limitation of Anti-Ballistic Missile Systems

In connection with the provisions of the Treaty Between the United States of America and the Union of Soviet Socialist Republics on the Limitation of Anti-Ballistic Missile Systems of May 26, 1972, hereinafter referred to as the Treaty, the Parties to the Treaty have, within the framework of the Standing Consultative Commission, reached agreement on the following:

1. Land-based, sea-based, and air-based interceptor missiles, interceptor missile launchers, and radars, other than anti-ballistic missile (ABM) interceptor missiles, ABM launchers, or ABM radars, respectively, shall be deemed, within the meaning of paragraph (a) of Article VI of the Treaty, not to have been given capabilities to counter strategic ballistic missiles or their elements in flight trajectory and not to have been tested in an ABM mode, if, in the course of testing them separately or in a system:

(a) the velocity of the interceptor missile does not exceed 3 km/sec over any part of its flight trajectory;

(b) the velocity of the ballistic target-missile does not exceed 5 km/sec over any part of its flight trajectory; and

(c) the range of the ballistic target-missile does not exceed 3,500 kilometers.

2. The Parties have additionally agreed on reciprocal implementation of the con-fidence-building measures set forth in the Agreement on Confidence-Building Measures Related to Systems to Counter Ballistic Missiles Other Than Strategic Ballistic Missiles of September 26, 1997.

3. This Agreed Statement shall enter into force simultaneously with entry into force of the Memorandum of Understanding of September 26, 1997, Relating to the Treaty Between the United States of America and the Union of Soviet Social-ist Republics on the Limitation of Anti-Ballistic Missile Systems of May 26, 1972.

Done at New York City on September 26, 1997, in five copies, each in the English and Russian languages, both texts being equally authentic.

FOR THE UNITED STATES OF AMERICA:
Stanley Riveles

FOR THE REPUBLIC OF BELARUS:
S. Agurtsou

FOR THE REPUBLIC OF KAZAKHSTAN:
K. Zhanbatyrov

FOR THE RUSSIAN FEDERATION:
V. Koltunov

FOR UKRAINE:
O. Rybak

Second Agreed Statement Relating to the Treaty Between the United States of America and the Union of Soviet Socialist Republics on the Limitation of Anti-Ballistic Missile Systems

In connection with the provisions of the Treaty Between the United States of America and the Union of Soviet Socialist Republics on the Limitation of Anti-Ballistic Missile Systems of May 26, 1972, hereinafter referred to as the Treaty, the Parties to the Treaty,

Expressing their commitment to strengthening strategic stability and interna-tional security,

Emphasizing the importance of further reductions in strategic offensive arms,

Recognizing the fundamental significance of the Treaty for the above objectives,

Recognizing the necessity for effective systems to counter ballistic missiles other than strategic ballistic missiles,

Considering it their common task to preserve the Treaty, prevent its circumvention and enhance its viability,

Relying on the following principles that have served as a basis for reaching this agreement:

- the Parties are committed to the Treaty as a cornerstone of strategic stability;
- the Parties must have the option to establish and to deploy effective systems to counter ballistic missiles other than strategic ballistic missiles, and such activity must not lead to violation or circumvention of the Treaty;
- systems to counter ballistic missiles other than strategic ballistic missiles may be deployed by each Party which will not pose a realistic threat to the strategic nuclear force of another Party and which will not be tested to give such systems that capability;
- systems to counter ballistic missiles other than strategic ballistic missiles will not be deployed by the Parties for use against each other; and
- the scale of deployment—in number and geographic scope—of systems to counter ballistic missiles other than strategic ballistic missiles by any Party will be consistent with programs for ballistic missiles other than strategic ballistic missiles confronting that Party;

Have, within the framework of the Standing Consultative Commission, with respect to systems to counter ballistic missiles other than strategic ballistic missiles with interceptor missiles whose velocity exceeds 3 km/sec over any part of their flight trajectory, hereinafter referred to as systems covered by this Agreed Statement, reached agreement on the following:

1. Each Party undertakes that, in the course of testing, separately or in a system, land-based, sea-based, and air-based interceptor missiles, interceptor missile launchers, and radars, of systems covered by this Agreed Statement, which are not anti-ballistic missile (ABM) interceptor missiles, ABM launchers, or ABM radars, respectively:

(a) the velocity of the ballistic target-missile will not exceed 5 km/sec over any part of its flight trajectory; and

(b) the range of the ballistic target-missile will not exceed 3,500 kilometers.

2. Each Party, in order to preclude the possibility of ambiguous situations or misunderstandings related to compliance with the provisions of the Treaty, undertakes not to develop, test, or deploy space-based interceptor missiles to counter ballistic missiles other than strategic ballistic missiles, or space-based components based on other physical principles, whether or not part of a system, that are capable of substituting for such interceptor missiles.

3. In order to enhance confidence in compliance with the provisions of the Treaty, the Parties shall implement the provisions of the Agreement on Confidence-Building Measures Related to Systems to Counter Ballistic Missiles Other Than Strategic Ballistic Missiles of September 26, 1997, hereinafter referred to as the Confidence-Building Measures Agreement, with respect to systems covered by this Agreed Statement and not subject to the Confidence-Building Measures Agreement on the date of its entry into force. Each such system shall become subject to the provisions of the Confidence-Building Measures Agreement no later than 180 days in advance of the planned date of the first launch of an interceptor missile of that system. All information provided for in the Confidence-Building Measures Agreement shall initially be provided no later than 30 days after such a system becomes subject to the provisions of the Confidence-Building Measures Agreement.

4. In order to ensure the viability of the Treaty as technologies related to systems to counter ballistic missiles other than strategic ballistic missiles evolve, and in accordance with Article XIII of the Treaty, the Parties undertake to hold consultations and discuss, within the framework of the Standing Consultative Commission, questions or concerns that any Party may have regarding activities involving systems covered by this Agreed Statement, including questions and concerns related to the implementation of the provisions of this Agreed Statement.

5. This Agreed Statement shall enter into force simultaneously with entry into force of the Memorandum of Understanding of September 26, 1997, Relating to the Treaty Between the United States of America and the Union of Soviet Socialist Republics on the Limitation of Anti-Ballistic Missile Systems of May 26, 1972.

Done at New York City on September 26, 1997, in five copies, each in the English and Russian languages, both texts being equally authentic.

FOR THE UNITED STATES OF AMERICA:
Stanley Riveles

FOR THE REPUBLIC OF BELARUS:
S. Agurtsou

FOR THE REPUBLIC OF KAZAKHSTAN:
K. Zhanbatyrov

FOR THE RUSSIAN FEDERATION:
V. Koltunov

FOR UKRAINE:
O. Rybak

Appendix G

June 1999 Joint U.S.-Russian Statement on Offensive and Defensive Arms

JOINT STATEMENT BETWEEN THE UNITED STATES AND THE RUSSIAN FEDERATION CONCERNING STRATEGIC OFFENSIVE AND DEFENSIVE ARMS AND FURTHER STRENGTHENING OF STABILITY

The White House
Office of the Press Secretary
Cologne, Germany
For Immediate Release June 20, 1999

Confirming their dedication to the cause of strengthening strategic stability and international security, stressing the importance of further reduction of strategic offensive arms, and recognizing the fundamental importance of the Treaty on the Limitation of Anti-Ballistic Missile Systems (ABM Treaty) for the attainment of these goals, the United States of America and the Russian Federation declare their determination to continue efforts directed at achieving meaningful results in these areas.

The two governments believe that strategic stability can be strengthened only if there is compliance with existing agreements between the Parties on limitation and reduction of arms. The two governments will do everything in their power to facilitate the successful completion of the START II ratification processes in both countries.

The two governments reaffirm their readiness, expressed in Helsinki in March 1997, to conduct new negotiations on strategic offensive arms aimed at further reducing for each side the level of strategic nuclear warheads, elaborating measures of transparency concerning existing strategic nuclear warheads and their elimination, as well as other agreed technical and organizational measures in order to contribute to the irreversibility of deep reductions including prevention of a rapid build-up in the numbers of warheads and to contribute through all this to the strengthening of strategic stability in the world. The two governments will strive to accomplish the important task of achieving results in these negotiations as early as possible.

Proceeding from the fundamental significance of the ABM Treaty for further reductions in strategic offensive arms, and from the need to maintain the strategic balance between the United States of America and the Russian Federation, the Parties reaffirm their commitment to that Treaty, which is a cornerstone of strategic stability, and to continuing efforts to strengthen the Treaty, to enhance its viability and effectiveness in the future.

The United States of America and the Russian Federation, recalling their concern about the proliferation in the world of weapons of mass destruction and their means of delivery, including missiles and missile technologies, expressed by them in the Joint Statement on Common Security Challenges at the Threshold of the Twenty-First Century, adopted on September 2, 1998 in Moscow, stress their common desire to reverse that process using to this end the existing and possible new international legal mechanisms.

In this regard, both Parties affirm their existing obligations under Article XIII of the ABM Treaty to consider possible changes in the strategic situation that have a bearing on the ABM Treaty and, as appropriate, possible proposals for further increasing the viability of this Treaty.

The Parties emphasize that the package of agreements signed on September 26, 1997 in New York is important under present conditions for the effectiveness of the ABM Treaty, and they will facilitate the earliest possible ratification and entry into force of those agreements.

The implementation of measures to exchange data on missile launches and on early warning and to set up an appropriate joint center, recorded in the Joint Statement by the Presidents of the United States of America and the Russian Federation signed on September 2, 1998 in Moscow, will also promote the strengthening of strategic stability.

Discussions on START III and the ABM Treaty will begin later this summer. The two governments express their confidence that implementation of this Joint Statement will be a new significant step to enhance strategic stability and the security of both nations.

Appendix H

National Missile Defense Act of 1999 (H.R. 4 ENR)

NATIONAL MISSILE DEFENSE ACT OF 1999 (ENROLLED BILL [SENT TO PRESIDENT])

H.R.4
One Hundred Sixth Congress
of the
United States of America

AT THE FIRST SESSION
Begun and held at the City of Washington on Wednesday, the sixth
day of January, one thousand nine hundred and ninety-nine
An Act
To declare it to be the policy of the United States to
deploy a national missile defense.

Be it enacted by the Senate and House of Representatives of the United States of America in Congress assembled,

SECTION 1. SHORT TITLE.

This Act may be cited as the 'National Missile Defense Act of 1999.'

SEC. 2. NATIONAL MISSILE DEFENSE POLICY.

It is the policy of the United States to deploy as soon as is technologically possible an effective National Missile Defense system capable of defending the territory of the United States against limited ballistic missile attack (whether accidental, unauthorized, or deliberate) with funding subject to the annual authorization of appropriations and the annual appropriation of funds for National Missile Defense.

SEC. 3. POLICY ON REDUCTION OF RUSSIAN NUCLEAR FORCES.

It is the policy of the United States to seek continued negotiated reductions in Russian nuclear forces.

Speaker of the House of Representatives.

Vice President of the United States and

President of the Senate.

Appendix I

Excerpts from President Clinton's Speech Deferring a Decision on National Missile Defense

The White House
Office of the Press Secretary
September 1, 2000

REMARKS BY THE PRESIDENT ON NATIONAL MISSILE DEFENSE

Gaston Hall, Georgetown University, Washington, D.C.

... When I became President, I put our effort to stop the proliferation of weapons of mass destruction at the very top of our national security agenda. Since then, we have carried out a comprehensive strategy to reduce and secure nuclear arsenals, to strengthen the international regime against biological and chemical weapons and nuclear testing, and to stop the flow of dangerous technology to nations that might wish us harm. . . . The question is, can deterrence protect us against all those who might wish us harm in the future? Can we make America even more secure? The effort to answer these questions is the impetus behind the search for NMD. The issue is whether we can do more, not to meet today's threat, but to meet tomorrow's threat to our security.

For example, there is the possibility that a hostile state with nuclear weapons and long-range missiles may simply disintegrate, with command over missiles

Excerpted from "Remarks by President Bill Clinton on National Missile Defense," *Arms Control Today*, September 2000, available on line at http://www.armscontrol.org/ASSORTED/clintonnmd.html.

falling into unstable hands; or that in a moment of desperation, such a country might miscalculate, believing it could use nuclear weapons to intimidate us from defending our vital interests, or from coming to the aid of our allies, or others who are defenseless and clearly in need.

In the future, we cannot rule out that terrorist groups could gain the capability to strike us with nuclear weapons if they seized even temporary control of a state with an existing nuclear weapons establishment.

Now, no one suggests that NMD would ever substitute for diplomacy or for deterrence. But such a system, if it worked properly, could give us an extra dimension of insurance in a world where proliferation has complicated the task of preserving the peace. Therefore, I believe we have an obligation to determine the feasibility, the effectiveness, and the impact of a national missile defense on the overall security of the United States.

The system now under development is designed to work as follows. In the event of an attack, American satellites would detect the launch of missiles. Our radar would track the enemy warhead and highly accurate, high-speed, ground-based interceptors would destroy them before they could reach their target in the United States.

We have made substantial progress on a system that would be based in Alaska and that, when operational, could protect all 50 states from the near-term missile threats we face, those emanating from North Korea and the Middle East. The system could be deployed sooner than any of the proposed alternatives. Since last fall, we've been conducting flight tests to see if this NMD system actually can reliably intercept a ballistic missile. We've begun to show that the different parts of this system can work together. . . .

One test proved that it is, in fact, possible to hit a bullet with a bullet. Still, though the technology for NMD is promising, the system as a whole is not yet proven. After the initial test succeeded, our two most recent tests failed, for different reasons, to achieve an intercept. Several more tests are planned. They will tell us whether NMD can work reliably under realistic conditions. Critical elements of the program, such as the booster rocket for the missile interceptor, have yet to be tested.

There are also questions to be resolved about the ability of the system to deal with countermeasures. . . .

There is a reasonable chance that all these challenges can be met in time. But I simply cannot conclude with the information I have today that we have enough confidence in the technology, and the operational effectiveness of the entire NMD system, to move forward to deployment.

Therefore, I have decided not to authorize deployment of a national missile defense at this time. Instead, I have asked Secretary Cohen to continue a robust program of development and testing. That effort still is at an early stage. Only three of the 19 planned intercept tests have been held so far. We need more tests against more challenging targets, and more simulations before we can responsibly commit our nation's resources to deployment.

We should use this time to ensure that NMD, if deployed, would actually enhance our overall national security. . . .

I want you to know that I have reached this decision about not deploying the NMD after careful deliberation. My decision will not have a significant impact on the date the overall system could be deployed in the next administration, if the next President decides to go forward.

The best judgment of the experts who have examined this question is that if we were to commit today to construct the system, it most likely would be operational about 2006 or 2007. If the next President decides to move forward next year, the system still could be ready in the same time frame.

In the meantime, we will continue to work with our allies and with Russia to strengthen their understanding and support for our efforts to meet the emerging ballistic missile threat, and to explore creative ways that we can cooperate to enhance their security against this threat, as well.

An effective NMD could play an important part of our national security strategy, but it could not be the sum total of that strategy. It can never be the sum total of that strategy for dealing with nuclear and missile threats. . . .

A key part of the international security structure we have built with Russia and, therefore, a key part of our national security, is the Anti-Ballistic Missile Treaty signed by President Nixon in 1972. The ABM Treaty limits anti-missile defenses according to a simple principle: neither side should deploy defenses that would undermine the other side's nuclear deterrent, and thus tempt the other side to strike first in a crisis or to take countermeasures that would make both our countries less secure.

Strategic stability, based on mutual deterrence, is still important, despite the end of the Cold War. Why? Because the United States and Russia still have nuclear arsenals that can devastate each other. And this is still a period of transition in our relationship. . . .

Now, here's the issue: NMD, if deployed, would require us either to adjust the treaty or to withdraw from it—not because NMD poses a challenge to the strategic stability I just discussed, but because by its very words, ABM prohibits any national missile defense. . . .

Nevertheless, at our summit in Moscow in June [2000], President Putin and I did agree that the world has changed since the ABM Treaty was signed 28 years ago, and that the proliferation of missile technology has resulted in new threats that may require amending that treaty. And again, I say, these threats are not threats to the United States alone.

Russia agrees that there is an emerging missile threat. In fact, given its place on the map, it is particularly vulnerable to this emerging threat. In time, I hope the United States can narrow our differences with Russia on this issue. The course I have chosen today gives the United States more time to pursue that, and we will use it. . . .

Apart from the Russians, another critical diplomatic consideration in the NMD decision is the view of our NATO allies. They have all made clear that they hope the United States will pursue strategic defense in a way that preserves, not abrogates, the ABM Treaty. If we decide to proceed with NMD deployment we must have their support, because key components of NMD would be based on their territories.

The decision I have made also gives the United States time to answer our allies' questions and consult further on the path ahead.

Finally, we must consider the impact of a decision to deploy on security in Asia. As the next President makes a deployment decision, he will need to avoid stimulating an already dangerous regional nuclear capability from China to South Asia. Now, let me be clear: no nation can ever have a veto over American security, even if the United States and Russia cannot reach agreement; even if we cannot secure the support of our allies at first; even if we conclude that the Chinese will respond to NMD by increasing their arsenal of nuclear weapons substantially with a corollary, inevitable impact in India and then in Pakistan.

The next President may nevertheless decide that our interest in security in the 21st century dictates that we go forward with deployment of NMD. But we can never afford to overlook the fact that the actions and reactions of others in this increasingly interdependent world do bear on our security. Clearly, therefore, it would be far better to move forward in the context of the ABM Treaty and allied support. Our efforts to make that possible have not been completed. For me, the bottom line on this decision is this: because the emerging missile threat is real, we have an obligation to pursue a missile defense system that could enhance our security.

We have made progress, but we should not move forward until we have absolute confidence that the system will work, and until we have made every reasonable diplomatic effort to minimize the cost of deployment, and maximize the benefit, as I said, not only to America's security, but to the security of law-abiding nations everywhere subject to the same threat.

I am convinced that America and the world will be better off if we explore the frontiers of strategic defenses, while continuing to pursue arms control, to stand with our allies and to work with Russia and others to stop the spread of deadly weapons.

I strongly believe this is the best course for the United States, and therefore the decision I have reached today, is in the best security interest of the United States. In short, we need to move forward with realism, with steadiness, and with prudence, not dismissing the threat we face, or assuming we can meet it, while ignoring our overall strategic environment, including the interests and concerns of our allies, friends and other nations. A National Missile Defense, if deployed, should be part of a larger strategy to preserve and enhance the peace, strength and security we now enjoy, and to build an even safer world.

I have tried to maximize the ability of the next President to pursue that strategy. In so doing, I have tried to maximize the chance that all you young students will live in a safer, more humane, more positively interdependent world. I hope I have done so. I believe I have.

Appendix J

Text of George W. Bush's Speech "New Leadership on National Security," 23 May 2000

NEW LEADERSHIP ON NATIONAL SECURITY

Washington, D.C.
Tuesday, May 23, 2000

Today, I am here with some of our nation's leading statesmen and defense experts. And there is broad agreement that our nation needs a new approach to nuclear security that matches a new era.

When it comes to nuclear weapons, the world has changed faster than U.S. policy. The emerging security threats to the United States, its friends and allies, and even to Russia, now come from rogue states, terrorist groups and other adversaries seeking weapons of mass destruction, and the means to deliver them. Threats also come from insecure nuclear stockpiles and the proliferation of dangerous technologies. Russia itself is no longer our enemy. The Cold War logic that led to the creation of massive stockpiles on both sides is now outdated. Our mutual security need no longer depend on a nuclear balance of terror.

While deterrence remains the first line of defense against nuclear attack, the standoff of the Cold War was born of a different time. That was a time when our arsenal also served to check the conventional superiority of the Warsaw Pact.

---

[4]The Bush-Cheney 2000 campaign speeches are available on line at http://www.georgewbush.com/News.asp?FormMode=SP&id=2.

Then, the Soviet Union's power reached deep into the heart of Europe—to Berlin, Warsaw, Budapest, Prague. Today, these are the capitals of NATO countries. Yet almost a decade after the end of the Cold War, our nuclear policy still resides in that already distant past. The Clinton-Gore administration has had over seven years to bring the U.S. force posture into the post–Cold War world. Instead, they remain locked in a Cold War mentality.

It is time to leave the Cold War behind, and defend against the new threats of the 21st century.

America must build effective missile defenses, based on the best available options, at the earliest possible date. Our missile defense must be designed to protect all 50 states—and our friends and allies and deployed forces overseas—from missile attacks by rogue nations, or accidental launches.

The Clinton administration at first denied the need for a national missile defense system. Then it delayed. Now the approach it proposes is flawed—a system initially based on a single site, when experts say that more is needed. A missile defense system should not only defend our country, it should defend our allies, with whom I will consult as we develop our plans. And any change in the ABM treaty must allow the technologies and experiments required to deploy adequate missile defenses. The administration is driving toward a hasty decision, on a political timetable. No decision would be better than a flawed agreement that ties the hands of the next President and prevents America from defending itself.

Yet there are positive, practical ways to demonstrate to Russia that we are no longer enemies. Russia, our allies and the world need to understand our intentions. America's development of missile defenses is a search for security, not a search for advantage.

America should rethink the requirements for nuclear deterrence in a new security environment. The premises of Cold War nuclear targeting should no longer dictate the size of our arsenal. As president, I will ask the Secretary of Defense to conduct an assessment of our nuclear force posture and determine how best to meet our security needs. While the exact number of weapons can come only from such an assessment, I will pursue the lowest possible number consistent with our national security. It should be possible to reduce the number of American nuclear weapons significantly further than what has already been agreed to under START II, without compromising our security in any way. We should not keep weapons that our military planners do not need. These unneeded weapons are the expensive relics of dead conflicts. And they do nothing to make us more secure.

In addition, the United States should remove as many weapons as possible from high-alert, hair-trigger status—another unnecessary vestige of Cold War confrontation. Preparation for quick launch—within minutes after warning of an attack—was the rule during the era of superpower rivalry. But today, for two nations at peace, keeping so many weapons on high alert may create unacceptable risks of accidental or unauthorized launch. So, as president, I will ask for an assessment of what we can safely do to lower the alert status of our forces.

These changes to our forces should not require years and years of detailed arms control negotiations. There is a precedent that proves the power of leadership. In 1991, the United States invited the Soviet Union to join it in removing tactical nuclear weapons from the arsenal. Huge reductions were achieved in a matter of months, making the world much safer, more quickly.

Similarly, in the area of strategic nuclear weapons, we should invite the Russian government to accept the new vision I have outlined, and act on it. But the United States should be prepared to lead by example, because it is in our best interest and the best interest of the world. This would be an act of principled leadership—a chance to seize the moment and begin a new era of nuclear security. A new era of cooperation on proliferation and nuclear safety.

The Cold War era is history. Our nation must recognize new threats, not fixate on old ones. On the issue of nuclear weapons, the United States has an opportunity to lead to a safer world—both to defend against nuclear threats and reduce nuclear tensions. It is possible to build a missile defense, and defuse confrontation with Russia.

America should do both.

Appendix K

President George W. Bush's Speech on National Missile Defense, 1 May 2001

National Defense University, Washington, D.C.
Tuesday, May 1, 2001

This afternoon, I want us to think back some 30 years to a far different time in a far different world. The United States and the Soviet Union were locked in a hostile rivalry. The Soviet Union was our unquestioned enemy, a highly armed threat to freedom and democracy. Far more than that wall in Berlin divided us. Our highest ideal was and remains individual liberty. Theirs was the construction of a vast communist empire. Their totalitarian regime held much of Europe captive behind an Iron Curtain. We didn't trust them, and for good reason. Our deep differences were expressed in a dangerous military confrontation that resulted in thousands of nuclear weapons pointed at each other on hair-trigger alert.

The security of both the United States and the Soviet Union was based on a grim premise that neither side would fire nuclear weapons at each other, because doing so would mean the end of both nations. We even went so far as to codify this relationship in a 1972 ABM Treaty, based on the doctrine that our very survival would best be ensured by leaving both sides completely open and vulnerable to nuclear attack. The threat was real and vivid. The Strategic Air Command had an airborne command post called the Looking Glass, aloft 24 hours a day, ready in case the president ordered our strategic forces to move toward their targets and release their nuclear ordnance.

The Soviet Union had almost 1.5 million troops deep in the heart of Europe, in Poland, in Czechoslovakia, Hungary and East Germany. We used our nuclear weapons, not just to prevent the Soviet Union from using their nuclear weapons, but also to contain their conventional military forces, to prevent them from extending the Iron Curtain into parts of Europe and Asia that were still free.

In that world, few other nations had nuclear weapons, and most of those who did were responsible allies, such as Britain and France. We worried about the proliferation of nuclear weapons to other countries, but it was mostly a distant threat, not yet a reality.

Today, the sun comes up on a vastly different world. The Wall is gone, and so is the Soviet Union. Today's Russia is not yesterday's Soviet Union. Its government is no longer communist. Its president is elected. Today's Russia is not our enemy, but a country in transition with an opportunity to emerge as a great nation, democratic, at peace with itself and its neighbors. The Iron Curtain no longer exists. Poland, Hungary and Czech Republic are free nations and they are now our allies in NATO, together with a reunited Germany.

Yet, this is still a dangerous world; a less certain, a less predictable one. More nations have nuclear weapons and still more have nuclear aspirations. Many have chemical and biological weapons. Some already have developed a ballistic missile technology that would allow them to deliver weapons of mass destruction at long distances and incredible speeds, and a number of these countries are spreading these technologies around the world.

Most troubling of all, the list of these countries includes some of the world's least-responsible states. Unlike the Cold War, today's most urgent threat stems not from thousands of ballistic missiles in the Soviet hands, but from a small number of missiles in the hands of these states—states for whom terror and blackmail are a way of life. They seek weapons of mass destruction to intimidate their neighbors, and to keep the United States and other responsible nations from helping allies and friends in strategic parts of the world. When Saddam Hussein invaded Kuwait in 1990, the world joined forces to turn him back. But the international community would have faced a very different situation had Hussein been able to blackmail with nuclear weapons.

Like Saddam Hussein, some of today's tyrants are gripped by an implacable hatred of the United States of America. They hate our friends. They hate our values. They hate democracy and freedom, and individual liberty. Many care little for the lives of their own people. In such a world, Cold War deterrence is no longer enough to maintain peace, to protect our own citizens and our own allies and friends.

We must seek security based on more than the grim premise that we can destroy those who seek to destroy us. This is an important opportunity for the world to rethink the unthinkable and to find new ways to keep the peace. Today's world requires a new policy, a broad strategy of active nonproliferation, counter-proliferation and defenses. We must work together with other like-minded nations to deny weapons of terror from those seeking to acquire them. We must work with allies and friends who wish to join with us to defend against the harm they can inflict. And together, we must deter anyone who would contemplate their use.

We need new concepts of deterrence that rely on both offensive and defensive forces. Deterrence can no longer be based solely on the threat of nuclear retaliation. Defenses can strengthen deterrence by reducing the incentive for proliferation.

We need a new framework that allows us to build missile defenses to counter the different threats of today's world. To do so, we must move beyond the constraints of the 30-year-old ABM Treaty. This treaty does not recognize the present or point us to the future. It enshrines the past. No treaty that prevents us from addressing today's threats, that prohibits us from pursuing promising technology to defend ourselves, our friends and our allies, is in our interests or in the interests of world peace.

This new framework must encourage still further cuts in nuclear weapons. Nuclear weapons still have a vital role to play in our security and that of our allies. We can and will change the size, the composition, the character of our nuclear forces in a way that reflects the reality that the Cold War is over. I'm committed to achieving a credible deterrent with the lowest possible number of nuclear weapons consistent with our national security needs, including our obligations to our allies. My goal is to move quickly to reduce nuclear forces. The United States will lead by example to achieve our interests and the interests for peace in the world.

Several months ago, I asked Secretary of Defense Rumsfeld to examine all available technologies and basing modes for effective missile defenses that could protect the United States, our deployed forces, our friends and our allies. The secretary has explored a number of complementary and innovative approaches. The secretary has identified near-term options that could allow us to deploy an initial capability against limited threats. In some cases, we can draw on already established technologies that might involve land-based and sea-based capabilities to intercept missiles in mid-course or after they reenter the atmosphere.

We also recognize the substantial advantages of intercepting missiles early in their flight, especially in the boost phase. The preliminary work has produced some promising options for advanced sensors and interceptors that may provide this capability. If based at sea or on aircraft, such approaches could provide limited but effective defenses. We have more work to do to determine the final form the defenses might take. We will explore all of these options further. We recognize the technological difficulties we face, and we look forward to the challenge. Our nation will assign the best people to this critical task. We will evaluate what works and what does not. We know that some approaches will not work. We also know that we'll be able to build on our successes. When ready, and working with Congress, we will deploy missile defenses to strengthen global security and stability.

I've made it clear from the very beginning that I would consult closely on the important subject with our friends and allies, who are also threatened by missiles and weapons of mass destruction. Today, I'm announcing the dispatch of high-level representatives to allied capitals in Europe, Asia, Australia and Canada to discuss our common responsibility to create a new framework for security and stability that reflects the world of today. They will begin leaving next week . . . part of an ongoing process of consultation, involving many people in many levels of government, including my Cabinet secretaries. These will be real consultations. We are not presenting our friends and allies with unilateral decisions already made. We look forward to hearing their views, the views of our friends, and to take them into account. We will seek their input on all the issues surrounding the new strategic environment.

We'll also need to reach out to other interested states, including China and Russia. Russia and the United States should work together to develop a new foundation for world peace and security in the 21st century. We should leave behind the constraints of an ABM Treaty that perpetuates a relationship based on distrust and mutual vulnerability.

This treaty ignores the fundamental breakthroughs in technology during the last 30 years. It prohibits us from exploring all options for defending against the threats that face us, our allies, and other countries. That's why we should work together to replace this treaty with a new framework that reflects a clear and clean break from the past, and especially from the adversarial legacy of the Cold War.

This new cooperative relationship should look to the future, not to the past. It should be reassuring, rather than threatening. It should be premised on openness, mutual confidence and real opportunities for cooperation, including the area of missile defense. It should allow us to share information so that each nation can improve its early warning capability and its capability to defend its people and territory. And perhaps one day, we can even cooperate in a joint defense. I want to complete the work of changing our relationship from one based on a nuclear balance of terror to one based on common responsibilities and common interests. We may have areas of difference with Russia, but we are not and must not be strategic adversaries. Russia and America both face new threats to security. Together, we can address today's threats and pursue today's opportunities. We can explore technologies that have the potential to make us all safer.

This is a time for vision, a time for a new way of thinking, a time for bold leadership. The Looking Glass no longer stands its 24-hour-a-day vigil. We must all look at the world in a new, realistic way to preserve peace for generations to come.

God bless.

About the Contributors

Charles Ball is a senior scientist at Lawrence Livermore National Laboratory, Livermore, California. He holds a Ph.D. in political science from the London School of Economics.

Ivo H. Daalder is a senior fellow in foreign policy studies at the Brookings Institution, Washington, D.C., and Executive Director of the Century Foundation Task Force on Organizing Government for Foreign Relations. He holds a Ph.D. from the Massachusetts Institute of Technology.

James M. Goldgeier is an associate professor of political science and international affairs at George Washington University. He also is acting director of the Institute for European, Russian and Eurasian Studies at George Washington University. He holds a Ph.D. from the University of California, Berkeley.

Richard J. Harknett is an associate professor of political science at the University of Cincinnati. He received his Ph.D. from Johns Hopkins University.

Timothy D. Hoyt is director of special programs and adjunct professor in the national security studies program at Georgetown University. He also is an adjunct professor at the U.S. Naval War College. He received his Ph.D. from Johns Hopkins University.

Robert Joseph is special assistant to the president, and senior director for proliferation strategy, counterproliferation and homeland defense. He previously served as U.S. Commissioner to the Standing Consultative Commission on Nuclear Testing; Principal Deputy Assistant Secretary of Defense for international security policy; and Deputy Assistant Secretary of Defense for nuclear forces and arms control policy. He holds a Ph.D. from Columbia University.

Kerry M. Kartchner is the U.S. Department of State's senior representative to the Standing Consultative Commission in Geneva, Switzerland. He holds a Ph.D. from the University of Southern California.

Jeffrey A. Larsen is a senior policy analyst at Science Applications International Corporation in Colorado Springs, Colorado. He received his Ph.D. from Princeton University.

Michael O'Hanlon is a senior fellow in foreign policy studies at the Brookings Institution, Washington, D.C. He also serves as an adjunct professor at Columbia University and Georgetown University. He holds a Ph.D. from Princeton University.

Bradley Roberts is a member of the research staff at the Institute for Defense Analyses (IDA), Alexandria, Virginia. He also serves as an adjunct professor at George Washington University. He holds a Ph.D. from Erasmus University, Rotterdam, The Netherlands.

Julian Schofield is completing his Ph.D. at Columbia University, and is an assistant professor at Concordia University, Montreal.

Dennis M. Ward is a professional staff member on the Governmental Affairs Subcommittee on International Security, Proliferation and Federal Services, United States Senate. He is completing a Ph.D. in political science at Stanford University.

James J. Wirtz is chairman of the National Security Affairs Department at the Naval Postgraduate School, Monterey, California. He earned his Ph.D. from Columbia University.

Index